THE CAVALRYMAN

THE CAVALRYMAN

John Ernest Conley
Major, US Army (Retired)

First Edition

ISBN: 978-1-7339838-0-8

Library of Congress Control Number: 2019904603
Library of Congress Registration Number: TXu 2-144-266

All views and opinions of the author are his own unless credit is given to others. Some names, dates and places may be in error or deliberately changed for the benefit or upon request by a trooper. Every effort has been made to contact copyright holders of images that appear in this book where possible. The author welcomes being advised of any errors or omissions and may amend future editions accordingly.

The author acknowledges that there are some differences in recollection of certain events. Time is indeed the archenemy of our memories.

Cover art compiled by the Author. It includes in part a photo provided by Reverend, Senior Medic Sergeant Cleophas C. Mims of Alpha Troop attacking in the infamous "Box Formation" and a sub-title by Mark Darrow.

Published by: John E. Conley, P.A.
              Conleyatlaw@aol.com

Dedications

This writing is dedicated to the magnificent
American Cavalrymen, alive, and those in the
loving hands of our Merciful God,
who honorably served their country in Vietnam.
It is further dedicated to the
warriors who preceded them,
assisted them, or followed them into harm's way,
who did their part to protect the freedoms,
of our families and friends against the
evils of Communism. These are the heroes of their time,
who placed their lives on the line for America, with
unselfish and unwavering performance of their duties under
the threat of an untimely, violent death.
And to their families
who carried the burden of the Troopers'
temporary or permanent absence from home.

*** * * God Bless you all * * ***

FORWARD

The Cavalryman, John Conley, was born to be a warrior, and excelled to the highest degree in the position of commanding officer of A Troop, 1st Squadron, 4th Cavalry. His leadership was of the highest order, and he proved this in that his troopers were completely loyal, inspired, dedicated with complete devotion to follow him in many fierce battles during combat operations against North Vietnam Regulars and war hardened Vietcong in and around Vietnam's dense jungles. He demonstrated great courage and always lead his soldiers by example. This cavalry officer was always the POINT OF THE SPEAR. The story he presents in this book is true and well worth reading.

Barney H. Forbes, LTC (Ret) U.S. Army

Captain Conley is a hard-punching, fearless officer who has commanded his Cavalry troop in combat in an outstanding manner. His predecessor was killed in action, so Captain Conley had no period of overlap or break-in. Yet he was completely in command of his troop from the moment he arrived on the scene. In fact, he received a congratulatory message from General Westmoreland (the first of two such messages sent to Captain Conley) for an action which occurred within a week of the time he took command. Captain Conley is cool under fire, is quick in reaction, and has good judgment. He has great potential for high rank and responsibility.

Thomas B. Tyree, LTC Armor, 1st Squadron, 4th Cavalry
(Efficiency Rating 12 July 1968 – See Appendix)

About the Cover

The cover photograph is Hardcore Alpha ("A") Troop in a Box Formation attacking from a clearing into heavy jungle after receiving enemy fire.

This formation was used where the lighter skinned Armored Cavalry Assault Vehicles (ACAVs) would be ineffective in crushing through the heavy jungle vegetation.

Normally six, on occasion nine, Tanks would form a tight line, almost bumper to bumper, and push the jungle down while firing 90mm Canister ammunition and automatic weapons at the enemy. The ACAVs formed multiple lines behind the Tanks and protected them from enemy in spider holes that would surface to attack the Tanks from the rear. They also protected the flanks of the formation with 50 Caliber and M-60 machine gun fire and provided rear security and protection from snipers. The Troop Commander and Platoon Leaders were directly behind the Tanks where they could best control the battle.

This formation had numerous advantages including visibility for pilots providing close air support, and the creation of a wide swath through the jungle for resupply or medical evacuation.

This Box Formation was not used where other combat formations were more appropriate as in open terrain or the rubber plantations. But it was extremely effective in digging the enemy out of their jungle fortifications and other heavily vegetated areas.

Unit Crest (left) and Coat of Arms (right) of the 4th U. S. Cavalry

1st SQUADRON MOTTO

"Prepared and Loyal"

1st Infantry Division Motto

"Duty First"

Overview

**Suffering from wanderlust,
John left home at 17 to join the Marines and
"Become a Man". Six and a half years later Sergeant
Conley attended the Army's Infantry Officer Candidate
School and was commissioned an
Infantry Second Lieutenant.
Then there was Airborne and Armor Officers training,
and he evolved into an Armor Cavalry Officer.
Like many other Cavalrymen in the Squadron,
duty to God and country merged into
a very personal rite-of-passage.
Challenged by the awesome trials of combat, and
conquering fear in the jungles of Vietnam,
this young mustang Officer became a leader
of awesome Cavalrymen, who affectionately named
him, "Kick-ass Conley" and "Killer Cong Conley".
Most everyone else called him "John".**

**John credits his success to God and his Mom and Dad
for their unconditional love, enduring patience and a
moral upbringing; and to the U.S. Marine Corps and
U.S. Army for their phenomenal training, and the
awesome Cavalrymen with whom he served.**

What is the Cavalryman?

**The Cavalryman
is a true adventure story
of an Armor Cavalry Officer,
who with his awesome, brave and loyal cavalrymen,
fought through Hell, known to others as Vietnam,
always asking the good Lord for assistance
to guarantee their success - - -
and it worked.**

You are about to see

The Soul of a Warrior

The Tip of the Spear

TABLE OF CONTENTS

ACKNOWLEDGMENTS

I gratefully acknowledge my many former troopers and superiors for nudging me to write this book, and to persevere in finding my comfort zone in this process.

This book was written and re-written at least three times until I realized the missing ingredient was recognition of the Divine assistance we received while fighting against soldiers who were on the dark side. Much gratitude is due to the Lord for not letting me back away from this project when it was most difficult. He is always there when the going gets tough.

I acknowledge my friend Lieutenant Colonel (Retired) Barney Forbes for reading my final draft, and for providing advice on certain important details. And I thank him for the very kind comments he made for the Forward of this book.

I am deeply indebted to Mark Darrow for editing this book. Mark, who was our very talented Forward Observer, placed Artillery wherever it was needed, during many fierce battles. He has provided equally exceptional and very professional guidance on the structure, organization and drafting techniques, where I needed his special expertise.

I am grateful to Colonel (Ret) William Haponski for the content of several of his books, and his advice on publishing my own. Colonel Haponski has published three exceptional books on his tour of duty in Vietnam as the commander of the 1st Squadron, 4th Cavalry. He has also provided a thorough history of the war in Vietnam by the French as well as our efforts to defeat the North Vietnamese and Viet Cong. I highly recommend "<u>Danger's Dragoons</u>," "<u>One Hell of a Ride</u>," and "<u>An Idea, And Bullets</u>" as mandatory reading in understanding that war. And he also has published yet another book, "<u>Autopsy of an Unwinnable War: Vietnam</u>".

I recognize my former compatriots for many pictures, documents and writings that have helped me put this story together, and for allowing me to tap into their memories. Assistance and encouragement were provided by: Colonel (Ret) Charles "Ben" Fegan, Colonel (Ret) Carl (Skip) Bell, Lieutenant Colonel (Ret) Fred Shirley, Lieutenant Colonel (Ret) Joseph Scates, Major (Ret) George Gram Poole, (former) 1st Lieutenant (Head Medic) Cleophas Mims, (former) 1st Lieutenant (Medic) Dennis Skiles, Command Sergeant Major (Ret) Natividad Escobedo, Command Sergeant Major (Ret) Colyn Crews, Command Sergeant Major (Ret) Bill Baty, First Sergeant (Ret) Terry Valentine, Sergeant First Class (Ret) Tom Reed, (former) Sergeant Dan Thompson, (former) Sergeant Mike O'Conner, (former) Sergeant Charles Jones, (former) Sergeant Alan Benoit, (former) Sergeant Fred Currier, (former) SP4 Bill Butler, (former) SP4 Richard Guerine, and many others. I thank you and salute you all.

And I recognize my darling wife, Stephanie, for putting up with my very time-consuming efforts to write this book for so many years. She experienced my discouragement at not quite finding the solution as to why I couldn't be satisfied with my aborted initial efforts. She was always positive and has been a pearl through it all.

Major Unit Locations

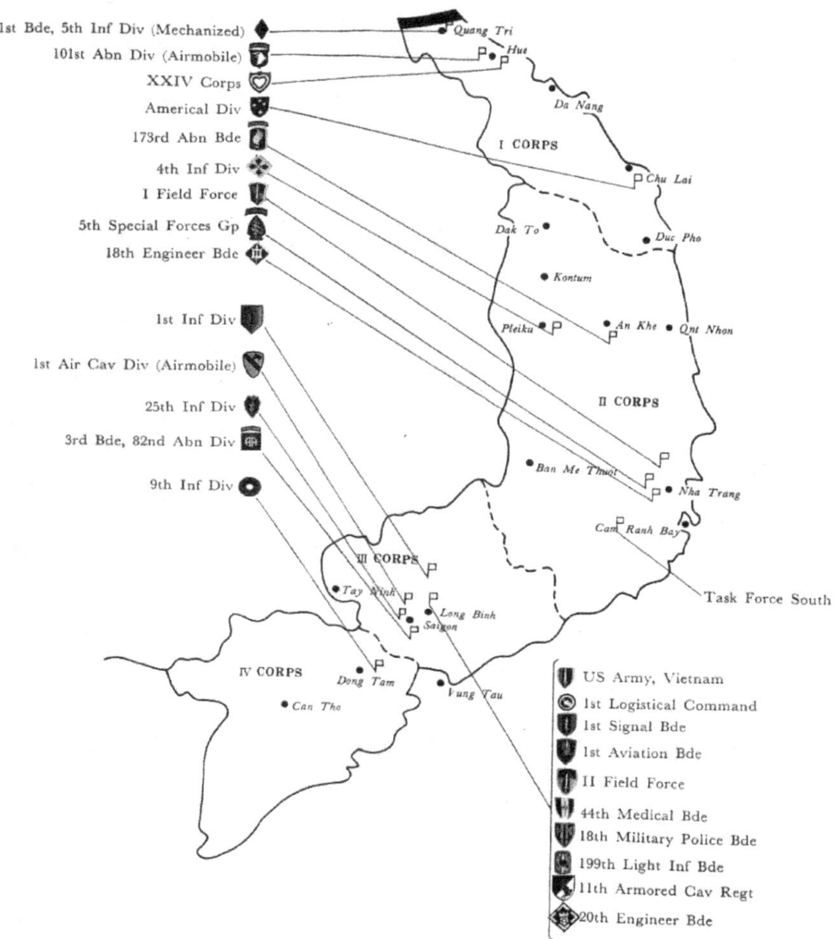

Unit Locations Early 1969

(shortly after I left Vietnam)

INTRODUCTION

This story follows the author, a junior Cavalry Officer, as I implemented my training and expanded my abilities during war. It was where I improvised, as emphasized in the Marines, to find new ways, not found in my military school training, to help us aggressively complete our missions, while simultaneously protecting the welfare of our troopers as best possible. This includes prayer and making our Lord an essential part of every mission.

This story discloses my background that brought me to the Republic of South Vietnam (RVN), and it reveals many personal and private thoughts and actions as I grew into a successful combat commander. The reader is allowed an opportunity to get into this officer's head and intimately understand the blood, sweat and tears experienced under these harrowing adventures and hardships of the hunt.

This is not intended to be a detailed historical account of the events that occurred in RVN, significant troop movements, or a detailed glossary of the equipment we used. That story has already been told elsewhere. This story tries to show how one officer was successful, because of the cumulative strengths of his superb troopers, Officers, Non-Commissioned Officers (NCO's) and young Enlisted Men (EM) mostly fresh out of high school, and a spiritual link forged with his Lord. Hopefully this testimonial will encourage future combat leaders to lean on the special spiritual resources available. On extremely challenging battlefields my distinguished warriors and I shared a special bond that non-warriors may never fully understand. But this story hopefully will help those interested to see this Cavalryman, and his courageous Cavalrymen, through a clearer lens.

But Reader beware - some antics of this Cavalryman could get most any officer in a heap of trouble, if his superiors timely learned of them.

They are not hard to identify, so they won't be discussed in detail or justified in any depth. Just recognize that I was an independent thinker and no saint. Neither the Good Lord, the Army, nor my Cavalrymen lost faith in me through it all. And some of the more regrettable actions, made quickly under unusual circumstances, could not be reversed, if I wanted to.

The events that follow have been examined and reexamined so the facts may be stated as accurately as possible. In some places names have been changed for good reasons. In other places names simply cannot be remembered. There also may be discrepancies in the sequence of actions depicted, and that can be blamed on the frailty of my memory.

This is a true story about a young man, who at an early age felt an obligation to fight for his country. Like many other leaders, my abilities were groomed on a solid foundation molded during my formative years and a deep-set desire to give my best efforts to my God and country. My leadership style was developed in the Marine Corps, as I advanced from a buck Private to the rank of Sergeant, and then being a Corporal and a Sergeant in the Army (a total of 6½ enlisted years) before becoming a Cavalry Officer---a mustang Cavalry Officer.

One may ask how success was measured in the jungles of Vietnam. It wasn't based on land conquered, but by body count. That being the case, the confirmed body count of my units and that of the enemy will be stated as this story progresses. But I will not give a running tally which seems overly morbid. If someone is so inclined, feel free to keep track of the dead and wounded for both sides. In doing so remember that the enemy drug their casualties away whenever possible, leaving only blood trails. We never tried to guestimate their wounded and their dead were sorely understated. We counted what we saw.

So, with no further hesitation, let's dive into my story.

PREFACE

Why This Book? - - Why NOW?

On Friday September 13, 1968, after a year and a half in the 1st Squadron, 4th U.S. Cavalry (the "Quarterhorse") of the famous 1st Infantry Division, I hated to come home in the middle of the turmoil and civil unrest America was suffering. I was extremely proud of what we had done. And was thankful for the assistance my Lord and Protector, Jesus Christ, provided to my men and I during the difficult combat we experienced. Our record was unsurpassed, and I wanted to shout it out. But bragging about military successes in the middle of such civil turmoil didn't seem appropriate or even possible.

It was better to ignore the barrage of disgusting stories told by nincompoops and combat soldier wanna-bees that disparaged the loyal, selfless participation of our warriors in this unpopular war. It was impossible to understand the highly visible and vocal citizens who condemned the men and women, who through their personal bravery, unwavering loyalty and unselfish sacrifices made it possible for their protests to occur at all. I could identify no good reason why John Kerry would throw his medals over the White House fence. And look what it has gotten him. Very sad.

Not dwelling on how my own actions and those of my honorable comrades, living and dead, were being misrepresented, I, like many others, simply buried my head in the sand. There will always be regrets at not having spoken out loudly at the time. But it didn't take a rocket scientist to know that a sane voice wouldn't be heard above the annoying chatter of the civil unrest. And I knew that to compete with the excitement of burning draft cards and discarding bras was just not possible.

Many accounts of the war related drugged up young soldiers with uncontrollable mental hang-ups, quenching their insatiable satanic appetites by raping and pillaging their way across Vietnam. BULLSHIT! I never saw any of this. I'm not saying that on occasion our soldiers never did unethical acts, but I didn't hear about any serious moral infractions from the professional soldiers I knew, except for very isolated cases. I found it hard to believe that when this conduct was discovered the perpetrators weren't severely punished. Liars have sold books and movies on this sensationalism, and some have told huge whoppers for the receipt of political and financial gain.

While pursuing a college education after returning home, I relished opportunities to reason with curious young adults who had been indoctrinated with maniacal images of the American military in Vietnam. They were nearly unanimously pleased to hear a combat veteran refute their liberal professors' stories that our soldiers conducted themselves dishonorably, "reminiscent of Jengus (sp) Khan" per Mr. Kerry. They were pleased to hear that the actions of the current generation of service members compared favorably to their counterparts from former times of strife.

Then while listening to a young Vietnamese dentist, who incidentally was born in Saigon in 1970, and her dental assistant, who had worked at the Miami VA Hospital, relate highly exaggerated, and obviously untrue tales of misconduct told by veterans, likely seeking self-aggrandizement, notoriety, or a higher Post Traumatic Stress Disorder ("PTSD") VA disability rating, I wanted to puke. It was then that I broke through my self-imposed cocoon of silence.

And I had been carrying a debt to our Lord to let others know that he was with us on the battlefield, and that soldiers in future wars should not lose sight of the importance of inviting God to accompany them into battle. He will still take sides against evil, as He did so many times in Biblical history. The power of prayer should not be underestimated.

This book is written as a memoir for my comrades who lived through this period of history; for other military to see what initiative and loyalty can result in when fighting a numerically superior enemy in his back yard; and a picture of the Cavalry at work. It is also written for my family and friends who have never learned what my troopers and I experienced in that far away land. This story follows the adventures of myself, a young mustang (former enlisted) officer, through my tour in Vietnam and the remarkable actions of my Cavalry troopers.

Part 1 concludes when my normal one-year tour is over. And Part 2 resumes when I return to Vietnam for an additional, very combat intensive half year, where my troopers and I dealt the enemy crushing blows. This is when I was most effective as a Cavalry commander. Part 3 has miscellaneous matters such as trooper comments, an Autobiography,

Efficiency Ratings, etcetera.

Until now I never gave recognition to the role our Lord played in my personal success and that of my Cavalrymen. How easy it is to accept the glory and not give credit where it is due, because it may cause some lesser people to sneer. And this is the very reason I was never satisfied with my initial efforts to finish this book.

Peering Back Through the Shadows

I've tried hard to bury the Vietnam war into the deepest recesses of my mind. Like many other veterans, I was deeply hurt by the reception received from an ungrateful nation upon returning home from those steamy jungles. We experienced the cold shoulder of indifference, and the all too frequent pretensions that military service lacked any meaningful virtue.

I'll forego most of my history prior to Vietnam although much can be found scattered throughout the text or at the end of the book.

In Vietnam many grew up fast and became better men, moving through their personal "rites of passage" into manhood as seasoned warriors. But in my mind, and many others, America's honor and dignity were lost for a while. And the guilt does not 'all' fall on the shoulders of our civilian leaders. There's plenty to go around.

There are many untold stories about our combat soldiers and their leaders who honorably met and overcame the awesome challenges they faced. But they didn't receive the recognition deserved for their battlefield achievements, both in the field and later at home. Let me pause to say that non-combatant soldiers were equally slighted but were indispensable to those combing the jungles to seek out and destroy the enemy.

Napoleon said: 'give me a million miles of ribbon (awards) and I will conquer the world.' It's unfortunate that not everyone learned this lesson. When some warriors are not appropriately recognized for their achievements, while others are, it adversely affects their morale. Deep inside I know that my own awards also belong to my troopers. I could have accomplished nothing without their loyalty and professionalism on the battlefield. They were slighted by a limited awards policy, and when these valiant soldiers returned home to cursing and spitting crowds, this added insult to injury and in many cases crushed their dignity. It wasn't fair and some never were able to overcome the pain.

The truth has never been fully revealed about the courageous young Americans of that war, who for the most part were drafted fresh out of high school, and that at the bequest of their country became wrapped in surreal struggles with death. Nor, to my belief, has the truth been adequately told as to the after-effects of the intense emotions they felt before, during and after those fierce combat engagements.

They named this injury post-traumatic stress disorder (PTSD), a handy term to package all the adverse psychological effects of war (formerly combat fatigue). In the Great War (WWII) the average combat soldier served far less time on the front lines than the Vietnam soldier. In Vietnam for the combat Infantrymen it was over 260 days packed into their one-year tour, and the Cavalrymen rarely had a break. And the front lines were 360 degrees all the time. The underbelly of that war, and all wars, is the gripping fear that had to be conquered, minute after minute, hour after hour, and day by day, crawling back and forth inside, keeping the animal within poised for another scrap, which could be the unfortunate last.

This was life in and around the jungles of Vietnam, while Ole' Glory was being stomped on, shredded and burned by our fellow citizens at home. Our returning soldiers wanted just a little respect. But there was far less than that to go around. And in my eyes the feeble attempts to right that wrong over the years has been far too little, too late. That's why Vietnam veterans greet one another with a greeting: "Welcome Home."

For myself, and others, as the years slide by, the haunting memories of battlefield memorial services linger just a heartbeat away. The rancid smells, sounds, and feelings of the battlefields are ever present; as are the choking red laterite dust; the ever-present pungent smell of diesel fuel; and strong odors suspended in the air from spent cartridges and explosives. The ugly odor of tear gas, rotting flesh, and the smell of decay under beautiful, lush green, magnificent jungle forests savaged by war remain vivid in our memories. And one can never forget the memories of the loneliness of separation from friends and family, and the finding of a new, surrogate, extended family of cavalrymen in the delicate balance between life and death, well within the borders of

Hell.

Only after leaving was there time to slowly consider the never- ending struggles we experienced and the challenge to maintain our sanity. We were preoccupied, grasping at survival during long days and nights, anxiously waiting for the sharp report of a sniper's rifle, or the explosion of a rocket propelled grenade ("RPG"), or the scream of "incoming" as the enemy mortars and rockets began exploding all around - - at times followed by a mass attack by a determined, drugged-up, screaming enemy. Nor was there time on the field of battle to consider the permanent effects of the sleeplessness caused by the concussion from nearby friendly artillery canons. Or the tenseness of night-time "thunder runs" with our armored vehicles charging along enemy-controlled roads to entice our adversaries into a fight. And there was always anxiety concerning the sudden day or night missions to rescue infantrymen, artillery support bases, or friendly villages defended by the Army of the Republic of Vietnam (ARVN).

We were always hunting for an elusive, mostly invisible enemy, while controlling our shredded nerves through an odd mix of prayer, anger, and an occasional beer. We searched the enemy's spooky, dangerous tunnels and learned bits and pieces from the few prisoners that were taken. And in any spare-time the Officers and NCOs were dreaming up special survival and combat tricks and tactics, not in anyone's play book, to make the enemy less aware of what the Cavalry might do next.

The suspense and tension of the hunt made our souls come

close to screaming. It was creepy and crazy. We survived on trust in our buddies and our bosses. Everyone's survival instincts were stretched far past even unreasonable limits. This is what fighting inside the threshold of Hell was like. We cursed the little sons of bitches that stalked us, while adrenaline rushed uncontrollably throughout our bodies, and we killed and killed some more until the demons ran away or were destroyed. We were unaware that in the process we were severely harming ourselves.

But there was a whole other side to this experience. A side that helps a soldier maintain his sanity. Somehow in this awful environment, most of us found a closer relationship with God. Within the crap we experienced, it's not surprising that we would either move closer to Him or discard our beliefs in His very existence. While buried in combat, survival is the preeminent focus, and prayer comes easy. For most, I believe they got closer to their Maker. But the experiences were also so horrific that some had a wedge driven between themselves and their Creator. Yes, there is much to gain in a war - - and so much to lose.

I assure you, I never have been accused of being a Saint. But still I was looked after by my Lord and Protector, Jesus Christ, throughout my life. Whenever the chips were down, He was there to lend a hand. Mostly it was a personal thing, but in Vietnam I asked Him daily to go with us when we moved out on our missions, and when we went into battle He was there. All of this will be shown in the story about to unfold.

Some critics will site some of my tales as evidence I was an awful sinner, and I will not disagree with them at all. But I did know who to trust. I experienced His awesome mercy. My troopers trusted me, and I placed my trust in them, the support troops, our leadership, and the Lord, and everyone came through.

I readily accepted the praise and credit for the tremendous outcomes of the battles we fought and was rewarded for my supposedly "unique leadership skills". But as the years have gone by, I've felt increased guilt for quietly accepting all the credit without saying a word about asking for Divine assistance to help me command my units against enormous odds. Confession is good for the soul and it's about time to fess-up to the reasons I was successful.

Some say that "God doesn't choose sides in war." I know better. We pray, and we fight, and we pray, and we fight again and again and again. But we speak far too little about this topic. Now you will learn a little more about the softer, better side of us tough guys, at least this one. This book is about awesome struggles and missed recognitions. Our soldiers received far too little recognition and the Lord received practically none. Hopefully what I have written will paint a more complete picture.

THE CAVALRYMAN'S

RITE OF PASSAGE

PART I

THEY CHARGED THROUGH THE GATES OF HELL

Chapter 1

THE CAVALRYMAN'S UPBRINGING

My background included the wilderness and animals and many other experiences that nurtured a curiosity suitable for a military life.

Spending so much time in the fields around home gave me a comfort with and understanding of many critters, and no fear of things that were different. As a boy I would lay in the fields and make friends with wild rabbits, robins, garter snakes, an occasional field mouse, and other animals in the heat of summer and even in the snow of bitter cold Michigan winters. Creatures who became familiar were given names and would receive an occasional treat if they showed an ability to bridge their instinctual fears to become friends. This boy especially enjoyed bringing out the personality of these little buddies as we learned to enjoy each other's company. You must understand that I was the younger brother to three sisters who played girly games. And if little brother was around, his part in their games was a motivator to head for the fields.

I learned to shoot using my father's Remington heavy hex barrel 22 caliber pump action rifle, while protecting wild rabbits from predator feral cats. There seemed to be an endless supply of these pests, courtesy of my best friend Bob's mother's kindness and generosity to strays. Unfortunately, they had to pass through the killing zone in my back yard to get into the field further south of my home to do their treachery.

The cats plus the mice in the chicken coop helped me hone some very accurate marksmanship. At night, my father and I would occasionally put a light down inside of a large chicken feed barrel, and as the mice would show their heads on the opposite side while entering the barrel, we would take turns, from a distance of about 15 feet, shooting the rodents. It was great competition and created a lot of shooting confidence. And in addition to pheasant hunting as I grew older these skills were further developed by spending over a year as a marksmanship training instructor in the Marines on Okinawa.

Even my dog, Boots, part Beagle and part Cocker Spaniel, who was raised with domestic and wild rabbits from birth, had an unusual relationship with wild rabbits. Quite regularly I would see old friends or their offspring leaving the safety and warmth of his dog house early in the morning to hop back to their field habitat. That didn't stop the dog from being a good hunter when taken away from the neighborhood, but no cat could have his friends or their bunnies for lunch if he could prevent it.

And the rabbits had nothing on me, as when I was a small boy of three or four years old, I was also found sleeping in the doghouse with an earlier friend - ole' Duke. Once when failing to respond to my father's call for supper, ***"Come'n Johnny,"*** that could be heard a couple city blocks away, the family was forming a search party to find me, when someone wondered why Duke was in his house in the middle of the afternoon. They found me sound asleep with my head on the dog, and the concern for my safety turned into laughter that woke me up. I was scolded because this was an all too frequent occurrence and I was told to stay out of the dog's house. No one worried about my communing with nature, but my mother was aggravated, as any other mom would be, by the worms, polliwogs, frogs or neat, interesting bugs that were often found when her hand inspected my trouser pockets at wash time.

But nature was only a piece of this boy's beginnings. With a father who was a superb maintenance man that had graduated from the Henry Ford Trade School during the depression, as his only son I grew up holding the light, while lying in the snow under the family car, during maintenance sessions, and I was involved in every maintenance procedure my father performed at home. Being the only son created a proficiency at repairing cars long before I was old enough to get an auto driver's license at the age of sixteen, a year before joining the Marines.

He always took the time to explain how what he was working on functioned. Dad worked at the Bundy Tubing Manufacturing Company in Warren, Michigan, just over the fence behind our home. In the evenings I listened dutifully to recaps of the maintenance problems he solved at the factory that day.

Dad never believed in letting anyone repair anything he owned, as past experiences had only brought costly disappointments. Perhaps it was also a pride thing. Or maybe he was just being too picky of other people's work. But it created a great opportunity for a boy to grow up learning how to figure things out for himself. By eight I could tear apart the lawn mower, make a reasonable analysis of its problems and do the repairs properly. And this growing mechanical aptitude resulted in many of the neighborhood friends bringing their bikes and other toys to our home for a dependable repair job, as opposed to bringing them to their own fathers.

At eleven I had a 280 customer Detroit News paper route and bought a Crusaire motor scooter from Sears & Roebuck to make the deliveries less difficult. This was my first credit account with a loan of $311, which made me very proud. Of course, my parents kept the card in their possession so I wouldn't learn any bad habits, and especially since they were the co-signers. I didn't get much chance to use my Crusaire for other than work as it was necessary to share in the three-year chore of helping my father build the dream home he had planned for many years, but which was delayed for about eleven years after a burst appendix depleted his savings on medical bills. Incidentally, it only cost $11,000 to build this 3-bedroom home with radiant heat in the ceiling.

Once the project started, my father began to suffer badly from asthma and emphysema, and I regularly found myself acting the part of an adult builder as his health progressively sapped his strength, but not his determination to finish the homestead. I lived in this home after its completion for a little over three years before going into the Marines. It was an awful experience to see my father suffer from an addiction to Chesterfield cigarettes and to ultimately die from emphysema at the young age of fifty-seven, four months after I returned from Vietnam. My father's demise was the most devastating injury I ever experienced, but there was some consolation in being there to hold his hands and receive a final squeeze of recognition as his last statement on earth.

As a child I loved wild places filled with interesting plants and creatures of never-ending varieties, but I knew things would change in the jungle. That's where I would experience really dangerous animals - - humans.

Chapter 2

AM I SMART ENOUGH FOR THIS?

Nobody knew of my lack of a formal education. I hid it well, but not from myself. I was fortunate to be a fast learner, and by exceeding normal expectations, the subject never came up. But I felt it deep inside.

I grew up strong and straight, but after quitting school to join the Marines this major educational deficiency dogged my self-esteem. I had a self-inflicted shortcoming of lacking a twelve-year formal education that caused a bit of an inferiority complex that I worked hard to keep hidden. My education had been best when it was hands-on, and whenever this occurred no one could do any better. Academic pursuits kept me bored, and boredom and a bit of wander lust was primarily what caused me to drop out of school. With my father's very reluctant blessing I entered the Marine Corps just after my seventeenth birthday. Obtaining a High School GED before coming home from the Marines was the fulfillment of a promise made to my father at the time of enlistment, but that was the extent of my education.

After five years in the Marines I worked in a security factory that was making the Lance Missile System and the long hours, seven days a week created the forecast that I wouldn't see daylight for several months with the short days of winter coming on. This was unacceptable. My thinking was to become a Marine Corps officer, but I needed to have a college degree for that. The Army was a good choice, as the recruiter said they would send me to obtain a college degree if I did a good job as an officer in Vietnam. And my education was adequate to go to the Officer school (OCS).

Although I obtained a GED and was later graduated by my hometown High School, having been a high school dropout and having no college was a badge of shame that I carried just below the surface. This continued to be a stain on my dignity even after I became an Army officer. The officers I was stationed with were college graduates and I frequently felt like the odd man out as they discussed their campus exploits.

I hoped no one would notice any deficiency in my education by constantly busting my ass to do better than other junior officers. This became my only acceptable level of performance, and it worked well to keep any potential critics in line. It was also a cattle prod when I tired, and I always had a reservoir of strength when others weakened. But I really had no idea of this benefit until years later when efficiency ratings showed a favorable pattern. But it made me shy away from many well-educated officers, and pulled me closer to my enlisted troopers, who didn't care about my education level, only my ability to be a good and fair leader.

The Orient had provided an unconventional education all its own. Vietnam was not my first time in the Far East. I knew the oriental people quite well, having served on Okinawa as a Marine, having taken a beautiful bride from Shuri, and making close friends with people from the nearby island of Hama-Higa, who would taxi my SCUBA diving club to some of the most gorgeous reefs on earth. A great memory was being one of the founders of the Camp Hansen Hydronaughts diving club and being its first Chief SCUBA Diving Instructor. Teachers of any kind were highly respected by the oriental people, which as a young Marine NCO, I enjoyed a lot. As a marksmanship instructor as well, this Jar Head (Marine) enjoyed a special teacher status among the island folk. But lacking a formal education troubled me, despite my different kind of education that could prove helpful in any war.

Westerners often seemed to not understand the oriental ways, but I had learned to feel comfortable with the people from this part of the world, and this was clearly a plus. My own family lineage was quite diverse including Scotch, Irish, Dutch, French, Belgian, and German. This all contributed to growing up with a good attitude, tolerance and appreciation of people from other cultures. I knew this would help.

Unlike the psychological discomfort I felt for a while when first landing on Okinawa at eighteen years old, I had no trepidation of the Vietnamese people, realizing fully well that many could have the face of a friend in the light of day, but quite the opposite after the sun set or when out in the jungle. I would take it as it came, treating everyone as a friend, while keeping a healthy apprehension of the possible other side of the coin.

I knew of the enemy's lack of concern for the sanctity of human life. A more philosophical view was held by many oriental warriors. The enemy was normally owned body, mind, and spirit by their government and totally devoted to ideas drilled into their heads from birth that we couldn't understand. Many were unable to balance these teachings against any alternative thoughts, since few were exposed to Western religious teachings. This was a mind-set that could never be fully understood by Westerners, and it created a formidable opponent.

The power of these ideas of duty and loyalty fostered by many years of absolute control and indoctrination made our enemy able to attack with wanton abandon into certain death. That selfless nonconcern for self-preservation was a match for many American military units and something to be taken seriously. And this Lieutenant would not make light of it.

I had an excellent enlisted military education in the Marine Corps learning how to destroy armored vehicles and fortified positions, followed by joining the Army and becoming a tank commander. Would my skin instinctively begin to crawl when approaching potential enemy killing zones, so I could timely alert my troops? I didn't know how long it would take to tune up many of these skills I had learned over the years. My education was unique and different from my fellow officers and hopefully I could quickly hone my survival instincts before any of my men were killed.

Perhaps the most valuable part of my education was a strong faith in

God that I acquired from my dear mother and a formal education in the Catholic school in grades 1 to 6. I knew He would be with me through thick and thin if I did my part and relied on Him for the rest of the problems we faced. This knowledge of the Lord made me confident that He would help when what I learned in the military schools wasn't enough. I had this hope and trust going into Vietnam.

On the plane I was facing the insecurities felt over the past year about whether I would be able to successfully lead men in combat. Preparing for war was a series of adventures and educational experiences, and the promise to myself to become an effective American warrior and leader of warriors was now at hand. The school of hard-knocks would have to do. I prayed it would.

[This is a good place to break from our story and revisit my 1ˢᵗ year as an officer. I had wonderful new adventures and several miserable training injuries during that period. I will also include a chapter on the help I could always depend on and my leadership growth and development. This, and some other background matters will help the reader to understand me better as my adventure unfolds.]

Chapter 3

MY YEAR BEFORE VIETNAM

After becoming an Officer I went to Jump School at Fort Benning, Georgia. The training was a lot of running and pre-parachuting exercises. After the training at OCS I didn't find this difficult and enjoyed floating through the air - - until I got to the ground on my 4th jump.

Bad Landing

I was doing great until I got to the second to last, qualifying jump and my foot found a hole to land in. Yes, I broke my ankle. After a couple weeks at home I went to Ft Knox.

Tank Trap

During the Armor Officer Basic Course, at Fort Knox, KY I had my fill of training when the tank I was commanding dropped into a tank trap the same dimensions as the tank, causing my loss of footing and slamming my face into the front of the cupola at over 40 miles per hour. With a healing ankle, fresh out of its cast, and now with a broken nose, accompanied by two black eyes, I was a mess. My poor parents, who were visiting me at the time, wondered what the future held for their son if he got this banged up during training.

Still healing from this accident, I was glad to arrive at the 2nd Squadron, 17th Cavalry Regiment of the 101st Airborne Division at Fort Campbell, Kentucky on the Tennessee border. Embarrassed at being a leg (non-airborne) officer in a gung-ho airborne division, finishing airborne school and obtaining those silver wings was my first priority.

The pain I lived with in my ankle didn't make this easy. But completing my jumps and earning the Silver Wings decoration for my uniform was thrilling. It was reminiscent of my Marine Corps promotion to Private First Class. I just knew everyone was admiring this addition to my uniform. I know I was. With all the trouble I went through to earn those wings, I felt like I stood out among about 10,000 other soldiers in the 101st Airborne Division, and everyone was surely watching.

Now as the Support Platoon Leader in the Squadron S-4, I learned about the Squadron's supply operations, and managed the Motor Pool and the assigned Squadron mechanics. And I found myself involved with a myriad of jobs including vehicle recovery during training maneuvers. I loved that part of the job.

My boss, Squadron S-4 Captain Ed Rose, quickly realized that my lack of a formal education was accompanied by an inability to write well. It was difficult, but I appreciated all the efforts he took to motivate me in this regard.

Being an officer in a support position, I also received an assortment of assignments as a Squadron legal counsel, first as a Defense Counsel. And then, because of the string of successes at this duty, I was elevated to Trial Counsel where, working just as hard on these duties, I produced equally good results. The problem as I saw it was that good men's futures depended on amateurs defending them, and the chain of command (the lieutenant's bosses) would try to unduly influence the integrity of the officers involved.

Like all Airborne troopers, I got a thrill out of jumping from "perfectly good airplanes." That couldn't ever be adequately explained. With about a dozen jumps from C130s and C141s, I looked forward to each chance to float over the earth under the T10 parachute like an eagle searching out the beauty of God's creation, while descending from the usual 1,200 feet used for training jumps. The landings were frequently rough, but I couldn't get enough of the majestic feeling during the descent once the parachute opened.

After eleven months, as a reward for having done a good job in the Squadron, I was sent to the Jumpmaster School just prior to leaving for the Panama Canal Zone on my way to Vietnam. Thank goodness for a thirty day leave at home, which gave me a chance to recover from an injured back I received on the last jump where I experienced watching my parachute deploy as I flipped through the risers to snap like the end of a bull whip as the parachute fully deployed.

Another Bad Landing

The final qualifying exercise was a night jump. It was night on the ground, but at 1,200 feet it was still twilight. This jump was also an equipment jump with a 90-pound PAE bag that looked a lot like an over-sized duffle bag. The bag was fastened to the harness and it was important to kick it out away from the plane as you departed the aircraft. I did that, but I kicked a little too hard. So, as a result I found myself looking back at the plane as the parachute deployed. Then as the chute popped open, I was snapped into the feet down position with an extremely sharp pain in the small of my back, which was so excruciating as to temporarily make it impossible to do anything except hang at the end of the risers while descending into the darkness below.

Surprisingly, in the dusk I could still make out some features on the ground, but I was moving too fast laterally to land safely. So, like I was trained, I started climbing the riser into the wind up toward the silk of the chute to slow my lateral movement. Suddenly I realized that the risers were reversed and as a result I was in trouble. I was sailing much faster over the rapidly approaching landscape. Quickly I released the riser and began to climb the opposite one hoping to brake the lateral movement. This caused me to oscillate to where the canopy was going to hit the ground before I did. Being about 40 feet or less above the surface, I released the PAE bag, which had a 40-foot lanyard. As the bag struck the ground it was only moments before the parachute also reached the surface.

I found myself suspended between the parachute and the PAE bag and hitting the ground in what could be called anything but a professional parachute landing. Using both hands I grabbed the quick release and disconnected a riser from the harness as rapidly as possible, but not until I had been roughly bounced along the surface at a high rate of speed. Coming to a halt, still tethered between the collapsed parachute and the bag at the end of the 40 feet of rope, I lay motionless as the pain gradually receded. Slowly I stood up and gathered the parachute just in time for a truck to stop by my position to assist. The pain in my back returned at every lifting event and throbbed mercilessly for the next few weeks. It seemed like with my propensity for injuring myself, I wasn't going to last much longer.

Then after a few weeks at home I left for Fort Sherman and The School of the Americas in the Panama Canal Zone. The training there was great. As for food, the students dined on specially prepared insects, snakes, sharks and other unusual delicacies.

Tunnel Ants

In the Jungle I slept in a hammock while a talented hoard of tiny ants erected a mud tube from the tree to my hammock's mosquito netting. They chewed a small hole through the net and bit the hell out of me while I slept, leaving itchy welts that lasted over three months.

Bamboo Fire Ants

Then there were the large bamboo plants, some which would render drinkable water, that did not quench your thirst because they lacked any mineral content, and an almost identical plant which exploded with its contents of red fire ants when smacked with a machete. You guessed it, I chose the wrong one.

I would rather forget some of these experiences, as I did find the training very interesting, especially the rappelling about 100 feet down the face of a waterfall, and an escape and evasion exercise where I was almost killed.

Chapter 4

ESCAPE AND EVASION

It started in a pretend POW Camp. Provided with a live white rabbit and a handful of rice, several in our group were too squeamish to prepare a meal. They appeared surprised that I had no problem killing, skinning and gutting the rabbit by hand. I broke it up into some rice being boiled in a large coffee can over an open fire. It was not pretty, but a nourishing meal, nonetheless. After gobbling down this gourmet lunch, the students were allowed to escape at around 0900.

Two other escapees and I linked up and decided to avoid the aggressors by leaving the training area. The aggressors would pursue the bulk of seemingly helpless POWs within this area. We had been told to stay within these boundaries because of extreme hazards. We interpreted this as a signal as to where the aggressors would be confined. Therefore, this was not where we wanted to be.

The Huge Mean-Ass Wasp

After entering the forbidden zone for about a half hour I stepped over a fallen tree next to a "Black-Palm" covered with needles that were difficult to remove from your flesh once you were pricked by them and they broke. I was being careful as I stepped over the Palm, but careful didn't appear good enough. With a sudden sharp shoulder pain, I thought I was stuck by one of the needles from the palm. Instinctively grabbing my left upper arm, I grasped a wasp larger than my little finger who was jabbing his stinger through the thick 101st Airborne Division, Screaming Eagle patch sewed to my left shirt sleeve. There were nine stings in all before the insect was thrown off. A sharp electrical pain shot from my shoulder to my finger-tips, back up my arm and across my chest in rapid pulsing sensations, leaving my arm totally paralyzed with no feeling at all. It just hung lifeless at my side. I knew I was in trouble.

With an estimate of over ten hours left before we would arrive at the trucks waiting at the far end of the training area, we chose to continue with our evasion plan in-spite of the injury. To backtrack into the training area had no guarantees of getting to the trucks any sooner. It was demoralizing envisioning myself in a hospital bed and with my career at an end. It was an awful depressing feeling. It was rough terrain and it was necessary to negotiate all the reasons why we were told not to go this way. Then came the meeting with fate. These don't happen very often in life and they don't reveal themselves in advance so that prevention or preparations can be made.

We found ourselves overlooking a sheer thirty to forty-foot cliff directly above a ten-foot wide running stream with a black volcanic bottom. Each of us had a length of rope that appeared long enough so we spread out to do hasty rappels. My two partners went around the curve to find suitable spots to go over the cliff. Failing to appropriately determine the risk of doing a one-armed rappel placed me in serious danger. I foresaw no problem using just one arm if I used my right hand as the anchor and kept my left side up hill with the rope going across my back and under my left armpit. **Wrong!**

The Fall

As I went over the edge, all went well for a few feet until my right foot slipped a little on a rock and I learned the hard way why two hands were absolutely required. Suddenly I was spinning and tumbling uncontrollably through the air, ass over tea kettle toward a rough landing on the hard, volcanic stream bed.

Though the air was heavy with the jungle humidity, I instantly envisioned the water being ice cold as it slid effortlessly across the lava bed and my mangled body. And it was only about six to eight inches deep, so I might be dead.

Sometime, however, during the prehistoric creation of this lava flow, God decided to put three roughly five-foot deep holes about 2 feet in diameter right in the middle of the stream, and one was right in my flight path. It was more than luck that I landed feet first, smack dab in the middle of the center hole. As I went down through the cold water, I landed feet first on a fine gravel bottom.

The hole was just deep enough for the water to cushion my fall, just wide enough to fit my shoulders inside, and the water was just shallow enough to allow me to stand on my tip toes and breath. I tried to grab the edge of this lava hole only to learn that it was razor sharp. Untold centuries of running water made the wall slightly wider below the surface and created a razor-sharp edge that made it impossible to get out of the hole without serious injury, even if I had the use of both arms.

I was very happy to see my partners running to my assistance. They were shocked as they scrambled around the bend in the stream and approached my water hole to render assistance. They were dazzled to not find me in an expected heap of broken body parts after the loud "AWE SHIT" they heard while I was falling. As they hoisted me to the surface, and for the rest of the day, there was a lot of talk about my being the luckiest man in the world, but I knew better, not why, just better.

Finally, after several more hours of persistent hard hiking through the jungle, the trucks came into view. And just as suddenly as my arm became paralyzed, with one sharp snap of electrical pain from my shoulder to my finger-tips, the paralysis of my crippled left arm and the pain was gone. Now how did that wasp know to attack me so viciously to set up the event at that stream?

Chapter 5

YES, I BELIEVE IN MIRACLES

Mysteries and miracles, I believe in them. It clearly has taken some extra help to keep me in one piece, and there was no doubt in my mind when I landed in that hole in the river bed that I had a full-time guardian angel. Perhaps more than one was required for that caper. And it caused me to be grateful and prayerful. I did things impulsively at times, without proper concern for my own welfare, and receiving unexpected help to survive when death came knocking was not a complete surprise. It also was like receiving a wake-up call when I got a bit too cocky. My occasional bawdy conduct prevented me from being known as a religious person, but for some unknown reason I could always count on some special help when it was needed. This was the third miracle I had experienced, reinforcing my knowledge of being looked after.

The first was at Crystal Pool in Detroit when I was an eleven-year old non-swimmer. I drowned and resigned myself to death. I remember watching the turquoise six-inch square tiles on the pool's wall until the air in my lungs was exchanged for water. Time stopped, but for how long I don't know. Eventually I saw a white cloaked arm reach down to my lifeless body to grasp my left shoulder. Then all consciousness was gone until I awoke while receiving Artificial Respiration or CPR face down over a log at the outer edge of the pool deck, while water gushed from my mouth and nose. I recognized the special help I had received. I looked around for someone wearing white clothing with long flowing sleeves, but no one fit that description.

The second miracle was when I was alone and absolutely lost at night in the snow, during an Operational Readiness Test in Germany. I had reached total mental despair, pondering a map that no longer meant anything, and a compass that was of no further assistance. Dead-reckoning, which was something that heretofore came naturally, was impossible on this plateau of white snow with vague tree lines in the distance no matter where I looked. And the sky was overcast with the moon and stars being absent, which added to the impossibility for me to navigate.

While snowflakes sprinkled the landscape, I felt chilled to the bone in-spite of my winter uniform. My confidence steadily drained away until it was gone, all gone, and I felt so very alone. I saw my reputation as an excellent diviner of location dissolve. And having the success of an important part of the Battalion's operational readiness test depending on my abilities, I took this very seriously. I had to get the information as to the whereabouts of the enemy's camp back to the Battalion's field headquarters by 2:00 AM. Now I saw my career and prospects at being selected to go to the officer's candidate school sliding out of reach.

Then, suddenly, at my lowest mental state, a place where I had never been before, dark with despair, a prayer formed on my lips pleading for help from Jesus. From deep in this despair, came a surge of energy like lightning that sprang through me shocking my sensibilities.

Everything suddenly became abundantly clear. Where I had been to the lowest of low, I was suddenly at the highest of high. The map and compass were no longer necessary. I, former Marine Sergeant Conley, with about 5 months in the Army, and 4 months in Germany, knew exactly where I was and where I was going. I instinctively and confidently struck out across the snow, without the use of map or compass, and within 45 minutes, and just in the nick of time, with only a couple minutes to spare, I brought the information concerning the enemy's camp to the Battalion Commander, Lieutenant Colonel (LTC) Fox. And with complete satisfaction, not even feeling the sub-zero temperatures, my spirit cared only to extend my gratitude to my Lord for His kindness. This was not my doing. I was helpless and was helped. This was as unexplainable as the hole in the lava riverbed being directly in my flight path.

Chapter 6

REFLECTIONS ON LEADERSHIP

Leadership had always been second nature; that is ever since I got my nose broken trying to get a fellow junior Marine on a troop ship headed for Okinawa to obey one of my orders. I was 18 years old and this happened shortly after I became a Non-Commissioned Officer (NCO), Corporal E-4. The lesson was a right fist and then a left to my nose in rapid succession. After the subordinate gave the first punches, I took him down and we fought on the deck of the USS Princeton's birthing compartment.

It was no consolation that this subordinate had to spend time in the ship's sick bay with a couple hurt ribs, while everyone else went ashore in Hawaii, and I found myself walking around Honolulu with two fresh shiners. I looked like a Racoon. Following this embarrassment, I started watching how other NCOs went about getting the willing obedience of their men. It was over two years before I had the opportunity to attend the Marine Corps NCO Academy at the Recruit Depot in San Diego to learn some finer points of leadership, about a year after being promoted to Sergeant, but by then I had pretty much learned the ropes and developed a leadership style that worked well for me.

And after attending the Army NCO School in Germany and Infantry OCS in Georgia my leadership style still favored the "persuasive" approach whenever possible, however no one doubted that when I turned "authoritative," most of the discussion was over.

But what was most troubling was the nagging question deep inside, *'Am I truly ready to shoulder such tremendous responsibilities when the chips are down, when faced with mass attacks or other encounters with the enemy?"* It ate at my sensibilities at every idle moment and had occupied a corner of my mind for a long time.

I saw no reason to fear the jungle, only the enemy in it. This was the third jungle for this soldier. Having trained in the tropical undergrowth of Okinawa as a Marine Corps Sergeant and at the Jungle Warfare School in the Panama Canal Zone, made me familiar with biting and stinging creatures and stinking, decaying vegetation. For whatever it meant, I had been designated a Jungle Expert in Panama, though I would refuse to wear that very attractive shirt-pocket patch until these skills were proven to the enemy who lived in these jungles from birth. And it was obvious that this would be a tough row to hoe.

Chapter 7

THE TROUBLED FLIGHT

Some advice was provided by my brother in law, Larry Summerfield, a Korean War Veteran, who said _"John, you will be all right if you survive the first shot fired at you in anger."_ This comment would prove to be spot-on, but at that moment, in that plane, nothing settled the vultures flipping around in my stomach, and I found myself counting down the hours until we would arrive - - and praying for strength and guidance.

With the life experiences already encountered, I felt that survival by myself in the jungles just about anywhere would be no problem. But this was different. Now there were young men to lead in combat. Training was over - almost eight years of it. _'Will the soldiers in my unit be well trained?' 'Who were they?' 'What kind of unit will I be in?'_ Being trained in infantry, anti-tanks, armor, and airborne units made the possibilities quite broad. _'Were any of the rumors true as to drug use by the troops, and even the officers?'_ I was too busy to consider that during training, but now I was clearly troubled. _'How would I respond to that first round fired in my direction?'_ And the questions went on and on and on.

Getting to Vietnam was an agonizing trip. The long flight across the Pacific Ocean, though not my first, was the most somber, and many anxious thoughts haunted every one of those 19 hours. Others on the flight seemed to share this bewilderment, or perhaps the anticipation of heading for a war zone from where they may not return home alive. With the belief they had the best training possible, there was still the nagging question as to whether they would be up to the task ahead. I tried to sleep, but this wasn't possible.

Chapter 8

No One Forgets Their Arrival in a Combat Zone

After a brief refueling stop at Clark Air Force Base in the Philippines, the plane surged on to Saigon. All noise being made by the passengers was suspended as we approached our destination. The *"fasten your seat belt"* signs were turned on by the pilot, followed a couple minutes later by a hydraulic squealing noise and a thudding of the wheels locking into place for landing. After a brief announcement of encouragement by the pilot, the charter Pan Am flight roared onto the tarmac, with wheels screeching, while the pilot pulled hard on its flaps and braked toward a stop. There was a strong rush of air with the plane giving its maximum stopping effort. The seatbelt strained against my waist as the bird came to a hurried halt at the Tan Son Nuit Air Force Base in Saigon. The pilot announced: *"Welcome to Vietnam"*.

As the door swung open the initial blast of pre-monsoon heat was breathtaking, causing everyone to gasp as it seared their lungs. After disembarking down a stairway that had been rolled up to the plane, the new combatants were hustled quickly into a building heavily surrounded by several rows of sandbags. Sandbags were everywhere. So were guns and people with guns. There were helicopters inside of protected positions enclosed on three sides by heavy pieces of corrugated metal intended for building airstrips and sandbags stacked up six to eight feet high.

There were aircraft of all kinds taking off and landing, loading and unloading military equipment and supplies, and happy soldiers heading home, who playfully teased the newcomers, saying anything from *"365 and a wake-up"* to "your all dead men". In the apparent chaos it seemed like everyone knew what they were doing. The thought struck, *'Will I be leaving this place in good health a year from now, or in one of those body bags being unloaded from a nearby C-130 aircraft.'* It was hot - stifling hot. Hot as Hell, and awfully humid. It took my breath away. *'Shit this is like an oven. Will I ever enjoy air conditioning again?'*

Inside the in-processing building I was surprised to get a choice of being assigned to the 101st Airborne Brigade, since my former assignment was in the Cavalry of the 101st Airborne Division or being assigned to the Cavalry Squadron of the 1st Infantry Division as an Armor Cavalry Platoon Leader. I thought I was headed for the 101st Airborne Brigade because of my former assignment, but my diverse experiences were for the first time resulting in a choice that was never anticipated. It was either the Cavalry of the 101st Brigade or the 1st Infantry Division. I understood what going to the Airborne Brigade would mean - - jump pay and prestige. There was also a lot of esprit in the 101st, but in this environment it was essentially an infantry unit with a cavalry mission. The notion of having heavy steel, good communications and big guns all around for the next year, with great mobility was more than appealing. And Mama didn't raise any fools. Choosing the Armored Cavalry assignment with the 1st Infantry Division was my first decision in Vietnam, and it would prove to be a brilliant one.

After the basic formalities of being issued jungle fatigue uniforms and a quick newcomers-briefing, the men assigned to the Quarterhorse (1st Squadron, 4th Cavalry, 1st Infantry Division) were put on a truck heading north with no idea how far they were going or how much risk existed in getting there. The 3/4-ton truck with a canvas rear covering over ten new troopers for cargo was moving fast and the driver recklessly swerved in and out of traffic. A look around the countryside revealed that I was indeed once again in the Far East. Everything was green. And there were assorted ferns and palm trees everywhere. There were folks wearing pointed straw hats and what looked like black or white silk pajamas working hard in the rice paddies and fields. Water buffalo were being used for most of the heavy lifting, while some people carried enormous loads on their backs. This display of strength would put many soldiers to shame. The stands of jungle were as impressive as others where I'd trained. These jungles were not for training though, or for enjoyment. This was for hiding the enemy. This was for killing.

The people looked smaller and frailer than those on Okinawa, but that was not a notion to foster for long. Initially it was impossible not to feel the same pangs of distrust experienced when first arriving in the Orient nearly a decade earlier. That would pass, but I wondered just how one could know who was friendly and who was not. *'This isn't going to be easy at all.' 'Crap. . . this is going to be damned tough.'*

There were many bikes, and Lambreta three wheeled motor scooter taxis, and many happily playing children in every small town. And then, somewhere north of Saigon, it happened.

We were passing the **Welcoming Committee.** Two smiling young maidens 18 to 20 years old in an open field pulled up their shirts to flash us new arrivals. They were braless and had beautiful, shapely breasts, which they were clearly very proud of. I was completely unprepared for this, and unfortunately had no beads to throw. I may have even blushed. They didn't blush. They were pretty, young women, and they had the ability to quickly overcome any language barrier. Everyone on that truck was impressed, and the crush to the rear for a good look nearly threw all the ogling passengers tumbling onto the dusty, rutted road. The women showed no fear, and despite our brashness they had a strange air of tenderness. Wherever lovely women appear in this world, a certain tenderness is appreciated, even if it is at times deceitful or treacherous. Any apprehensions we might have had, eased off with the power of a smile from this welcoming committee.

The truck tossed and turned and bounced in all directions for nearly three quarters of an hour and then after such a violent ride it suddenly came to a halt at a Quonset Hut that housed the 1st Squadron, 4th Cavalry's Headquarters in the Phu Loi basecamp about eleven miles north of Saigon as the crow flies. Next to the Quonset Hut was what appeared to be an organized, heavily sand bagged structure with a small rectangular sign by the entrance that read *"TOC"* (Tactical Operations Center).

Chapter 9

WELCOME TO HELL!!
FEBRUARY 7, 1967

After reporting in to the Squadron S-1, Administration office, I was assigned to Bravo ("B") Troop. Someone was told to lead me to the Troop area and my sleeping quarters (hooch) that wouldn't be seen by me again for about five months. During my trek between buildings toward "B" Troop, I saw more hooches, and smoky, stinking barrels (55-gallon drums cut in half) of shit behind outhouses, that were being soaked with diesel fuel and burned. I arrived at "B" Troop and met the Troop Executive Officer (XO), 1st Lieutenant Tom Brandon (Bravo 5). After dropping the bags off I followed the same trail back to the Officer's Mess/Club with the XO, which was just across a dirt street from the Squadron Headquarters, to have dinner and meet fellow officers that were in the basecamp.

On the way it was great meeting Sergeant (SGT) Nealey who had been stationed with me as a fellow NCO in Crailsheim, Germany a couple years earlier. Crailsheim was a former WWII German prisoner of war camp that was converted into an American Post that housed two Armor Battalions. It was reassuring to know that SGT Nealey was the Communications NCO for "B" Troop, in charge of keeping the Troop's radios working properly. Knowing SGT Nealey's abilities from Germany was comforting, and as for the three primary functions of the Armored Cavalry, to shoot, move and communicate, Communications, the life blood of this armored cavalry unit, could not be in more capable hands. Without good radios the risks would be overwhelming for an armor unit.

As it turned out SGT Nealey took a special interest in the Second Platoon, and in April he caused the assignment of a budding radio repairman, still a jewel in the rough, Private First Class (PFC) Fred Currier to the platoon. Though Currier didn't know much about radios at the time, he had a good head on his shoulders and could be depended on to figure communications problems out in a hurry. This was a very significant favor, and although I never saw SGT Nealey again after the 1st week of April, this friendly gesture was never to be forgotten.

It was getting late, so we grabbed a bite in the Officer's Mess for starters, then had too many strong mixed drinks in a row, made by a very capable Club Officer, Warrant Officer (W-4) Krusac, who didn't spare the booze. Krusac was also the Squadron Maintenance Officer and did a terrific job there as well. All the while I was meeting the officers of the Squadron Headquarters, those from Charley ("C") Troop that were in from the field, and from Delta ("D") Troop (Air), which provided direct helicopter close air, reconnaissance and firepower support, etcetera, to the line troops and other elements of the Division, as well as having the LRRP (Long Range Reconnaissance Patrol). The "B" Troop Commander was not there at the time and I didn't meet him until April.

The enemy gave his special welcome. I took it personal that he felt it necessary to introduce himself at this time. Mortar rounds started exploding all around the base camp, and Tom scrambled back to the Bravo Troop area with this new Platoon Leader in tow. By this time, it had become dark and I felt like a blind man being led by a race horse, tripping and stumbling in the pitch-black darkness back past the smelly outhouses, through a deep ditch, between many buildings that had become nothing but vague shadows, and to the Troop arms room where my 45-caliber pistol and holster were issued. I quickly moved toward the Second Platoon which was across the muddy street, parked side by side in even deeper mud. It's amazing how quickly you can sober up from all those strong drinks.

While at the Officers Club I had been told that the 2nd Platoon's Platoon Sergeant, Sergeant First Class (SFC) John L. Coker, was

highly skilled and had been the Platoon Leader for several months. I
knew from prior experiences that this had
to be more than a mere coincidence and
gave a moment of prayerful thanks. With a
choice to be an Armored Cavalry Platoon
Leader and ride into battle, finding an old
friend as the Troop's Commo NCO, and
then having a top-notch Platoon Sergeant
made me feel truly blessed - - so far. But
what would happen next? In the pitch-
black night and the deep mud, I had no idea
what was about to happen.

The Squadron Headquarters had a mission
for the Second Platoon to head for the
countryside where they thought the mortar
rounds were coming from. I hadn't met

SFC John L. Coker

anyone in the Platoon at that point, but the men all seemed to be
expecting me and displayed a positive and polite attitude to their new
Platoon Leader. Perhaps SGT Nealey had built up my image a little
during the past few hours as I felt none of the animosity frequently
experienced by newly arriving, green Second Lieutenants. I found
myself trudging into the blackness toward the sound of armored
vehicles revving up. Stumbling across the street, with no light
whatsoever and not a star in the sky to help, it was obvious by the
scurrying shadows and the racket being made that the troopers knew
exactly what they were up to.

The Platoon consisted of 3 M48A3 Tanks and 7 ACAVS (Armored
Cavalry Assault Vehicles - M113s converted for combat) Once by the
tanks and ACAVs, I called out, *"Point me to Sergeant Coker's track."*
After a few points and nudges, I met my best friend for the next several
months. Being new but not stupid, my instructions were, *'Sergeant
Coker, you'll keep running the Platoon until I figure out what the
Hell's going on, and don't ever be shy about giving advice at any time
in the future. I don't want to do anything stupid that gets any of our
men killed.'* From all appearances Sergeant Coker appreciated that this

new Lieutenant was going to be a team player from the start instead of one of those know-it-alls, with an ego bigger than their brain or experience, which often got someone killed before they learned the lay of the land and tricks of the trade.

When I found my ACAV, B-26, I immediately went to work figuring out the commo (communication) system and got my CVC helmet on my head just in time to be told to move the Platoon out. SFC Coker, on the B-20 ACAV, who also had an auxiliary radio receiver and the ability to switch readily between the higher command's frequency and the platoon frequency, was quick to respond with a *"Roger"*. And the Platoon responded with precision into the darkness as he said *"25 ("B-25 Tank"), move out."* I sat down on a couple cases of C-rations that were stacked up and tied down on the left rear corner of the ACAV, and we were on our way.

I felt a sense of bewilderment at that point. This new life was unfolding a bit too fast and not at all as I would have anticipated. Thankfully those drinks had not made me overly groggy. Struggling with the map and with the help of the M-60 machine gunner, and a red lens flashlight, I had things somewhat sorted out about the time we arrived at the mortar firing site a couple kilometers east of the Phu Loi basecamp.

The site had been abandoned and the threat was gone, so the Platoon was ordered to stay there the rest of the night. We formed a tight perimeter and two LPs (Listening Posts) were placed in the direction of the jungle less than a couple hundred feet to the north of our position.

There was a little moon-light so I took the opportunity to cautiously move around to meet the track commanders and many of the troopers before getting any rest. I was concerned that visiting the Officer's Club for drinks before meeting my men and becoming familiar with the Platoon's equipment could have placed me in a precarious position had a battle developed. At that time no one had any idea where we were headed at day-break so I spent the rest of the night becoming familiar with my Command Track and its maps and equipment, meeting the troopers, and even getting a little rest.

My decisions and training had brought me into this war zone. I was now the Platoon Leader of a combat unit, and I was beginning an adventure that would become a monumental influence throughout my entire life. A life, where the horrors of the battlefield had once been a romantic story. But it was being replaced by the survival of the fittest, at least for the next year. My ability to become the fittest would soon be tested - - daily.

I got lucky. My track commanders were professional and proficient NCOs and my troopers were well trained. I was able to assume command of my platoon feeling confident that they were ready to fight. And then we headed north, deeper into Hell.

Chapter 10

MOVING INTO THE DEVIL'S LAIR
FEBRUARY 8, 1967

First thing in the morning, before sunrise, with less than 24 hours in country, we were directed to secure a convoy headed north up QL-13 (Thunder Road) with the lead elements of the Division, proceeding into the Junction City II campaign, starting along the Cambodian border near what was called the Fish Hook (not to be confused with the Parrots Beak) and sweeping south. The operation was to place a squeeze on the 9th Viet Cong Division that controlled the jungle and rubber plantations on the west side of the 1st Infantry Division's Area of Operations (AO) and the east side of the adjacent 25th Infantry Division's AO. The north end of this operation butted against Cambodia about 100 kilometers north of Saigon.

Our Platoon joined the convoy where the road going north out of the Di An basecamp intersected with the east-west road that ran south of the Phu Loi basecamp (Route 313) and intersected QL-13 (Thunder Road) in the city of Phu Cuong. The convoy would then proceed north on Thunder Road through Ben Cat, Lai Khe, and on to An Loc and Quan Loi. South from Phu Cuong on QL-13 would go to Saigon on the route taken by the truck the day before, that delivered me to the Phu Loi basecamp.

SFC Coker already advised me on how the platoon had secured these convoys in the past and two of the tanks jumped in front of the convoy, while the rest of the Platoon spread out between the trucks when directed as it passed the intersection. The plan was to keep two tracks together and the third tank with an ACAV at the rear end of the procession. This convoy had close to a hundred vehicles, but the road up to Lai Khe, except for a few sensitive areas, was fairly secure. And we would be staying in Lai Khe overnight.

SSG Helmut Grossinger, B-25

Five minutes after joining the convoy we were moving through a large village half way to Phu Loi's southern gate. The children stood by the adults and happily waved at the convoy. SFC Coker pointed out that this was a sign of no Viet Cong being present, as if they were in the village the parents would hold the children close to their sides and not allow them to act friendly. Another few minutes and the Phu Loi basecamp was passed. In another ten minutes we made a right turn in the city of Phu Cuong, which was the last major city we would see until Ben Cat about thirty-five miles to the north.

As we approached Phu Cuong, Sergeant Coker pointed out a long grey warehouse about a hundred meters to the right of the road. Using the track call-signs he said, *"Two-six this is Two-zero." "Roger Two-zero,"* was my reply. *"Do you see that long building with the swastika on it?"* He was referring to the large Buddhist symbol in the middle of the slanted roof that looks like a mirror image of a Nazi swastika. *"25 (Helmut Grossinger) was here before,"* he said as he chuckled. Quickly the lead tank commander, Staff Sergeant (SSG) Grossinger responded, *"You know that's Buddhist!"*

SP4 Robert Coad,
Loader B-25

Grossinger was one of the best tank commanders I would ever know. He was formerly in the German Army and had a great sense of humor. SSG Bates on B-24 and SSG Adams (sp) on B-27 were also terrific.

SSG Grossinger had a colorful family history, as his father had been a Panzer Commander in the Austrian Army during WWII. There were a few jovial comments from other track commanders and the swastika moment was history. Having already spent a couple years in the Far East I had seen these symbols before, so no one was able to pull my leg on this. It was good clean fun and there would be more as time progressed.

The road was dark red laterite and it didn't take long before the heavy red dust was deep into everyone's lungs and hanging in their mouths and nostrils. Preferably the vehicles would have traveled at dust distance, which would allow them to stay just outside of the dust trail of the vehicle to its front, but for the first 15 kilometers north of Phu Cuong there was no breeze, so the dust just hung over the road. Dust distance would have made too much distance between the vehicles for safety, therefore that driving technique would have been unreasonable. It was such a relief when a breeze started taking the dust off the road again. By that time everyone was gagging from the nasty, thick mud in their lungs.

We traveled roughly 45 miles the first day. As we moved north there was some tension when we passed on the right side of the Hobo Woods and the bottom of the Iron Triangle, which were large enemy controlled jungle strongholds that housed formidable Viet Cong (VC) units. These VC units controlled the countryside and the few villages that remained along the road.

The Engineers had done a lot of work along the sides of the road cutting the jungle back at least a hundred feet or so on either side. What had not yet been accomplished was the removal of the trees and stumps that had been pushed down and dug up by the bulldozers. And this gave far too many great firing positions for the enemy RPG and Recoilless Rifle gunners. Nervous? – Hell Yes!

SFC Coker was very familiar with the route and placed everyone on alert as we moved through this area. Soon we entered Ben Cat city with many areas heavily sandbagged to include the old French fortress. This made it clear that we were now in territory that was subject to an enemy attack at any moment. Once past Ben Cat it was only a short drive to the Lai Khe basecamp, which was the First Infantry Division's forward base of operations.

We entered Lai Khe from the south. There was an airstrip along the right side of the road being used to helicopter lift soldiers into the infantry's search and destroy operations. A flight of Huey helicopters was taking off as we passed, and a large contingent of infantrymen armed to the teeth were awaiting an airlift.

SGT Crews cleaning 50 Caliber machine gun

Just past the airstrip was a long parking area about 100 feet wide bordered on the east and north by organized rows of rubber trees that were part of a rubber plantation. By this time, I had taken some control and started to feel like a Platoon Leader. There was about an hour and a half of daylight left as we backed the tracks side-by-side up to the rubber trees with the guns facing the north/south road.

All the track commanders knew what needed to be done and the crews pulled vehicular and weapons maintenance while they traded off getting a hot meal at a nearby mess hall. A gasoline truck came by in

Coker and Crews studying their maps.

about a half hour to top off the ACAVs and a diesel truck refueled the tanks. We had no responsibility for perimeter security duties that night, so only a minimal watch was necessary.

Stripping off my shirt and taking a whore's bath felt great as I removed the thick layer of red laterite from my sweat soaked body. A vendor came by on a three-wheel Lambreta motor scooter, just in time, providing an opportunity to buy a small red plastic pan they called a "douche bucket," or a "Peter Pan," so I had a place to wash up other than in my helmet.

Once the maintenance chores were complete, someone visiting one of the troopers announced that there was a small Club at the end of a nearby building just inside the rubber trees to our north. A few of the troopers and I decided to get a drink to cut the dust we had breathed. So, off we went.

Chapter 11

A COLD BEER BREAK BEFORE PROCEEDING DEEPER INTO DANGER

The room wasn't more than 20 feet long by 15 feet wide, with a small bar, a few tables, about ten to fifteen chairs and four or five bar stools. There were probably ten or so bottles of hard liqueur and plenty of beer. A cold beer was sure nice after that long, hot drive, but only after having a double shot of Jack Daniels to cut the laterite I'd been breathing. I settled in at a table near the door and relaxed.

Into the second beer, Brigadier General James Hollingsworth came through the door, saying *"at ease,"* so everyone could remain seated. It was a bit of a shock as he was wearing civilian clothing. BG Hollingsworth, who was the Assistant Division Commander for Maneuver, came straight to the bar and ordered a drink. He made a comment that *"drinking with the Armored Cavalry brings back some of my best memories."*

The General had gone into North Africa during WWII as a Second Lieutenant, Tank Platoon Leader in the 2nd Armored Division on November 5, 1942, just 56 days after I was born. He spent five years with the same unit and left it as a Lieutenant Colonel. The General didn't stay long at the Club and was gone, but his attitude toward the Cavalry was clear. And it provided a reason to relax a bit, as a Cavalry platoon leader in an Infantry Division, learning that the second in command of the Division understood our capabilities and vulnerabilities.

After a relaxed evening inside the perimeter of Lai Khe, with considerable anticipation of the move north into territory that had been controlled by the VC for the past several months, sleep didn't come easy. Laying on a cot that was stowed in my track, since the platoon lost its last Lieutenant, proved to be very comfortable, but the sound of artillery constantly firing into the night, and the anticipation of what lay ahead left me tossing fitfully for a long time. I gazed at the stars overhead and called out in my mind, *"Jesus, help me be the best Officer I can be, and protect me and my men from what lay ahead."* In the hands of my Maker, prayer soon faded into the sweet calm of sleep.

Chapter 12

MOVING INTO CRAZYLAND
FEBRUARY 9, 1967

Before daylight everyone was at the mess hall gulping down a hot breakfast and making final, frantic preparations for moving into the wild territories beyond Lai Khe's north gate. You would have thought it was a wagon train readying itself to hit the trail into Indian territory a couple hundred years ago. The Engineers had swept the road for mines for about the first half kilometer from the north end of the basecamp and an Armored Cavalry unit had started to run the road north at about 0600 hours. We picked up the convoy and passed the north gate start point at 0630 sharp. Everything went smoothly with no enemy to deal with.

The movement was uneventful, and the platoon was ordered to drop out of the convoy near a Night Defensive Position (NDP) about 7 - 8 kilometers north of Lai Khe, near where there once was a village known as Ap Bau Bang to post a section of the road until the convoys all passed on their trek north to An Loc and Quan Loi cities. Another Cavalry platoon replaced the Second Platoon of "B" Troop as convoy escort at this point, and there was nearly no slowing of the convoy with the security changeover. This became nearly a three-week operation and my first experience working with an Infantry Battalion as a Cavalry Officer. I was thoroughly familiar with Infantry tactics, having gone to the Infantry Officer Candidate School (OCS) at Fort Benning, Georgia, and having spent five years in the Marine Corps.

The convoys had all cleared our section of the road by 1600 hours and between 1700 or 1800 the platoon was ordered into the NDP at Bau

Bang. SFC Coker had informed the platoon that over 400 Viet Cong (VC) had been killed here with a large number left hanging on the wire, as well as many being killed inside the perimeter, during a mass attack on the NDP a while back. This was before the Tanks were placed into the Cavalry platoons instead of being used primarily as stationary security on basecamp perimeters.

Upon pulling into the NDP I reported to the 1st Battalion, 18th Infantry Regiment's Battalion Commander. Little did I know that I was meeting one of greatest Infantry Battalion Commanders to set foot in Vietnam. Lieutenant Colonel (LTC) Dick Cavazos appeared professional and congenial, and welcomed me as if I was a key member of his unit. I was never to experience an Infantry Battalion Commander quite like this one again and was surprised how well my Cavalry platoon was treated for the time of our attachment. LTC Cavazos' father was the foreman at the Kings Ranch in Texas, and it was obvious that this was a special officer that was going somewhere with his career. *(He retired as a four star General and passed on to a better life on October 29, 2017.)*

The Battalion Commander professionally discussed the defense plan and how to best use the Cavalry. I was surprised to have an Infantry Battalion Commander initiate this first conversation with *"Lieutenant, where do you think the best locations will be to position your tracks."* I inquired, *"Colonel, do you know where the main VC force attacked this NDP previously."* When it was established that it came from the southwest, I made a recommendation which had the southwestern part of the perimeter tank heavy. The proposal was accepted. I put two of our three tanks on the south and west sides, and the majority of the platoon's ACAVs were positioned in those directions as well.

As luck would have it, I spotted an Infantry officer of the 1st Battalion, 18th Infantry, who was in my OCS class at Fort Benning, GA, Second Lieutenant Christiansen, the Recon Platoon Leader. He was getting his men ready to go on an ambush patrol about a kilometer north of the NDP as my platoon moved into positions around the perimeter. We didn't have time to talk then but would later.

LTC Cavazos advised me that fuel and water were available, but the water (in the water buffalo trailer) might not be as plentiful for the next several days. Also, hot food was being held for the Platoon at his field mess truck. The men were filthy after riding up that red laterite road and parched from sitting in blocking positions along QL-13 for most of the day under a burning sun. So, while some cleaned weapons and pulled maintenance on their vehicles, others ate or stood watch, and still others took whore's baths and re-filled each track's 5-gallon water cans from the water trailer. Everyone was in a bit of a hurry, as it was getting dark fast, and that was when the VC, like vampires, would go on the prowl.

Chapter 13

FIRST NIGHT RESCUE

As the sun set, many of the troopers were washing up and were therefore partly or completely undressed. Suddenly there was a sound like popcorn popping in the distance. The call from LTC Cavazos was quick that Chris's platoon had been ambushed and we needed to rescue them. My first of many Infantry rescue missions had begun. The platoon had been on these missions before and immediately started getting their tracks ready to begin a significant night mission. At that point I was rinsing the laterite and soap off my body. I started to rummage through my bag for a clean uniform but was all thumbs. There was no time to get proper, and lives were at stake. So, my focus quickly changed, and I had to do the necessities, <u>NOW</u>! It didn't matter that I was naked as a jay bird.

Not having a crystal ball to foresee the problems we could be facing and wanting to keep my troopers as unscathed as possible, I turned to my religious side with a brief prayer. *'Jesus, please ride with me. Lord I could get us into something that's beyond my abilities to handle, but with You at my side I'm certain we won't come up short.'* The butterflies were then shaken out of my system.

There was a little squawking when I threw on my shoulder holster, flak jacket, and CVC helmet, climbed onto B-26 and immediately ordered the platoon, *"Crank 'em up; move 'em out." "All tanks to the front. Let's get on the road and head north - fast."* That would be the last grumbling I'd hear from my troopers as they now knew what I expected in an emergency. My driver reacted smartly, and the track lurched backward out of its position, twisting to the left, then forward and into the column as the second ACAV behind the third tank. Under cover of darkness all ten tracks bolted north from the NDP in a tight formation.

[As a side note, my *prayer was my private, secret ritual. A quick prayer to a trustworthy, loyal Lord and Friend settled my nerves in preparation to move around this treacherous landscape. I firmly believed that, regardless of the politics back home, the battle against the evil Communists was a moral and necessary fight, and that the Lord was with us. And that we were warriors doing His will. I recognized my frailties and asked for divine assistance to fill in the gaps in my abilities when we were in jeopardy, and it worked well. I made it a point to place my trust in the Lord when going into battle, and believe the payoff was big.*

Over time I added implements of personal security by carrying a small bible, wearing a Catholic scapular around my neck, and in my left breast pocket there was a miniature Buddhist prayer book about one inch long, a half inch wide and less than a half inch thick. I carried this at the request of a dear sister in law's mother on the island of Okinawa, who gave assurances that it was not necessary to believe in Buddhism in order to be protected. And in another pocket, there was a horseshoe, which said Aloha Hawaii, gifted by another concerned friend, Patrick C. "Happy" Marciel, who lived in Honolulu. Now with all the accouterments of security, the job was up to myself, my men, and the favor of our Lord. It seems a bit odd, but these trinkets I carried became insurance of a sort helping to settle my mind, so I could function effectively with little concern for my personal safety once a battle began.

Carrying these special security items may seem a bit nuts, but there were many others to look out for, and I also knew that concerns for my own personal safety could prove fatal to others. Some troopers carried letters or pictures from home or sniffed perfumed letters from their wives or girlfriends and other rituals to help maintain their mental balance when times were tough and scary. Troopers also forged close friendships with one another . . . something Officers were unable to do.

Being a Platoon Leader didn't allow such luxuries as close friends, although a closeness was developed with my NCOs - especially my Platoon Sergeant, and later my First Sergeant. Being a Platoon Leader was akin to being head of a family and those in a parent role must maintain their authority, which would be undermined by too close of a friendship with their charges. But it got lonely at the top - - very, very, lonely.]

SSG Grossinger on B-25 was in front as usual, followed by B-24, commanded by SSG Bates, then B-27, commanded by SSG Adams (sp), then Sergeant (SGT) Bernadine, B-23, followed by the command track, B-26, then SGT Catus on B-21, SP5 Augusta (sp) on B-22, SFC Coker on B-20, SP5 Perez (sp) on B-28, and SGT Crews on B-29. As the formation charged north the artillery began to provide enough illumination munitions to allow reasonable visibility for a quick advance without headlights. With luck on our side a breeze moved the heavy red dust to the right of the road allowing the vehicles to stay less than fifty feet apart and to travel nearly 40 miles per hour. There couldn't have been better conditions for a fast advance to the battle site.

We weren't too worried about mines, as the sun had just fully set, but we were alert to a possible ambush. The troopers instinctively knew what to do. The tracks stayed close together and moved as fast as possible. The tanks stayed to the center of the road and followed in each other's tracks to limit the amount of road that was traveled, to avoid mines that might have been hastily laid.

The ACAVs put their left track in the left footprint of the tanks. This placed the ACAV's drivers and gas tanks, which were on the left side of the vehicles, safer from receiving the brunt of the concussion from a mine. With the tracks of an ACAV being narrower than that of a tank, the 1st ACAV swept the road with its right track. That's why the command track was not the 1st ACAV behind the tanks.

The daylight was gone as we cleared the perimeter. We followed Route QL-13 north in the spooky, shimmering light from the artillery flares. Every man was poised for a fight. There was no guesswork as to where the fighting was because of the exchange of tracer ammunition from the automatic weapons and the flares illuminating the enemy positions. As we approached the ambush site I was talking with Chris on the radio. Sergeant Grossinger picked a spot just north of the distinct east-west trail where the ambush patrol had set up its positions. The tanks turned to the left on line and spread out to give room for the ACAVs to do the same and move on line between the tanks. There was a tank on each end of the line and one in the middle of the advancing tracks. Every man was itching for a fight but had to hold their fire until the danger of injuring or killing friendly soldiers was resolved.

Unable to fire our machine guns and certainly not the 90mm tank guns until we got on line with the Infantry platoon, the Cavalry platoon rushed carefully toward the chis-crossing tracer ammunition, red from Chris' machine guns and green from Charley's (VC). Just as we pulled on line with the infantry, two flares lit up the sky behind the enemy. The Infantrymen rolled from side to side to keep from getting run over and then started entering the rear of the ACAVs.

This was one of the smoothest rescue operations I would experience in Vietnam. And I attributed its success to the discipline and professionalism of Lieutenant Christianson and his platoon, and the ability of my Cavalry troopers to execute commands boldly, carefully, and accurately, to quickly get into positions to support the Infantrymen without putting them in any significant danger from friendly overhead fire. And I really couldn't blame myself much for this efficiency. SFC Coker had the track commanders and troopers well trained to respond as a team long before my arrival.

Once the Infantry Recon Platoon Leader said, *"the tracks are past my men,"* I said, *"okay, open fire,"* although I was uncomfortable doing this with the chaos going on around me. That command to the Cavalrymen was authority to bring sheer havoc down on the source of those green tracers and other assorted enemy ordinance (RPGs and mortars) that were now trying to impede the rescue.

While the Cavalry laid waste to the jungle to our front, the Infantrymen scrambled into the ACAVs. Within a couple minutes Lieutenant Christianson announced, **"were all aboard."** I ordered my platoon to *"slowly back out to the road but keep your fire on Charley."* At the road SSG Bates on B-24 and SSG Adams (sp) on B-27 took the lead heading the Cavalry platoon south. This time Grossinger covered the rear until we were disengaged and racing back to the NDP with the darkness illuminated by a few artillery flares popping open along the way.

Time was suspended for a while, and it seemed like only a couple minutes before a hole was opened in the perimeter concertina wire for us to pass through. It was comforting to get back inside of the perimeter's security and the tension slid back to a feeling slightly akin to returning to the comforts of garrison life, which of course didn't exist. We pulled our tracks into the positions they had previously been in, but it was too late to put out listening posts forward of the wire for fear of the VC spotting these positions during the movement. The Platoon bedded down with 50% awake and on the alert all night long. So ended my third night in Vietnam.

Only a couple of the Infantrymen had been wounded, but not seriously. It had been a perfect rescue and LTC Cavazos made some great comments about the Cavalry, and the professional and eloquent way he gave his praise made everyone very proud of that action. Not a single enemy soldier was seen, but it was a victory nonetheless to accomplish this night rescue without a single fatality being inflicted on the ambushed Americans by either enemy or friendly fire. And with the devastating fire placed on the enemy positions, there was no doubt many of the enemy were killed or wounded. Also, it was fortunate that my platoon suffered no casualties.

While unloading from the tracks, the Infantrymen realized that the Cavalry platoon was poorly dressed for battle and saw fit to comment about it for several days. But they appreciated the quick reaction and had a lot to say how they felt about the Cavalrymen not wasting time getting proper for the fight before coming to their rescue. We took the ribbing in good humor. I was one of the naked cavalrymen they were referring to. Although this set well with those being rescued, some of the remarks were a bit bawdy. While unloading the Infantry Platoon, Lt Christiansen asked, *"Is this how you **always** dress for a fight?"*

When he said it, I suddenly felt vulnerable to the voracious appetites of the mosquitoes that were staking claim to my hide. There is no telling just how much of a blood donation was made that night before our uniforms were back on. And we were bit in some very private places. When Christiansen made his remarks, I immediately started scrambling for my clothes, which were outside the track in my duffle bag by my plastic pan that lay spilled on the ground from the sudden departure. It all made an interesting impression on the Infantrymen and within my Platoon as well. Comments were made like, *"We will get naked (or drop our drawers) for the chance to rescue some grunts (Infantrymen),"* or "this platoon sure knows how to keep cool during a fight.

Chapter 14

THE BASTARD TRIED TO KILL ME
FEBRUARY 10, 1967

The next day the mission started by sweeping the road for mines. The platoon had about a kilometer to sweep to the south of the NDP. Two ACAVs were on the right of the road, three on the left (including B-26) in echelon and two on the road behind one another. One Tank led the ACAVs on the right of the road and two on the left side. And the two ACAVs on the road were just behind the troopers walking along with their mine detectors. It was serious and dangerous business. Soldiers were doing this on roughly 30 miles or so of road north of Lai Khe to An Loc, unless there were tanks running the road on Thunder Runs throughout the night. This was a daily exercise to get ready for the convoys that were moving supplies and equipment north. Once the sweeping job was finished the Platoon would outpost the road again, all day.

It was hot as Hell by 8 A.M. and the flak jackets were heavy and sweltering hot. On the right (west) side of the road there were rubber trees in perfect European symmetrical parallel lines, just wide enough for a tank to nicely fit between the rows of trees. On the left side, less than 100 feet from the road, was an old railroad berm about eight feet high, with occasional small tunnels going under it, and with other larger breaks every hundred meters or so where the railroad tracks had been removed and the berm was bulldozed flat. The berm was a formidable barrier which our tracked vehicles could not cross, and the tunnels were overgrown with high grass and bushes.

Riding on my perch on top of B-26, and wearing a flak jacket, the heat gradually made me drowsy and my back was starting to ache. So, I arched my back for a stretch. My head was suddenly spun to the right by a Rocket Propelled Grenade that Charley apparently thought to thread through my ears. Thank goodness for the need to stretch. Perfect unplanned timing. Thank You, Lord. I never have lost the sensation of that rocket's heat on my left cheek, as it sped about an inch past my face. Whenever the thought occurs of that meeting with destiny this shocking experience is relived. The round struck a rubber tree across the road, destroying the tree with its explosion. The initial reaction found me diving head-first into the ACAV through the large open hatch on top of the track.

"Okay Lieutenant, what do you do now?" screamed in my head. This was a question frequently asked during officer training after a hypothetical situation was stated. Without prompting, or perhaps on the order of SFC Coker, the ACAVs had placed a barrage of machine gun fire all along the railroad berm to kill anyone hidden in the brush. I couldn't see anything from inside the ACAV and felt vulnerable to a second RPG shot. So up I came like a Jack in the Box, never to retreat to that deceptively protective shell again.

I became a genuine combat Cavalry Platoon Leader at that moment. I commanded a drive to the next break in the railroad berm, about 100 feet or so up the road. The tracks on the east side of the road went through the gap in the berm and flooded the area with 50 caliber and 7.62mm machine gun fire, as well as several High Explosive Plastic (HEP) rounds from the 90mm Tank guns. In addition, the Infantry called in some 105mm Artillery fire from the same fire support base that had provided the illumination the previous night. But no one knew if any VC were winged. And no bodies or blood trails were found when the Infantry swept the area.

Fortunately, no one was hurt and being a "genuine" combat Platoon Leader now felt good, to a degree. It was a starting point. With this brief skirmish I bonded with my men. They were watching closely to see exactly what I would do when that first attempt was made on my life. They were satisfied with what they saw, and in their eyes their new Platoon Leader had now assumed command.

No longer did that question exist, although others would plague me for several months. The question as to how I would respond when that first shot became personal evaporated into thin air. This was now 'my' fight, and with that crucial question resolved I felt that I could find a way to do this job. From that experience forward I put my leadership role on like a new sports coat. Fear had been overcome and I learned that my mind could think clearly in conditions that would panic many good men. It was obvious that there was a lot to learn and there had to be better ways to do business than being surprised like this. And if we couldn't stop the surprises, we were somehow going to have to make it very expensive for this enemy, even on his own turf. Praying helped, but I no longer had one foot in the war and the other one back home. I was fully dominated by the job at hand - most of the time.

After sweeping the assigned section, the platoon's mission was to outpost the road and be prepared to assist any convoy passing through the Battalion's tactical area of operations. The Infantry companies had assigned patrols working the area near the road and the NDP, and it was necessary to stay prepared to support their activities if necessary, as well as guard the road. Spread out along the road in the hot, humid air, while wearing a 30-pound flak jacket, and CVC helmet, made for a very tiring day, and it was unreasonably boring. This daily routine quickly became monotonous except for an occasional thrill of some minor enemy contact or the increased possibility of such.

Upon returning to our positions on the Bau Bang perimeter we had a little excitement. SSG Bates (B-24), a very serious and professional Non-commissioned Officer, had a pet monkey on his tank that had a bad habit of riding on the main gun. Shortly after B-24 was moved into its position there was a cook-off (the round in the 90mm main gun fired because of the heat of the gun tube). The monkey had been perched on the gun tube and received the full concussion of the muzzle blast. The last time that monkey was seen, he was staggering into the jungle holding his head with both hands. He never returned.

I never favored monkeys on the tracks who could easily learn to pull a hand grenade pin after watching a trooper do so in battle. This of course would destroy the track and everyone on it. He also could key the radio's hand mike and block all use of the platoon's radios. "Monkey see, monkey do."

I quickly lost the thrill and anxiety of that first night at Bau Bang after returning from the rescue mission. But the second night, after nearly being killed was totally sleepless. I knew that Charley had a barrel of tricks and I was overly excited from being baptized by fire that morning. That night I stood my own watch and the watch of at least another crew member. I watched through the starlight scope and was almost certain things were moving in the brush to the front of our position. The movement turned out to be nothing more than some busy nocturnal ground animals looking for their next meal - - this time. The night proved uneventful and the nervousness was just a prelude of more horrors to come.

Chapter 15

THE ACAV BURNED TO THE GROUND

Within the next couple weeks, as the Platoon moved out of Bau Bang to sweep the road B-29 hit a mine. It was a huge pressure detonated mine with a bamboo trigger designed so it would explode under the center of the track. The mine was buried next to a high explosive (perhaps a dud artillery round), which caused a huge explosion.

It was deafening. All three persons on the ACAV were injured. The driver and the M-60 machine gunner had to be dusted off for deep cuts on their legs and loss of hearing. The track commander SGT Colyn Crews was blasted high into the air and landed on top the ACAV. His back and legs were injured, and he broke a couple toes. His total deafness lasted for several days. He was taken to the Infantry's Aid Station, but being a superb NCO, he chose not to be evacuated as the pain eased somewhat with pain killers by late in the day. He was put on the Platoon Sergeant's ACAV until a replacement vehicle was brought to the field in about two weeks.

B-29 had instantly burst into flames beyond anyone's ability to control. SFC Coker was fast on his feet and ran up to the track and extracted the crew before there were any fatalities. He tried to control the fire with a fire extinguisher but was unable.

The picture became indelible. The basic load of ammunition exploded violently, and the ACAV, made of an aluminum-magnesium alloy, was so hot from the burning gasoline, C-4, claymore mines and other munitions that it melted in front of us. It was very demoralizing. Huge globs of white-hot metal slopped their way down to the ground and the vehicle's floor. Amid the after explosions and the tremendous heat was the sound of popping and snapping of the igniting machine gun ammunition. When it cooled there were silver melted pieces that had come loose from the track and were on the roadway around the wreckage. The whole mess was pulled off the roadway to be later buried when a bulldozer came by in a convoy.

There was nothing that could be done but watch in horror as B-29 burned and melted. It was painful, but it welled up instincts I never was to fully understand. For us to survive, I knew we must somehow find the enemy before they struck again, and we needed to do a better job of mine sweeping to avoid such catastrophes.

As soon as we could, we restarted mine sweeping the road to get ready for that day's convoys. We increased our listening posts at night, in front of the tracks, and were allowed to put out ambush patrols near that railroad berm. SGT Crews led these patrols despite his hearing issues.

Chapter 16

THIS CRAP HAS TO STOP - NOW!

There was another incident where a track was seriously damaged by a command detonated mine, but I can't recall which ACAV it was. The VC was hiding in a tunnel under the railroad berm again and activated the mine when the track was directly over it. I don't recall any injuries, but it angered me that Charley was using a tunnel under the berm to attack us, and we hadn't learned from it the first time.

It was time to stop this crap. Any action, no matter how routine, must somehow anticipate the least and worst possible enemy actions. It sounded easy, but we were Charley's prey, and the prey was normally the victim from ambushes that could come at any time, and from places that were tough to anticipate. The predator had significant advantages.

I knew that my anti-tank training had to provide some clues on how to read Charley. But what were they? Nothing apparently could be trusted. What appeared the least threatening could be the most. This was mixed with not wanting to act paranoid and cry wolf at every stand of brush. The problem was very troubling.

Every trooper knew his job. Each one was as nervous as the others on how the next contact with the enemy would occur. Only Charley knew. The cavalrymen were all confident that after a fight began, they could regain fire superiority. It was the initial contact that was feared most of all and this created the most stress. Surely there had to be some techniques which would increase the platoon's safety. I spent a lot of time pondering this, and there was a lot of dead time available while sitting along the dusty road securing convoys for several hours a day to think and pray about it.

Part of the solution was a no-brainer. The priority was to look ready to fight more than anyone else. That meant <u>neat looking tracks</u> inside and out, <u>closed flak jackets,</u> no matter what the weather was like, and <u>radio discipline. Uniform spacing between the vehicles</u> during movements was extremely important. Every trooper had to <u>look ready and anxious to fight</u> at every moment. With the heat, humidity, boredom, and a lack of so many creature comforts, this was very difficult. The men and their tracks looked a little disorderly. This could be worked on so as not to look like an undisciplined ragtag outfit which could embolden Charley. SFC Coker had a good handle on this prior to my arrival, but I knew that this had to be frequently reemphasized.

<u>Reaction procedures</u> needed refining too. Any attack on the platoon required an <u>immediate, violent counter-response</u> without hesitation, followed by a report as to what was happening. And any attack on the platoon required an immediate assault by all Tanks and ACAVs directly into the problem without any command. In other-words go back to the basics - <u>Look sharp, be sharp, and respond aggressively!</u> That became the model to follow. It wasn't really a major change, but it became our standard. It was what the enemy would least expect.

Charley anticipated a lull on the part of a unit being attacked which gave him an opportunity to inflict severe damage, then tactically disappear during the time it takes for a plan to be developed and executed. The troopers were given the requirement and trust to respond to an attack without saying *"mother may I."* I saw the initial response to the enemy as the most essential moment of any fight. Taking control of the battlefield without hesitation was essential. Whether it was one gunner or a unit sized ambush, <u>an immediate counter-attack would throw the surprise back into Charley's face</u>.

Generally, the VC prepared "L" shaped ambushes in the jungle (and an occasional "U" shaped ambush) and on a road he would normally be on one side and try to knock out the front vehicle or two and then the rear vehicles, to lock the unit into his killing zone. In either case he would be looking for a quick kill and a quick escape if he lost the momentum. It was our job to get out of the killing zone and into his face as fast as possible.

In two of the attacks we experienced so far, the enemy had been hiding in one of the small tunnels under the railroad berm. I hadn't learned fast enough, and this was much too costly. What Charley did was exactly what I may have done as an anti-tank assault-man. With the entire area likely having tunnels, Charley could do his dirty work and quickly jump into a secure hole in the ground until it got dark. We had very little time to catch this bastard unless we caught him in the act. This became a wake-up call that I would never forget.

From that point on we would reconnoiter every suspected enemy position either by machine gun bursts or by an M-79 grenade launcher (40mm grenades). To save on ammo I began to keep a track right up close to that berm, so the track commander, driver or gunner could carefully examine any clumps of brush where an enemy soldier could be hiding, as we passed it. The closeness would make it difficult for the VC to act or move without being seen. And when in doubt we could toss a grenade or fire into the suspected hiding place.

My former antitank training was kicking in and it would gradually become a part of my normal thinking. But attention to the basics of soldiering and aggressiveness was just as important. Keeping alert and ready for a fight, all the time, would serve us well throughout the rest of my Vietnam experience. No one learned all the tricks of the trade in service schools, like staying on top of potential enemy locations when you couldn't stay safely away from them and aggressively responding into every attack without orders. These tidbits of combat leadership were a good start.

Chapter 17

SEALING AND MED CAP MISSION

Confrontations with the enemy stopped, but all was not sheer boredom. One day when there were no convoys, the platoon supported the Battalion's mission of securing and searching a village about two kilometers to the west of QL-13 on the east-west trail to the west of where Lieutenant Christiansen's ambush patrol had been ambushed. Now the Cavalry platoon would tote the Recon Platoon to a blocking position as part of our mission.

While the Infantry Battalion airlifted into LZs (Landing Zones) that facilitated their movement to encircle the west, north, and east sides of the village, the Cavalry and Recon Platoons headed west and then northwest on the tracks through various open areas in the jungle and undergrowth shown on the 1:25,000 scale pictorial map, to positions locking in the likely escape route on the south side of the village. The Infantry Recon Platoon was a bit surprised as to how quickly the Cavalry made it to the intended destination. And I had a golden opportunity to show off my own skills of rapidly moving an armored unit through some formidable terrain with relative ease and pinpoint accuracy. I felt a little like a show off, but it was fun and certainly broke the monotony.

The men were elated at doing something other than sweeping for mines and out-posting the road and rather enjoyed this mission through rough terrain, full of huge red ants with enormous vice-grip jaws and scratching branches as we pushed our way through the undergrowth with as much stealth as a freight train blowing its whistle. It was clear that an armored unit wasn't very quiet, but speed and accuracy compensated a great deal. It was an interesting mission too. The surprise of a Cavalry platoon being where it wasn't expected benefitted the mission and our morale. As we deployed, Chris spread his platoon out between our Tanks and ACAVs along the south side of the village just in time to see the rest of the village being sealed by the remainder of his Battalion that was airlifted into nearby LZs (Landing Zones).

Most everyone was a bit surprised at how smoothly the village was sealed. After it was searched by a combination of U.S. infantrymen and Vietnamese soldiers, a Med Cap (Medical) team was flown in to provide care to the residents. Only a few suspects were taken away for questioning, all males between the age of twelve and twenty, and there were very few of them present.

For the most part, the village was populated only by women, children and old men. The medical activities seemed a splendid diversion from the business of killing, trying to avoid being killed, or sitting bored fifty feet off the side of the laterite road, roasting in the sun, breathing heavy red dust, and watching for the enemy's sudden appearance. It was very special - - all except for the dental work.

It was not hard to sympathize with the miserable dentist who extracted rotten teeth buried within beetle nut laden mouths. Beetle nut is a grotesque deep red color narcotic that was the only readily available protection from the pain of rotting teeth that these natives could obtain. It was always sickening when one of the otherwise beautiful maidens chewing this crap blessed us with an open-mouthed smile. Nasty, Nasty, Truly Nasty.

This Med Cap mission concluded our attachment to LTC Cavazos' Battalion. Working with the 1st Battalion, 18th Infantry was enjoyable. It was an opportunity to see just how rough the Infantry had it, and the importance of the Cavalry and helicopter support on the battlefield. Without available Armor, Artillery and Air resources for support, the American Infantry would be in the same handicapped position as the French when they tried to tame the jungles of Vietnam.

Having previously been an Infantryman, I had a unique appreciation for well-trained, combined arms (Infantry and Armor) teams for successful civil/military activities in this unusual theater of operations. This adventure with the Infantry would be the last attachment to the Infantry for more than a couple days at a time that the platoon would experience while I was the Platoon Leader.

Chapter 18

A FRESH NEW MISSION

Suddenly, without warning, the platoon was ordered to move north with a convoy to the city of An Loc and then west along the Cambodian border about fifteen kilometers via a deeply dusty road paralleling a portion of the Cambodian border known as the Fish Hook.

No one questioned why it was necessary to be in such a hostile place. That was a job for the Generals, although there were moments for concern. My platoon was just expected to do their job, and to stay alive if we could. By day Cavalry units escorted convoys of supply trucks and engineer vehicles to An Loc about 100 kilometers or so north of Saigon, and at that point the convoys were escorted West, deep into the hostile wilderness, and too close to the Cambodian border for comfort. Some of the convoys would turn Eastward at An Loc to resupply Quan Loi.

This extensive movement of equipment and supplies was needed to build and reinforce an outpost with a helicopter landing pad deep in the middle of Charley's territory, in an extremely dangerous part of Vietnam, which could not be easily defended for long once the Junction City II operation ended and the 1st Infantry Division pulled its main forces South, back to its forward operating base of Lai Khe, about half way to Saigon.

On every campaign north to An Loc, or beyond, supplies and artillery ammunition were also delivered to Quan Loi. Quan Loi was a French plantation owner's residence and airstrip. It was located on a peninsula that jutted out from the huge rubber plantation in a roughly northeasterly direction. This peninsula housed an important communications relay station and was protected by Infantry, Armor, and Armored Cavalry, and housed Artillery units that harassed the enemy and supported units operating that far north.

Once we were as far as An Loc, "B" Troop's Second Platoon, became a convoy escort, working from an NDP a little south of An Loc west to the construction site along the Cambodian border, and with side trips to Quan Loi. When we brought convoys back from the Fish Hook or Quan Loi to our NDP, convoy escorts would take them south to Lai Khe. It was a Cavalry escort relay exercise. Cavalry escort platoons would spread themselves out among about fifty or so vehicles, and then they would go as fast as possible to their next relay point, all the while hoping they would not come under attack.

Along Thunder Road at suspect locations friendly units were pre-positioned, and Artillery NDPs were strategically located to support the movement of supplies and equipment to and from Lai Khe. And Infantry units kept the enemy activities disrupted by search and destroy missions, and most importantly, they were ready to assist if there was a major assault on a convoy. The convoys were normally overflown by Forward Observers in fixed wing aircraft, who were also skilled high-performance aircraft pilots, and could quickly provide air or artillery support if the need arose.

The dust that accumulated on the nearly fifteen kilometers of bad road from An Loc along the Cambodian border was often more than six inches deep by 0700 to 0800 after the pre-monsoon rain water evaporated in the early morning heat. Charley planted mines along that stretch of road nearly every night. Some of the mines were command detonated, while others were buried along the road or edges of the roadway ready for the pressure of a wheel or track to detonate its explosive charge. If a mine was missed on a morning sweep it was almost certain to violently end someone's life or permanently maim them.

There were essentially four mine laying variations that Charley used on the roads - - an anti-tank mine with a pressure trigger; the same mine rigged to be command detonated by a VC hiding nearby; an antitank mine buried next to a dud (unexploded) artillery shell or bomb, so both would explode at the same time by what's known as sympathetic detonation; and a ratchet mine that had a triggering device which activated when the first vehicle drove over it and exploded when the third vehicle made contact with it. The ratchet mine was intended to explode under the Platoon Leader's track. These must not have worked very well because I never experienced any of the rachet types. The ones that exploded in the middle of a column were normally command detonated or simply mines that were missed by the other vehicles.

And then there were some areas that remained un-swept where there was less likelihood of a mine. The first Tanks down the road verified the non-existence of mines in these areas. But even where the road had been swept, none of it was to be trusted. Unlike Thunder Road, the foliage along this northern route had received very little of the defoliation treatments, and ambushes were likely from the dense growth at locations hand-picked by the VC for the advantage afforded by the terrain and the ability to scurry away after striking a blow at us. It made everyone feel like a target, all the time.

Two trips to or from An Loc and back and sometimes one to Quan Loi was about all that was possible in a single day. It left everyone drained after pulling the necessary personal, weapons and vehicle maintenance before the sunlight faded. And when it was raining cats and dogs this was much more difficult. But even after putting out the rolls of barbed concertina wire in front of the armored vehicles and sending out a couple two man listening posts (LPs) forward of the wire, someone still had to stay awake on every track behind its primary weapon throughout the night.

The Platoon Sergeant's and the Platoon Leader's tracks kept in touch with the LPs by using a series of clicks of the radio hand mikes (microphones) as code, so that the men outside of the perimeter did not have to talk, and it was also useful to help them stay awake. There was

Hell to pay when an LP fell to sleep, and a decision had to be made as to whether someone would go through the wire to see if they were asleep or if they had been silently killed. And of course, no one wanted to crawl straight into an enemy trap. This was one of the scariest assignments. No one intentionally fell asleep on LP duty, but tiredness and laying quietly on the ground among the natural soft noises of the jungle was intoxicating. There was, however, a motivation to stay awake. For the trooper who fell asleep on LP, there were many shit details to help him learn to resist the urge to doze in the future.

The LP job was very important, as was the sentinel on each track. Should the VC get past the Platoon's ten armored vehicles and about thirty-eight troopers, whoever they were protecting would be hamburger. It was a heavy responsibility for a 24-year-old officer just about a year out of OCS, although being a mustang with six and a half years of enlisted experience in infantry, armor and anti-tank units in the Army and Marine Corps helped a lot.

Training and experience-wise I was better off than most yearling Lieutenants. I found that my previous enlisted experiences kept my mind constantly spinning for ideas to do everything I could to stay a step ahead of Charley's tricks. And I still thank God for the handful of awesome NCOs that kept our troopers, who were almost all freshly out of High School, focused on the details of our responsibilities. And I can't say it enough that these young troopers were awesome. Not at all like the young men wandering around the Malls back home with no apparent purpose in life.

Chapter 19

TIME FOR PROMOTION

I was anxiously waiting for promotion orders to arrive which would be dated April Fool's Day of 1967. I couldn't get my mind off that butter bar (gold insignia of rank of a Second Lieutenant) and how nice it would be when it was replaced by a nice silver one on my dress uniform. Although I may never see a dress uniform again, I wouldn't look like an inexperienced fledgling ever again once that insignia was changed.

The first job as a First Lieutenant (1LT) would be to find someone to replace the sewed-on dim brown camouflaged rank insignia on my jungle fatigues with black ones. But that seemed of little importance. My black grease pencil used for marking on my plastic map case would suffice to improvise the correct rank on those fatigues until there was an opportunity to get new ones sewed on. And I was ready for the change.

Then one day during the first week of April 1967, after running our last convoy for the day between An Loc and the remote base, the platoon was ordered to go to an NDP a couple kilometers from that remote base located under gorgeous trees towering over a hundred feet above the jungle floor. This triple canopy jungle could have been Paradise except for the Armored vehicles scattered under the forest and the pungent smell of gasoline and diesel fuel hanging in the air from the refueling process.

During this brief stop of a couple hours, this yearling Second Lieutenant met his Troop Commander, Captain James Skillings, for

Fred Currier in Rubber Plantation

the first time, and was promoted to First Lieutenant. I was surprised to see Brigadier General James Hollingsworth in that NDP to provide his congratulations. This is also when Fred Currier joined the platoon.

(Years later I was fortunate to have lunch with Major General Hollingsworth first in Korea and again on a River Boat out of New Orleans, with him and his lovely wife, Jeanie, while attending an annual Society of the 1st Infantry Division reunion.)

We then returned to the remote outpost and this is where we would provide security until the next day's convoys. The nights here were very nerve racking. I spent a lot of time examining our very dangerous environment, and wondering why I chose to be where I found myself.

Chapter 20

A NIGHT NEAR CAMBODIA

It was a dark, pitch black night and this young Platoon Leader was in the cupola of Bravo-26, sitting quietly behind the 50 caliber machine gun straining my eyes into the night, and damning the evil, total blackness we faced.

There was nothing but bitter darkness to the front, to the sides and to the rear. Rarely does one experience the total theft of light. All of it was absorbed by the dark green jungle to the front of my ACAV. No matter where I looked, even down into the crew compartment of our track, there was nothingness except for an occasional blip of light on the face of the radio, which was our lifeline if a fight erupted. The immediate world appeared gone except for the steel gun shield on either side of the machine gun to my direct front, which swept to the left and right around the track commander's position on three sides, and the hand grips and firing mechanism held loosely in my hands.

Yet this coal dark night was capped by a beautiful starlit sky. It was a dome sparkling with the magnificence of the Christmas lights I enjoyed just a few months earlier at home on the other side of mother earth. And there wasn't a speck of distortion from fleeting lights suggesting human habitation. Nor were there any occasional aircraft, characteristic of the sky above my home and family in Michigan. There was a feeling of having fallen through a black hole into Hell, and somewhere within those stars above was the Earth I knew, and a way back home - - if it could ever be found again. I thought, *'Lord, what happened to my frigging world?'*

A sharp pang of loneliness shot through me as the sky suddenly became clouded and the downpour began. The thoughts were strange as the heavy rain stopped and restarted again. When it wasn't raining the air stunk of rotting foliage, like the stirred up, ripe, decaying vegetation in a mulch pit full of worms. And there was persistent and heightened nervousness (called fear) that always had to be dealt with when we stayed overnight in this remote location. Concern for suddenly being attacked by a hoard of screaming devils. There was fear of the unknown - cold, ugly tremors of icy chills through my mind and body. These were unhealthy emotions that soldiers fight until

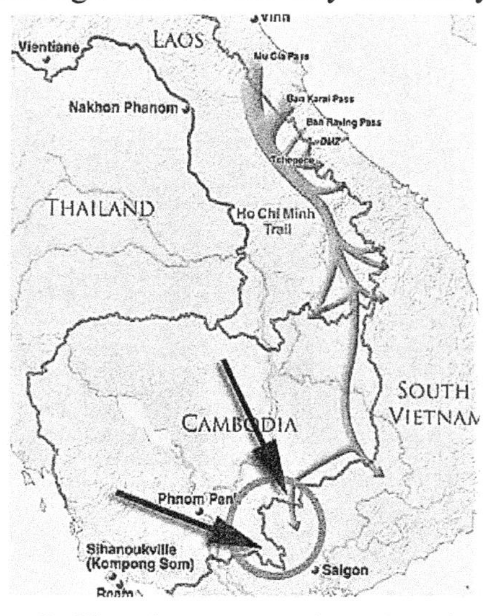

Infiltration Routes into South Vietnam, Top arrow is through Fish Hook

they learn to bury them deep inside, lest they go nuts. Usually that feeling was suppressed, but not in this location.

Cambodia was just too damned close. And we were facing the Fish Hook on one of the major infiltration routes to attack Saigon. The NVA (North Vietnamese Army) didn't even have to go out of their way to cause trouble. We were right in their path. The tension was enormous as we were told to anticipate a major attack. The evening's monsoon showers gave the enemy a golden opportunity to sneak up to the edge of the jungle undetected. The rain made the troopers drowsy and a very vulnerable

Fish Hook in relation to Saigon

target. If Charlie didn't attack us now, they were missing a golden opportunity.

Peering into the jungle at night with the naked eye was impossible. This eerie blackness seemed like the perfect home for souls of the damned. With only about 50 feet to the Jungle's edge, I mentally grappled into the blackness for the presence of the deadly little bastards, moving stealthily about this nether land, lusting to end this Platoon Leader's life and that of my troopers in a split, violent fraction of a second. I determined that the VC could see us from that dark jungle, although we couldn't see them at all.

Concentrating into the abyss was lonely, boring work and everyone had to take their turn. On these long nights, those on watch were always fighting a nagging pull into slumber, to stay alert after a long day of escorting convoys on heavily dusty roads, breathing the dust until we were chocking. And the boredom taxed one's ability to the breaking point to stay alert. Even prayer served to make me drowsy. Staying awake was tougher to do at first, and the difficulty never did leave entirely. There was always a longing for quiet, peaceful rest. No one knew that as a result of the stress of this war they had likely seen the last peaceful night's sleep they would ever experience again.

During the unrelenting evening showers of the approaching monsoon season there was good reason to worry that the enemy could at that very moment be slinking toward the perimeter, using the noise of the rain slapping on the heavy vegetation to muffle the sounds of their advance. They could be stepping carefully along the trails that came out of the jungle just a short stone's throw in front of our tracks.

I couldn't help but recall my own learned ability to sneak up on wild animals as a boy, and I imagined the VC as having developed this art to perfection, since stealth and surprise were their most formidable tactics against the overwhelming firepower they faced. And this, after all, was their jungle. The place where they grew up and trained for such an opportunity. These long, miserable wet nights were filled with unrelenting stress that could be cut with a knife.

Sitting behind the 50-caliber machine gun, at the ready with the first round from the ammo box loaded and ready to fire, while most of my mind stayed focused on the task at hand, a part of it couldn't help but wander.

After the rains lessened, I sat nervously in the darkness waiting for the enemy to make their move, while reminiscing about home and my first child, Irene, who was a bright little two-year-old. Suddenly, a noise to my front jerked me back to the present danger.

As the weather cleared, there was an abundance of drizzling noises from the remains of the downpour, which included the sounds dripping from my helmet's edge and off the barrel of the 50-caliber machine gun to tease my imagination. Nothing could be seen, and as the drizzles slowed to a stop everything returned to a deathly quiet. There were also sounds from the occasional movement of crew members in their troubled sleep on the ammunition boxes stored within the ACAV, which served as a mobile bunker that gave as much safety as the aluminum magnesium skin of the ACAV could provide - not that much.

An ACAV provided reasonable safety from small arms fire if the cavalrymen were fortunate enough to be inside when a fight erupted; unless the fight started with an RPG striking the ACAV. The shape charge on the front of an RPG focuses the energy of the explosives through the side of the vehicle shooting white hot metal to viciously slash around the inside of the track killing or maiming the crew and igniting the ammunition - sometimes even melting the track to the ground. And an RPG was also an effective weapon to take out our Tanks.

From time to time there was also the rushing squelch noise from the radio over the CVC helmet's earpieces. My nerves shot skyward upon hearing any sudden noise. There were even times when I knew that my heart was beating far too loud, and that this could lead Charley through the darkness straight to my position.

*While I was stationed on Okinawa, I experienced that feeling five years earlier when skin diving and suddenly finding myself about thirty feet from a pair of eight-foot-long, pure white, lean and mean sharks in the East China Sea. I was convinced that fear made my heart beat like a drum, which was a dinner bell the sharks could easily hear. I felt this also during these tense periods in the jungle. And this gave a mental flash of certainty that the dreaded enemy had arrived. Like Edger Allen Poe said in <u>The Raven</u>: **"Suddenly there came a tapping, as of someone gently rapping, rapping at my chamber door."** Was this death knocking, knocking, knocking at my door?*

Frequently, just a sparkle from a luminous insect would cause a mental surge of panic. The crackle from an animal playing along the jungle floor could be Charley coming our way - any noise made my heart leap into my throat and it instantly snapped all my finely-honed defensive instincts to alert. My pulse tripled, and the adrenaline charge was instantly felt streaking through my veins, while I hastily searched every inch of this dark, deadly landscape for signs of Charley's presence, hoping that in my lethargy I didn't let an enemy soldier or unit approach.

I listened to the night noises as I scanned the area, letting my night vision search for movement in the darkness. Then I searched every inch of landscape within the view of our starlight scope. I carefully examined the trail that went back into the jungle and tried to look around the trees for shoulders, toes, clothing, edges of hats, or weapons that would give Charley's presence away. Every inch of every piece of the landscape in front and to the sides were carefully inspected. I called for a sit-rep (situation report) from each track, just to be sure every sentinel was alert, and checked-in with the listening post almost to the front of my position.

After fully regaining my alertness, and determining that the ruckus was of no concern, part of my mind gradually wandered again to examine just what brought me to this strange, angry land where one could smell and taste the beautiful green, rotting forest, with its treacherous little men lurking in the darkness behind this incredibly lush vegetation, watching for an opportunity to violently send us all to Hell. Perhaps they were already nearby. Although the platoon's tracks were invisible to my naked eye, I knew exactly where the other six ACAVs and three Big Boys (Tanks) were located. I had placed part of them about 150 feet apart along the east side of the perimeter looking down the road that the convoys were using. And on the north side of the perimeter the remainder of the tracks were facing Cambodia, which was only a few hundred meters through the thick forest. A feeling always nagged me that we were either being watched or slowly being stalked.

Charley's ability to swiftly move about undetected was well known, and frequently when the land mine clearing teams started their sweeping operations in the morning, mines were found in places that should have been observed by night vision devices a very short distance from adjacent defensive positions. No one doubted that Charley ruled the darkness. And for those responsible for securing the perimeter, the darkness was nearly maddening. Was I going mad?

The naked eye could see only the black nothingness of a blind man. The twisted jungle to the front was completely invisible. All was deep black and threatening. And it would have struck overwhelming fear into any man except for periodically using the battery powered starlight scopes. These were light enhancing optical devices that weighed roughly five pounds and were less than two feet long and a few inches in diameter.

Somehow this device allowed sanity to exist where there would have otherwise been none. In using it, I could look to the flanks through a green haze and see two of the adjacent armored vehicles on either side, with the closest vehicle being clearly visible and the second one more obscure. When using this device, it was even possible to see a little way up the trail directly in front of the track that led toward the border, and everyone on watch patiently searched for the movement of these dangerous little men that had been predicted to take a stab at overrunning the new base while we were there. The starlight scopes, however, being battery operated, couldn't be used too often, although there was a mental pull to do so. Every sentinel was tensely awaiting a mass attack by the enemy, who could gamble that the defenders would not respond quick enough as they stormed the perimeter's defenses. And we were so very close to the jungle they could be on us before detected.

When it was my turn to sleep, I found that the daunting responsibility for the welfare of my men, and the base we were protecting, made rest next to impossible. The night passed slowly. It was a tremendous relief when daylight returned, and the night fears receded. Every night along this border was just as nerve racking and it was such a relief when the sun showed its face, even though every day was also subject to the enemy's deadly surprises as well. It was joyous when our assignment changed.

Chapter 21

CONVOYING ALONG THE
CAMBODIAN BORDER

Along the Cambodian border, daily, after the road was swept for mines in key suspect areas, the platoon was split up in a convoy headed for An Loc. The standard operating procedure we had adopted was that when the convoy came under attack the armored vehicles closest to the ambush would fiercely engage the enemy, immediately attacking into their strength, while the convoy continued to move as fast as possible, trying not to stop if possible until past the killing zone. As more armored vehicles arrived on the scene they would join in the battle until the enemy was destroyed.

After passing the ambush site the convoy would slow down until the armor was finished kicking butt and rejoined the convoy. The platoon varied the pattern a little so as not to give away any tactical advantage to Charley, but it couldn't be varied too much and still provide the necessary protection. Fortunately, most ambushes were sprung while the road was being swept for mines and the out-posting of the road usually kept Charley at bay while the convoys passed through. But there were always gaps in the out-postings which still allowed opportunities for ambushes. My platoon was confronted by only one ambush, and some ineffective sniping another time during this period until the Junction City II campaign was completed.

I forced myself to stay focused on the chores at hand, always fearful of an ambush, and unhappy about needing to eat enormous amounts of dust while running these convoys. Soon after the platoon stopped at the NDP where I was promoted, we began alternating convoy security missions with another platoon. The convoys were now getting fewer and fewer, as most of the equipment and supplies were already moved into place or removed from the forward areas. This was where I met the other "B" Troop Platoon Leaders on the day I was promoted to 1st Lieutenant. My promotion orders were dated the first of April, but it took nearly a week for them to get to Vietnam. But that really wasn't too bad. And after the promotion I had a couple opportunities to perform some missions with the Troop Headquarters for about a week before the end of Junction City II.

During that brief period of working under the Troop Commander, the platoon continued to run convoys, but mixed it up with some search and destroy missions where we would join up with Infantry units and try to catch the Viet Cong in their tunnel hideouts or in villages, which for the most part were under Charley's control in this far out area on the fringe of the 1st Infantry Division's Area of Operations. But for the most part the Junction City campaigns had driven the enemy south away from the area we were searching, and we were only finding tunnels and ammunition.

On April 7 or 8 at about 10AM, while the platoon was about a half hour down the dusty road from the remote site, escorting a convoy toward An Loc, I received a call on the radio from an Air Force Forward Observer (FO) with a call sign of "Red Barron" in a spotter plane somewhere above the Division's operations. The Red Barron said he had intercepted a Red Cross message that my wife had a baby. Nothing more, just "a baby and its weight." Concerned about the brevity of the message, I asked the FO to get more information, and he said he would try, and went off the air.

There was considerable tension during the next ten minutes or so until the Red Barron came back to announce the baby was a healthy little girl, and the mother and baby were doing fine. This was Maria Toyoko Conley, my second daughter. The baby was born on the 7th of April.

[*My first child, Irene Marie, was born while I was in Germany a couple years earlier. I was called away from shivering in my M-60 Tank in near zero weather, while I was trying to make the heater work, to the Red Cross office to be informed of her birth. This was very nice of the Red Cross. What one normally remembers is the Red Cross bearing unfortunate news of the serious illness or death of a family member back home. This was quite different.*]

The kind of news I received was terrific and it served to timely break the boredom and monotony of the convoy work. This is not the last encounter I would have with the Red Barron. There would be two more over the next year and a half that became very memorable. Quite a guy!

Midst the giddiness of the moment, radio discipline went to Hell in a hand basket. There was far too much laughter and chatter on the radios. Charley apparently mis-interpreted this chatter as an indication of poorly disciplined soldiers and went for it. That was his mistake and they were quickly overrun (estimate 15 VC casualties). It did, however, put a stop to the frivolity and radio discipline was restored. Fortunately, we took no losses or damage.

Perhaps the platoon's discipline was why the Second Platoon was chosen to stay up north at Quan Loi when the Junction City II campaign ended. We knew how to conduct business without supervision, plus I was the oldest Platoon Leader, age wise, in the Squadron. Although I did not have that much time in country, I had an efficient unit with very skilled and competent Non-commissioned Officers and a Platoon Sergeant that could operate on his own at any given moment. Most Platoon Leaders speak highly about their Platoon Sergeants. They boast that they have the best one in the Army. But I was sure that SFC Coker was the best of the best. And he had been an effective Platoon Leader of this platoon for nearly six months before I arrived.

In any case, the Junction City campaigns were not that eventful for us.

For the most part the cavalrymen seemed a bit dismayed at being used primarily in defensive roles, out-posting the roads or providing convoy security. Perhaps that was necessary. The few occasions we had an opportunity to take an offensive role were exciting. But little opportunity was provided for that so far. Whenever we had an opportunity to show some initiative and demonstrate how the platoon could be a vital part of an Infantry mission, except for our experiences with LTC Cavazos, I felt that the Infantry had been shortchanged in their training on how to use armor.

The platoon was used as a blocking force on occasion, but that also was a minimally effective use of a cavalry unit's capabilities. It seemed like the Infantry felt most comfortable in using the armor as mobile bunkers. Perhaps they were nervous of all that firepower while they were running helter-skelter on the ground. In any case we were pleased to receive the mission to Quan Loi that could possibly lead to some independent actions.

Chapter 22

A FINAL MISSION WITH THE TROOP

The Troop had one more mission with the Headquarters and its two platoons before our detachment to Quan Loi. It was a search and destroy operation through the Dutchman's Rubber Plantation about five or six kilometers south of An Loc on the west side of Thunder Road. The Troop came off QL-13 to the north of the rubber trees and skirted the plantation. The 2nd Platoon was given a mission to search the southwest side of the plantation.

We searched the area systematically and eventually found a large underground tunnel complex about 300 meters southwest of the rubber trees in a lightly wooded area. There were booby trap trip wires galore. We carefully cleared over 20 well placed booby traps before sending volunteers, including myself, into the tunnels. We were surprised to find a significant stash of ammunition.

We pulled about fifty 60mm mortar rounds out of the five tunnel entrances, along with a large pile of small arms ammo, a couple hundred pounds of C3 explosives and 20 or so assorted anti-personnel and anti-tank mines. While the tunnel entrances were being blown shut with C4, the munitions were being organized for destruction.

Scout Section Leader SGT Bernadine discovered a huge 250-pound bomb that didn't explode on impact. It was only about 75 meters away, so all the enemy munitions and explosives were carefully moved and stacked around the bomb, which took nearly an hour. A mat of American C4 explosives was then carefully placed over the pile, so that when the C4 was detonated everything would explode in place as opposed to flying all over the landscape.

The C4 was fused to blow in 3 minutes. Once the rest of the platoon was moved to a safe distance, SGT Bernadine ignited the fuses and high-tailed it to the platoon's position. He no sooner arrived when the explosives detonated. The roar ripped through the afternoon air like thunder and the ground shook violently. A huge fireball rose to at least 100 meters above the detonation and it spilled an ugly, dirty black cloud several hundred meters into the sky before it started to dissipate.

We then drove east between the rubber trees, and after the last unit moving south passed and the other "B" Troop elements jumped onto the convoy's tail, Bravo 26 moved north to An Loc and then to Quan Loi.

Chapter 23

FREEDOMS OF THE DETACHED PLATOON

Bingo!! We found ourselves detached from the Squadron and our Troop and heading for Quan Loi, while the 1st Infantry Division rolled down the road south to Lai Khe, leaving the Thunder Road above Lai Khe pretty much in Charley's hands again. I didn't know that this detachment would be for over three months. The attachment to Quan Loi was a grand new adventure, and a strange independence to be part of the guardians of an airstrip at a Frenchman's plantation home. The military Officer in charge of the defense of Quan Loi was a full Colonel known as Dixie North. The site had a major radio relay station, known humorously as Dixie North's erection, for the huge antenna erected at that location.

The plantation owner's residence included a small fixed wing aircraft airstrip and an opulent Frenchman's home that sported a very large Romanesque swimming pool adorned with statues and arches, complete with beautiful growths of ivy clinging to the walls of the home and stone arches around the pool.

Quan Loi Plantation Home

The Frenchman's swimming pool was a gorgeous blue ceramic structure with sparkling water. It was roughly 50 yards long by about 25 yards wide and was surrounded by a wide deck capable of handling a large party, and it all was buried within plush landscaping maintained by several workers of the household staff. There was a wide walkway that went up to the plantation house with a series of cement steps broken by flat walkways and flowery decorative plants all the way to the home.

There was a privacy fence about seven feet high that extended around the swimming pool and the west side of the garden and home which was adjacent to the artillery positions.

Occasionally I could see a pretty blond lass in her late 20s to mid-30s take a dip by observing from the top of my track.

When we pulled into the base camp that surrounded the airstrip, the platoon was placed on the north side

The Swimming Pool

of the perimeter facing a huge gully, over a kilometer across and at least a hundred feet deep. It was filled with dense jungle forest that appeared to have never been molested by the war and which stretched to the east for a couple kilometers down to where the landscape opened into terraced rice paddies down to a river. And you could see well above the tree tops of this pristine landscape to the rubber trees on the opposite side of the gully.

The positions for the tracks on the perimeter were fixed, with berms that were bulldozed to protect the fronts of the vehicles and part of their sides. These positions were spread about 100 feet apart, which was a concern at night, especially on dark rainy nights. The positions were forward of a dirt road that went completely around the perimeter, except for the Platoon Leader's ACAV's position which was behind the road and almost backed up to the privacy fence by the swimming pool, and the Platoon Sergeant's ACAV which was behind the road, near the Artillery Command and Control Center.

Close to B-26 I had a small tent and a cot to sleep on, a folding chair and a wooden folding desk, which was the extent of the luxuries enjoyed.

On the north-east end of the Platoon sector was a well built out-house which was enclosed on three sides with plywood about four feet high. The open side faced the gully so one could sit and enjoy the view of the beautiful, green jungle tree tops while they relieved themselves. This shit house was fully equipped with two halves of 55-gallon drums beneath the seats, which were pulled out, doused with diesel fuel and burned out daily, often as a punitive assignment.

Lt John Conley
at Quan Loi

On the Platoon's right flank was an Engineer tank platoon, five tanks from Dreadnaught Bravo, "B" Company, 1st Battalion 34th Armor, minus a couple tank platoons that were attached to other units. We were attached to this Tank Company with Captain (CPT) Claude L. Clark as its commander. The elements of his Company at Quan Loi were his headquarters, one tank platoon (his second platoon), two Quad 50 Gatling guns mounted on 2½ Ton trucks, two 40mm (anti-aircraft) Dusters, and his maintenance platoon. CPT Clark had to frequently fly out to look after the detached part of his company and his duties did not allow him to venture out on missions outside of the Quan Loi base camp.

His Second Platoon Leader, SFC Perry, was an excellent leader who was anxious for an opportunity to do more than protect the Quan Loi perimeter. CPT Clark regularly gave me the opportunity to use his tank platoon when patrolling the huge rubber plantation and jungle and bamboo that surrounded our new home. The men of both platoons were eager to work together. and building tactics to suit such a force was interesting for everyone. Who would have thought that a young Platoon Leader would find himself with such independence and a mix of armored units to command? CPT Clark had some kind words to say in a special efficiency rating he wrote for me. (See appendix)

Quan Loi was just a few miles east of An Loc, which was a large city protected by South Vietnamese (ARVN) units. The platoon rarely visited An Loc except on some Sundays when we would escort a Vietnamese Catholic priest to his services when the VC were milling around the area looking for trouble. We also had an opportunity to take the priest to a few villages when he needed protection to do his duties.

Fr. Chin (sp) and some parishioners in a Montagnard Village

The town of Quan Loi was a village on the outskirts of the base camp and in a small group of buildings cold beer and female companionship was available. Usually on Saturday or Sunday the platoon would kick back a little from patrolling the plantation and enjoy these amenities, a few troopers at a time.

The plantation home, airstrip and all military positions were on a high ground peninsula jutting northeast from the rubber plantation, overlooking a steep drop off facing jungle on the east and south side of the peninsula to terraced rice paddies down to a river and over to the village. The jungle went around the north side of the peninsula and

105mm Howitzer positions

into the deep gully facing our positions. The jungle there was so dense in the drop off in front of our positions that there would be no way to detect enemy movement until Charley was in our laps. I never was advised of any of our Infantry units venturing into this area which made this a quite dangerous location. Dixie North was a very nice person, who got along with everyone at the base camp. It was believed that he reported to the highest commanders in the country, and the 1st Infantry Division had the job of providing security for the airstrip and communications facilities. Dixie North respected all the attached units, and he never tried to pretend

175mm Long Tom

that he knew how to employ his armor elements more effectively than the officers commanding those units, and consulting a lowly lieutenant was not beneath his dignity.

8-inch Howitzer

On the south side of the plantation house was a Battalion of heavy artillery composed of 8-inch Self Propelled Howitzers and 175mm Long Toms that would keep the ground rocking almost every night, firing harassing fire and to provide a protective umbrella for the American and Vietnamese long-range patrols in the area. There were also 105mm Howitzers to provide shorter range support and more rapid fire. The Infantry Battalion that protected the remainder of the perimeter also had their Mortars linked into the fire support plan.

Oh, what a glorious, comfortable, wonderful night it was on the rare occasions that the big guns were quiet. How we learned to sleep with those guns going off over our heads is a mystery. And what a pleasure it was to leave the perimeter on our daily patrols to get away from that ear shattering concussion. Probably all the Cavalrymen's ears were damaged spending all that time next to those huge artillery pieces, and they would surely be destined to many years of restless sleep caused by the loud, sharp report of the artillery.

Midway down the platoon's section of the perimeter were the bath house tents. We tried to get in from patrols daily in time to wash off the red laterite before the bath house closed. This was not always possible. On the way in we would go to the water point and fill our 5-gallon containers with freshly treated water, as well and go to the POL Point to refuel the vehicles to be ready to move out at a moment's notice. But washing that red laterite off the body was close to heaven on earth.

The troopers enjoyed one huge benefit by being located by the Artillery units. This made it possible to get two hot meals daily. The Dreadnaught Bravo cooks were also working in the Artillery mess hall, and everyone knew how necessary it was to have a hot meal ready for the armored combat elements when they returned from a mission. The cooking was first class and best of all close by. Everyone was very gracious and never gave any crap when the platoon got in late for dinner. They always would check to see if the Cavalry had eaten before closing the mess line and made it a point to save plenty if they hadn't.

The Artillery Fire Control Center was easy to work with, and they made plotting artillery checkpoints to adjust artillery from on the daily missions enjoyable. This was one of the most important priorities following breakfast.

Chapter 24

THE PATROLS

We could simply have swept a section of the road daily for mines and out-posted the road to protect the traffic, or perhaps run a few escort missions between Quan Loi and An Loc. But that would be terribly boring and there would soon be a loss of readiness for a fight if one came along. Since both Dixie North and CPT Clark understood that concern, I was given the opportunity to plan and execute daily missions to the limits of the rubber plantation and beyond so long as we stayed inside of the area where we could be supported by the 105mm artillery battery (the 105mm artillery fan).

We had a great time working with the Dreadnaught Bravo tank platoon. At first, I didn't mix the units together, but gradually over the first couple weeks the additional tanks provided a great opportunity to experiment. By mixing my ACAVs with the Dreadnaught tanks, I could create two cavalry platoons. Both SFC Coker and the tank platoon leader, SFC Perry, were top notch, experienced Non-Commissioned Officers and they were ready to play around with the interesting possibilities. It sure helped keep the boredom under control.

Except for one day a week, we would leave early each morning on a mission to make our presence known in and around the rubber plantation. Our area of operations would be assigned daily, and it usually included a section of jungle or bamboo that bordered the vast plantation. Just like the rubber trees further south, the trees here were planted European style and a tank would fit nicely between the neat rows of trees.

The tactics we used were to move to the assigned area and shift through various standard formations (line, column, and echelon) between the rows of rubber trees. Mines were a major concern and if workers were not seen in an area, the ACAVs would very carefully follow the tanks with the left track of the ACAVs trailing the left track of the tank to reduce some of the risk. Sometimes the pucker factor became so extreme that it was necessary to travel in a column, single file with two tanks leading and one in the rear. *The term "pucker factor" represented the tightness of one's rectum with extreme nervousness, with the maximum pucker factor being capable of pinching off the head of a needle.*

Generally, we could move fast in the rubber plantation, except for areas where there were berms that made me very nervous, as to cross them required the tanks to come nearly to a halt and expose their underbelly to any enterprising enemy. If Charley was behind the next berm with an RPG Launcher, a tank with its belly exposed would be an easy, more vulnerable target. One answer to this problem was to put tanks in adjacent rows of trees, and alternate moving one tank across the berms at a time and cover its vulnerabilities as best possible with the others.

When the extra tanks were attached, we played with the formations. While leaving the rubber and going into the bamboo or jungle, I'd put the tanks nearly bumper to bumper in front of a row of ACAVs. That made it possible to make good headway through heavy undergrowth and push it down into the face of anyone who had plans to attack a tank from the front. Gradually I learned that we could move quickly from any formation into this new "Box" formation and back into a standard formation when the terrain opened-up again.

With a half dozen tanks up front and everyone else behind them, this new formation gave a great deal of security. And I always knew where everyone was while going through extremely dense vegetation. The cavalrymen on the thin skinned ACAVs protected the rear of the tanks from snipers or VC in spider holes who could shoot an exposed tank commander in the back. The ACAVs also created some depth for flank and rear protection of the formation.

The Box was a specialty formation, and of course it was not suited for open terrain where the ACAVs could be better used on line with the tanks or in an echelon formation. But I could never overlook the benefits of having ACAVs behind the tanks to protect the tank commander's rear. If it was a combined Infantry/Armor assault formation, the infantry could likely serve the purpose of walking behind the tanks to provide that security. But we never had the opportunity to try this idea out. We had tanks and ACAV's and this worked just fine.

I liked this Box formation more and more as we used it. Being able to see all the fighting vehicles eliminated the risk of the accidental shooting of friendlies if Charley jumped up between the tracks. I was later to learn more and more very important advantages of the Box. A large clearing was made while pushing through the thick jungle, which facilitated aerial resupply and the landing of med-evac (dust-off) helicopters. It was also easy to see the whole unit from the air, making close air support and adjusting artillery from the air a piece of cake.

Most of the time though, conditions were such that we used the standard formations, and the real benefits of the Box would have to wait until we were in heavy Jungle or bamboo. I would not learn how to most effectively use this formation until I controlled "B" Troop during the first days of the 1st Tet Offensive the following year, and when I later commanded "A" Troop.

Chapter 25

THE WATER DISASTER

Suddenly, an unexpected problem began. Every member of the platoon had the Montezuma's Revenge and it didn't want to ease up. Everyone at Quan Loi seemed to have the same problem to some degree or another. As the weeks progressed so did the diarrhea. When in a column every fifteen minutes the platoon would have to herringbone (turning every other track 45 degrees to the left and right), and half of the troopers at a time would dismount and crap beside their tracks. (If we had today's Modern Volunteer Army and female soldiers were in the platoon, we would obviously have had a tougher time dealing with these issues.)

Day after day this continued. Some seemed to start building a tolerance. Others, including myself, just kept getting worse. Soon I had lost about thirty pounds and began feeling severe exhaustion from the ordeal. Conversations would be rudely interrupted by loud groans from within, and my extremely sore rear end didn't seem to understand the abuse. Fearing it was amoebic dysentery motivated me to fly to the Lai Khe field hospital to have it examined.

Surprise photo at shit house by a 2nd Platoon trooper. Paybacks were Hell!

At Lai Khe, I was treated to all the general tests, which showed nothing. But the problem almost immediately disappeared. So, after sleeping on clean sheets for two days I flew back to Quan Loi. The diarrhea returned immediately with a vengeance after my release from the field hospital, and it was soon determined that it was caused by too much chlorine being used in the water purification process. The problem went away when the water was treated properly and so did the need for the extraordinary supply of petroleum jelly. The cramping and pain stopped, and my groaning innards were very grateful.

Upon my return from Lai Khe I learned that my platoon had been tested by Charley the night before and had performed marvelously under the capable command of SFC Coker. I was a little put out at having missed the Viet Cong company sized probe right into our sector of the perimeter. Only one of my men was slightly wounded. Charley had used Bangalore torpedoes to blow holes in the perimeter wire and put pieces of wood across the wire, but it did them no good. The battle lasted about an hour and the enemy drug their dead and wounded away leaving no way to know for sure what damage was inflicted on them. But the estimate was placed at 20 enemy killed. I was very proud of how my men performed while I was away, but I felt guilty and pissed at missing the fight. This increase in Charley's activity doubled my determination to push outside the rubber plantation into his lair.

Chapter 26

IT'S KICK-ASS TIME

It seemed a little screwy at first, but I wanted to find a way to bait Charley into a fight. Call it payback if you want to, but I was more dedicated after the VC attacked my platoon in my absence. My NCOs and I put our heads together and brain-stormed for a workable scheme to trick them into a fight.

Soon, my platoon, plus the Dreadnaught Bravo platoon, left Quan Loi at 0630 one morning with the Company's two 40mm Dusters (anti-aircraft weapons tracked vehicles), and two 2 ½ ton trucks that had quad fifty (50 caliber) guns mounted in the truck beds. The quad fifties were covered with canvas and it must have seemed a bit unusual to the onlookers when our unit turned up a road through the rubber plantation toward the western part of the plantation which ended on the edge of the jungle. It was a sucker play. But would it work?

Anyone viewing this would hopefully believe we were bringing what appeared to be cargo to the edge of the jungle in those covered vehicles. It just had to draw some interest. Several plantation workers saw the unusual column approach to where the rubber trees ended. Before entering the jungle, we stopped to pull a little maintenance, eat lunch and hook tow cables from the front of the trucks to the rear of a couple ACAVs.

Then, after about an hour to give Charley a chance to hastily bring some forces into the area, I gave the command to head north. Three tanks were in the lead with Staff Sergeant Grossinger up front. He was fast, very fast, and when his tank came under fire, you would hear the 90mm main gun on his tank report with three quick, well aimed shots of canister ammunition in such close succession it almost sounded like an automatic weapon. Grossinger insisted on being the point tank and nobody argued that they were better suited for the job.

My ACAV, B-26, was the second track behind the lead three tanks. A couple tanks were in the middle of the ACAVs and the remaining tanks were at the rear. The 40mm Dusters were also evenly spread out in the column. The quad fifties were midway between the middle and the rear tanks, and the front and middle tanks. This must have been a confusing sight for Charley. We moved through clearings in the jungle and slowly worked to the northwest. The Artillery was ready to support.

There was dense jungle on the left and lighter growth on the small rise to the right side of the formation when the excitement started. We were hugging the thickest jungle on the left, so we could see down into the darkness and not be surprised from that side. Contact came from the right side as a rocket propelled grenade was fired at the front tank and Grossinger cut loose. Almost at once a barrage of enemy small arms fire started, and both platoons responded with overwhelming firepower. But instead of attacking into the strength, this time the canvas was pulled from the quad fifties and Hell fire was unleashed on Charley.

It was a sight to behold as the vegetation was mowed down by the 50 caliber guns along with any Viet Cong who dared to lift their heads. The artillery was quickly adjusted as a blocking force behind the enemy and moved toward the platoons as a gun ship worked the jungle on our left side. The 40mm Dusters cut loose on the right flank and had a great time flooding the area with anti-aircraft ammunition. The tanks and ACAVs herringboned and fired into the left and right sides of our formation. We pounded the area on both flanks for about ten minutes. That should have sent the message I had in mind, so our heavily armed combined arms unit returned to the plantation which was about a half hour away.

There is probably some Charley still wandering around that piece of jungle, even today, in a daze saying "Oh Shit! Oh Shit!" We all had a ball, and I felt a lot better after getting a good piece of our enemy. This was payback. Hopefully they would catch on to that message.

Chapter 27

INTO THE BAMBOO

One day we planned a swing through the southeastern border of the plantation. It was only with my own platoon, and it brought us in contact with a new kind of vegetation. The whole southeastern border of the rubber plantation appeared to be ancient bamboo that towered into the air nearly 20 feet with a variety of sizes up to 3 and 4 inches in diameter. It was a solid light green wall immediately bordering the neat rows of mature rubber trees.

Suspicions were aroused as there weren't any workers harvesting the rubber or even passing through. The bamboo had well used paths extending from the plantation's edge, although the maps showed no villages or other reasons to justify such foot traffic.

It was just too quiet for comfort and everyone seemed to be feeling the same creepy feeling of being watched. I pulled the platoon a couple hundred feet back into the rubber trees and formed a perimeter with the tanks facing the bamboo. We took some time to eat lunch and examine the maps. The peace was suddenly interrupted by an explosion from an RPG round that overshot the vehicles, and an intense barrage of small arms automatic fire.

There was a mad scramble to remount the tracks. No one was hurt as the platoon had about finished lunch and everyone was either on their track or milling around them at the time. We quickly formed on line in the rows between the rubber trees and attacked into the bamboo. I called for artillery support, as we moved beyond the rubber trees.

It became obvious that the tanks had little problem progressing forward, especially while firing the Canister rounds, which weakened the heavy bamboo stands. But, the lighter ACAVs were not as capable, and in addition to the crews being beaten up by the bamboo falling over their tracks, with their abundant supply of huge biting red ants, the lighter vehicles were lagging behind. Besides having the problem of losing sight between the tracks, I had an immediate concern for the lack of protection afforded to the backs of tank commanders from spider holes that were driven over.

This was just the kind of enemy tactic I learned about as an anti-tank assault-man in the Marines, and it made my skin crawl. It was good that there wasn't much chance yet for RPG gunners to get a shot at a track with the bamboo being pushed into their faces, but the risk of a back shot was nerve racking, and it smelled like trouble.

I backed the platoon out quickly and reorganized into a Box formation with 3 tanks up front, almost bumper to bumper, and with ACAVs following each outside tank, and with my ACAV behind the center tank. With the artillery now working to our front we moved forward again. We found it about as easy to move through the bamboo as through the thick jungle in this formation, and just as secure. It was a lot easier and safer to enter this rough vegetation in this unorthodox formation, rather than try to get into the Box while bamboo or trees were pounding down on the tracks with their basic load of biting insects and possible deadly bamboo vipers.

As we progressed through the bamboo, we reconnoitered the front and flanks with machine gun fire to keep any enemy gunners in their holes. But the exercise was otherwise uneventful, except for some ant nests in the bamboo that the troopers would have rather not disturbed. What we were learning though was new tactics that weren't in any manuals and were tailored to thwart Charley's tactics and the environment we were working in. We did, however, find a lot of evidence of large units moving south. This was reported to Dixie North who passed it on to the Division. We never received any feedback.

Chapter 28

KEEPING CHARLEY OFF-BALANCE

It was our job to test Charley at every opportunity but tricking him into a fight was not easy. These jungles were tough. The enemy spent much of his time hiding under the ground. He moved at night through jungle trails and picked his targets based on his logic, not ours. But his logic was basic animal. We had the equipment, he had the cunning, and we had to adapt.

A few patterns could be seen, and they were consistent. The minute we dropped our guard a bit, the VC were there, like rattlers coiled to strike. Always lurking in the shadows. Always watching, but rarely ever seen. Always ready with an effective new tactic. A sign of their presence could be found in well walked pathways where there was no apparent reason for it. Occasionally a bunker complex was discovered, but they were normally abandoned. They were like pre-established motels that only the enemy knew about, which they would use when moving through an area. These defensive positions were already in place. No putting out wire. They just quietly dropped into the holes and moved again when they saw fit to do so.

Getting Charley to expose himself was nearly impossible if he wanted to be invisible. And this phantom enemy proved very hard to hunt. It was necessary for everyone to stay alert, 24 hours a day, 7 days a week, every week, and always be the predator and try to keep Charley off balance. It was a chore to keep up a good defense while staying on the offense as much as possible. But if that's what getting home in one piece meant, then that was what we would do. We were in the business of making our tactics at least meet his head on. His moves needed to be anticipated and our tactics needed to conform to the way he wanted to fight, or to trick him into believing he had the upper hand.

So, the platoon was always required to be ready, and I rethought the tactics learned in the Marines on how the Chinese Nationalists innovated to destroy Japanese tanks by surprise. I listened to the many stories of past enemy actions that my troopers had experienced and ran this through my mind over and over, and over again.

This was not much different from the early American Cavalry roaming around the West, with the Indian tribes blending into the wilderness and sneaking up on their prey. Prey we were, and predators as well. Rabbits, with the best weapons and equipment in the world, hunting invisible wolves, who could appear at will with razor sharp teeth to make our day. The training we had did not go far enough.

How could it have been possible to understand this primitive mind. We were dealing with the deadliest animal on the face of the earth. He was stealthy, unpredictable for the most part, dedicated to their mission of killing Americans, and fully knowledgeable of our tactics. And there were no limits on the terror they could use. If it was possible for the human mind to create a horror, it was acceptable in their world. But not in ours. We would never comprehend their savagery, and the few times we saw the product of their most evil imagination would create a lifelong impression. And there was a fear of knowing that they were watching, always watching, and you had no idea where they were.

Chapter 29

MISSION IMPOSSIBLE

Quan Loi was on high ground and a river flowed in a deep draw to the north and to the east. To the northeast the map showed the heavy jungle opening into low ground with terraced rice paddies on either side of the river for over a kilometer of low, wet ground. Where the ground rose again to the north of the river there was a sizable village with a road leading north to a larger town. All of this was remote territory where it was apparent that there were few if any visitors from our side. A small river flowed easterly into one that was large and clearly non-fordable. I was searching the map to find a surprise target. And I thought I found it.

An aerial photo of the area northeast of Quan Loi on the opposite side of the rice paddy laden gully showed a grown over trail going all the way from QL-13, starting between An Loc and Loc Nihn, north of An Loc, and meandering through fairly young jungle re-growth, ending at the village north of the paddies. This village was the only logical place where the people lived who harvested these extensive terraced rice paddies. Following the map and aerial photo further to the east showed a possible way to get through the river that merited inspection if we wanted to plunder this year's rice crop. Hopefully, Charlie hadn't already taken the rice up the road to the north of the village.

I took the platoon on a swing through the rubber and located an old abandoned road that moved north toward the river. Traveling parallel to the road we pushed a single path to within sight of the river. There was a high and dry level area to the left and right of the road that ended at a bombed-out bridge. Dismounting with a half dozen troopers, we walked to the water's edge. On the left side of the blown bridge the water was deep. To the right side the stream split leaving a sturdy little island between what became two shallow streams. The first stream had a spot that was a couple feet deep where the water moved swiftly. The bottom was surprisingly firm with what appeared to be a stone base covered with silt and the site had a dead tree hanging across the water. After crossing over it was clear that the island could support tanks. About 50 meters further to the east we found a flat open area of shallow water that was almost stagnant. The bottom was mushy and about 100 feet wide, but there was a place firm enough to cross the second leg of water. It was possible to now do the impossible, to cross that river, secure the village, extract the rice that appeared in the aerial photo, if it was still there. Perhaps a Med-Cap operation and even a fight with a surprised enemy could be had. There were not many chances to surprise anyone with an armored unit, but the map revealed that we could sneak through the jungle to the east of the unused road north of the blown-out bridge under cover of noise from artillery. We could finally put that noisy artillery to good use. The decision would be that of Dixie North.

It felt good to present this Cavalry discovery to Dixie North. It was rare that a Cavalry platoon had such independence to create a significant plan from nothing. And I was truly surprised to see some genuine excitement over this discovery. The plan quickly developed. Since the area to the east and north of the village was right at the edge of the 105mm artillery fan coverage, the Colonel decided to move four self-propelled 8-inch Howitzers to the flat spot by the river just to the left of the road by the blown-out bridge. Those 8-inch crews could drop artillery on a dime and that could be very important. An Infantry platoon would provide their security while the Cavalry crossed the river. More Infantry and a Medical Team would be ready to fly to the village once the area was secured. And they would haul away the rice we found.

It rained hard the next two days and then the opportunity came. We were on the road heading east at 0500, before the sun came up and the workers started to mill around the plantation. The plantation was deserted and having broken our pattern of movement, we proceeded unobserved to the river. About a half hour after arrival the artillery was ready to fire, and the Platoon started to cautiously cross the river and submerge itself into the triple canopy jungle beyond. Dixie North and the artillery were monitoring the platoon's progress by a series of predetermined checkpoints which were smoothly crossed.

We were all in awe at the most beautiful, pristine, unmolested forest we had ever seen. There was no sign of life. The canopy towered well over 100 feet above our slowly moving column. Huge mahogany trees joined hands above the mold laden surface leaving large gaps to travel through without any need to run over any of the gorgeous ferns and other unique foliage. It was so quiet and unspoiled. There were no signs of war here, which made me very nervous, and we gently worked our way between the magnificence with our war machines, trying not to bring the damage of war to this paradise, while fully knowing that this was a great place to hide a huge enemy unit.

As we moved to within 1,000 meters from the northeastern edge of the village, I called for Artillery fire in the dense jungle along the unused road north of the bombed-out bridge to mask the sound of our movement. Once we were east of the village, the platoon came out of the jungle and charged northwest across the road that went out the northeast side of the village, spread out and moved into the village throwing the citizens into a panic.

There was rice everywhere, tons and tons of it ready for someone's market and most of it was already bagged for shipment. All of it was planned to be shipped north, deep into enemy territory very soon. Our planned activities were going to cause a bit of a stir in the enemy village barely in sight up the road. Within a half hour the Infantry was on the ground and the helicopters were hauling out the rice and bringing in the Med-Cap team. The people were completely cooperative and passively sat by and watched the activity. There was no anger shown, no emotion at all, and it was crystal clear that we Americans appeared to be a strange and unusual lot to them. They were going to lose the rice anyway, and at least this way they didn't have to do the work of bagging the rest of it.

When the infantry had the village in their control, I took part of the platoon to the northwest to observe the destroyed vehicle that was on my aerial photograph. It was the burned-out hulk of an M113 personnel carrier that had hit a mine on the driver's side. The markings were burned off and I felt it best to stay clear of it because of possible booby-traps. While we checked out the burned-out track from a distance Sergeant Bernadine took his track, B-23, and the other ACAV in his Scout Section a little way up the road to watch for any enemy activity to the north of the village.

Just after the Med-Cap team left the village and all the rice and Infantry were extracted, Sergeant Bernadine, reported that there was a small amount of dust seen on the road in the distance moving our way. This prompted me to move the platoon into positions about fifty to seventy-five feet from the road, on its west side, spread out over about 100 yards and backed into the trees. We sat quietly with the engines on idle waiting to pounce on Charley.

Then we received an order from Dixie North to get the Hell out of there. The platoon was on the wrong side of the river and there was suddenly a lot more dust coming down the road. I called for artillery and the 8-inch howitzers started firing on the road disbursing those vehicles. Under the cover of the Artillery, we quickly crossed the road and went back into the cover of the jungle to backtrack toward the river.

Entry into the beautiful, triple canopy jungle brought with it an unusual sense of safety and serenity. But that was clearly a feeling that needed to be resisted. Nothing was known of this area, but Charley would know it all too well. So, we moved quickly, but cautiously. As the column neared the ford and was making a curve to the left, a beautiful peacock suddenly appeared an equal distance from all the tracks about 50 feet to the east. The suspense and tension were tremendous at that point, although we were within sprinting distance of the river, and about to break out of this jungle paradise. As we were making the semicircle turn to the left, I saw that all guns were pointed at the gorgeous bird with its plumage spread triumphantly. Acquiescing to some primal urge affecting all the men at once, I whispered over the radio - *"fire"*. In an instant the beauty was gone, my heart immediately dropped from this senseless execution that could only be accounted for by a stroke of sudden madness, and I knew this should never have happened. I would have to control this new-found impulse in the future.

Getting over the river was uneventful, as was the movement of the Artillery and Infantry back to Quan Loi. It was an exciting day and we were a very proud Cavalry platoon. We had our way with the enemy at last, and we knew Charley would have to try to provide a payback, but for the moment this platoon was on top of the world. And best of all, we pulled it off without anyone being injured. We never mentioned the peacock. Everyone knew that this meaningless killing was wrong. I never asked anyone what that shared evil urge was. The platoon received a tremendous amount of praise at Quan Loi and it felt great to be looked up to by the officers of all the units involved.

Chapter 30

MORE PATROLLING

While traveling in and around the plantation over the next few weeks it became evident that an enemy buildup was going on. The people were getting less friendly, indicating that they were worried and likely being watched. The VC transportation routes through the jungles around the rubber plantation were much more traveled. And the plantation was being serviced less and less by the workers. I reported the evidence we were experiencing. It was our job to search and report.

As we wandered around the plantation, we had interesting creature experiences. Charging between the rubber trees early in the morning created a special spider hazard. Intricate, beautiful webs would be spun between rubber trees, and at the dead center would be a single huge yellow and black spider. With his legs spread on the web the spider would be roughly six inches across with a body over two inches long. Although they were often the exact height of the tank commanders face while standing in their cupolas, and a few did get into the tanks, the troopers never suffered any spider bite casualties, probably because they were so scary and impossible to ignore.

Then there were walking sticks over six inches long and completely unafraid. And praying mantises over four inches long. And beautiful birds of all varieties of color. What a strange land this was.

The natives we met were interesting people. Frequently the tracks would be approached by young boys and girls with wares to sell, and on occasion vending their bodies. Although I was no prude, I did not want these people around our tracks for discipline and safety reasons. You never really knew who they were working for. With the tracks separated during road posting duties, it was hard to keep the men from playing with the young ladies, and they looked more and more attractive as the weeks and months passed and the testosterone raged.

The Montagnards were natives with a Cambodian decent. They were friendly, tough mountain folk and never appeared to have any love for our enemies. They stayed separate and lived in small villages away from the cities tending their gardens, hunting and scavenging a living. Their women usually did not wear tops and had some of the most beautiful breasts imaginable. The men often had white fungus growth all over their bodies and chewing Beetle-nut was necessary to control the pain and discomfort they experienced. Learning of this body fungus would save my life in a couple months. Beetle-nut was an effective narcotic to kill all pain and was often chewed to kill the pain from rotting teeth. A smile was not a pleasant matter. But the people were simple, wonderful folk. I had a hunch that the Montagnards could all be trusted, but the stakes were too high to gamble on that notion.

I enjoyed catching animals in the jungle when the opportunity surfaced. It was not uncommon to catch large snakes, or possums with gorgeous striped furry coats, and other animals while disturbing the wilderness. As a rule, I would keep an animal alive until we arrived at a village and then kill the animal and give it as a gift to the village chief. These gifts were well received. It was necessary to kill the animals. The natives had no refrigeration, so animals had to be eaten right away or they would spoil. Killing the animals made it impossible for them to be taken away by enemy soldiers moving through the area for a later food source.

Chapter 31

THE PACHYDERM

As time went on we searched in and around the plantation and enjoyed short visits with the Montagnards. As we looked north eastward across the treetops of the deep ravine in front of our positions about 4 to 5 kilometers, we could sometimes see the smoke from their village fires. To get there, it was necessary to travel along narrow roads in the plantation or go between the rubber trees and over multiple series of berms in the plantation. Although it would take only about an hour by road, for the most part we needed to stay off the roads to avoid setting patterns that would invite Charley's land mining enterprises.

No one envisioned any risk to the natives we associated ourselves with just because we showed each other some mutual courtesy and kindness. The children liked the candy we provided, and the troopers looked forward to earning those smiles and their laughter. It clearly reminded them of the brothers and sisters that they missed so sorely back home. And this was an excellent location for getting rid of certain C-rations we really didn't care for. And these folks were very appreciative of our friendliness. It was also awesome how much the old men enjoyed an American cigarette. We enjoyed our brief stops at this village. We never expected to see it all turn into tragedy. But it did.

Our mission one day was to search the area north of the Montagnard village, so we planned to pass it on the west side of their grass huts and sweep north about 500 meters through dense jungle growth, in an arc to the west, into an area that had been strip burned to prepare it for farming. After we entered the jungle and pushed through the heavy vegetation for about half an hour, we stopped for a short lunch break.

When all became quiet with the engines turned off, we heard a braying sound nearby off to our left and down in a shallow gully. A few troopers were dismounted and cautiously followed the sounds. At the bottom of the gully, the jungle opened into a tiny clearing where a baby elephant was staked out. There was no question as to by whom - Charley. He was friendly and gave the troopers no difficulty as they led him back to the tracks. The friendly little cuss was a little over 5 feet tall at the back and looked quite healthy.

We looked for the little guy's caretaker, but we couldn't find one. So, I had him hooked by his rope to the rear of an ACAV and we proceeded to follow a small trail through the jungle that was going in our intended direction. For the next hour we moved slowly through the jungle, and then left the trail as a non-fruitful venture, and we continued the arc to the west that was pre-planned. The landscape went gradually down-hill until we crossed a heavily vegetated, soggy stream bed with young bamboo growing in and around the water. As we started going up the opposite bank, we realized that black leaches were all over our bodies.

Thank God for disciplined troopers. The aerial photograph I was using showed the burned off jungle straight-ahead, so we pushed for it with a lot more enthusiasm than we had all day. Within minutes the platoon was clear of the jungle, and after herring-boning the tracks half of the troopers on each vehicle were permitted to strip. Panic was hard to control as it became apparent that the leaches were all over our backs and chests and their bloody carcasses were already 2 to 3 inches long, and quickly growing. This was an incentive for those with their shirts still on to help scrape the nasty blood suckers off the backs of their comrades with their k-bar knives. The second group nearly ripped their shirts off when it was their turn. Some of the troopers inspected the elephant and we were back on our mission in about twenty minutes.

As we came out of the burned area and through a small strip of jungle, we could see the Montagnard village off to the east. It was getting late and the question needed to be resolved as to what to do with the elephant. After clearing it with Dixie North over the radio, I gave the animal to the Montagnard village chief. That proved to be stupid. I had given Charley's beast of burden to a peaceful village of friendly families. Then we quickly headed back to Quan Loi. Upon arrival we gassed up, cleaned our weapons and ate a hot dinner at the Artillery mess hall.

After cleaning up, it was already dark, and we were in our defensive positions for the night. It was a clear, quiet night with no hint of any adventurism by the enemy. Then, between midnight and one in the morning the sky lit up in the distance over the Montagnard village. Through the binoculars I could see the high flames and green tracers. A chill came over me. My stupidity was apparent. The village was being attacked because of the baby elephant. And we were helpless to defend them.

Helicopters were dispatched to look the area over. Artillery could not be fired into the jungle north of the village as this was the only place where the villagers could find safety. My platoon readied itself and in about a half hour the order was given to move out. I had gone to the Artillery Fire Control Center and prepared for illumination along the road to the village and established checkpoints along the way to quickly call in artillery fire. Upon receiving the order to move, the platoon with a couple extra tanks from Dreadnaught Bravo headed out of Quan Loi and onto the road. Movement was deliberate and fast along the roads through the plantation up to the areas that I had identified as possible ambush or mine sites. Being cautious it took nearly an hour and a half to arrive at the village. It was still burning.

Ten to fifteen villagers were coming in from the jungle. Bodies were strewn throughout the burning ruins of the village. The horror of more than thirty butchered friendly people will never be forgotten, nor will the smell of their burning flesh or the crying of the survivors. Guilt rose up inside of me for not recognizing the obvious risk of dropping the elephant at the village. That was immaturity and stupidity. I learned about such brutality in school. What a short memory. It was all real. Disembowelments and systematic torture. Such disgusting behavior by one human being to another. I was sickened and wanted to leave immediately, but I knew that we had to stay until the sun came up and the Infantry and Medical personnel were inserted. The next couple hours were an eternity and hate found a home in me. I prayed but it didn't seem to help. My heart was hardening.

Chapter 32

END OF THE QUAN LOI MISSION

From that day forward my dedication to destroy this enemy was renewed and strengthened. We charged back and forth through the plantation and the surrounding area, but Charlie stayed clear. My platoon continuously found evidence of enemy movement to the south on trails outside the plantation, and crossings between the rubber trees, and we kept a steady flow of information to the Division. It was obvious that Charley was moving men and supplies south. But the enemy stayed clear of any combat.

Our worst enemy became boredom and I was aware of where that could lead. Keeping one's guard up became difficult and straight thinking was not always easy. After one long day of patrolling we returned to our perimeter positions to find the shower point closed. The tracks were covered with mud and everyone was caked with laterite.

As I pulled into my position outside of the plantation house's privacy fence, I could observe the beautiful, crystal clear Frenchman's swimming pool glistening in the moonlight. For a morale booster, I had my driver back up to the fence and after the troopers cleaned their weapons and prepared their tanks and ACAVs for the next mission, and finished their meals, I invited them to climb on my track to shinny over the fence, so they could get cleaned up in the pool.

It was wonderful. The night was lit up by the Milky Way watching down on the scene. One by one the troopers entered the water with their bar of soap and bathed in the Romanesque surroundings. While floating around the pool you could see arches and columns covered with lush ivy. The caretakers had created a paradise inside of Hell itself. And none of them would be back until the morning. Ah! The bliss of it all. The stars carried my mind back to a home far away where the meanness seemed nearly non-existent. Where my family and friends were enjoying the summer sunshine and fortunately not experiencing the primitiveness of this angry land.

After a nice swim/bath I opened a package from home and found a small tape player with a tape recorded by my wife, my father and mother, my sisters Virginia and Eunice, and my brother-in-law Russ. But most of all I enjoyed a couple songs by my two-year-old daughter Irene including <u>"Twinkle, Twinkle Little Star"</u> in Japanese and in English. It went *" Pica, pica hoshio, antawa itai nondisca; Annani takaye soyano ye; Dia mundo mizuyo ni; Pica, pica hoshio, antawa itai nondisca. "* A tear came to my eye as a stab of depression, like a bullet, struck deep into my heart. I tried to shunt this out of my mind, but the song, in my daughter's baby voice kept coming back. *"Pica, pica ho .... "* I still hear it when the thought occurs.

Morning brought a loud, shrill shriek and what could only be translated as the worst Vietnamese vulgarities imaginable. I climbed onto the fence and saw screaming caretakers around the pool glaring in shock at what looked like a cesspool with red laterite bubbles the size of baseballs floating on a bed of slimy red liquid. And worse, the wet streak on the wood fence made it obvious where the culprits came from. Carefully retreating in defilade below the privacy fence's top, I called the platoon on the radio and gave the order to move out a little early onto our patrol. Leaving early and coming back late for the next week helped avoid confrontation with the Frenchman's employees, but it did not avoid an awful ass-chewing for this indiscretion. Although it was a timely morale booster, the repercussions came quickly. My butt-chewing was severe, although through it all I harbored a chuckle beneath my every breath. At this point in time the swimming pool was off limits to the Americans and our (my) infraction was totally unreasonable.

July 4, 1967

Shortly after this bathing incident I did get into the plantation house. It was quite the surprise, as I thought I was on their permanent shit list - - not their party list. Wow! What an experience in opulence, for SFC Coker and I to attend the French plantation owner's 4th of July party. It was a finger food and booze event which was obviously designed to impress. It certainly impressed me with all the little Vietnamese servers carrying goodies to the guests. As soon as my glass was near empty, a full one materialized. And the food kept coming, and coming, and coming. It was as though a couple of the little gremlins (waiters) were assigned to each guest. It was fantastic!

I was a bit surprised that the swimming pool was totally cleaned up and looked great. I thought I might hear something about our bathing caper in the swimming pool when I spoke to the pretty blond French woman, but all was quiet. Not even a dirty look. And I was watching for some reaction. But nothing happened.

On July 10, 1967 I was instructed to be sure we brought all our personal belongings with us when we went on patrol of the southwestern part of the plantation. Where the plantation ended, there was only about 300 meters of secondary jungle growth, underbrush jungle, to a vacated Artillery fire support base along Thunder Road just south of An Loc. The Division had been working the area to the west of QL-13 again and they had opened the road to An Loc. The operation was ending, and the Division was moving back south. Someone decided that the 2nd Platoon of "B" Troop had been operating independently for too long, and the vacated fire support base was chosen for the switch of cavalry platoons.

It was nearing noon when we arrived, precisely when the 2nd Platoon of "A" Troop was coming off Thunder Road. The platoons formed a hasty perimeter and the platoon leaders pulled their tracks side by side to briefly coordinate. A-26, 1st Lieutenant Gordon Smith, an experienced Platoon Leader, was quite pleased to be attached to Dixie North. While I pointed out the trail on the map to get to Quan Loi, pleasantries were shared, and I warned of the buildup that was taking place and my worries that Quan Loi could soon be attacked. LT Smith however had heard the prevailing stories and expressed excitement at receiving this mission, commenting that he heard it was like R&R (Rest and Recuperation).

LT Gordon Smith

It's odd how one learns to read people and circumstances over time. When the Frenchman's aircraft left the plantation, the pucker factor went way up. It was a clear signal that Charley was active in the area. Everyone paid close attention to these type signals.

I told Gordon of the Frenchman's daughter flying out that morning. She had been the only French resident of the plantation house for some time. I didn't feel like I was very convincing in stating the threat level, but I was sure that it wouldn't take very long before he was on top of it.

Our mission was now to return to the Phu Loi to trade in the Platoon's ACAVs, which were the oldest gasoline driven ones in the Squadron, for brand-new diesel-powered tracks. We wished each other the best and moved in opposite directions. There was a sadness in my heart, but a tough mission lay ahead, and the big question was whether the oldest gasoline powered tracks in the Squadron could make this long trip without a breakdown.

Chapter 33

HORRIBLE MISFORTUNES OF WAR
JULY 10-11, 1967

The whole Division had already moved south and the road was wide open. From time to time the platoon had a chopper overflying its formation. The movement was fast. Probably over 40 miles per hour was averaged all the way to Lai Khe. Most of the way there was a gentle air movement to the east which allowed the tracks to hold their interval at dust distance with no more than 25 meters between vehicles.

In Lai Khe we refueled, took a short C-ration lunch break, and were back on the road within an hour continuing the journey south. When we were approaching Ben Cat, we received an order to turn east toward Phuc Vihn to engage a small enemy force about five miles southeast of Ben Cat. The Platoon pushed hard toward the coordinates we were given and swept a small patch of jungle finding

SSG Bates (lft), SFC Coker (rt)

no enemy. Charley was apparently not in the mood for a scrap, so we headed south on Highway 1A which brought us to a point just to the east of Phu Cuong and west of Phu Loi. A few more kilometers and we were home.

We had left Phu Loi on February 7, 1967 following the mortar attack and returned a couple hours before dark on July 10th. The platoon was now seasoned from top to bottom. And all these old, gasoline driven ACAVs came in under their own power. That was remarkable for a trip of about 90 klicks (kilometers). This was a testimony to the maintenance men of Dreadnaught Bravo, and to the discipline of our own troopers. In addition to changing to the new ACAVs the platoon was losing SFC Coker and replacing him with B-24, SSG Bates as the new Platoon Sergeant. Sergeant Coker would be sorely missed.

And there they were, seven beautiful, new ACAVs in the center of the parking area. A wonderful site to behold as we ended this trip. Each driver pulled up next to the ACAV with the corresponding identification markings already painted on them. Without any order being given, instead of waiting to be cleaned up or eat a hot supper, the troopers immediately started tearing out everything in their old tracks and outfitting the new vehicles. They had to be ordered to break from the work to eat. The job was less than half done when darkness set in. Some work could be done after dark, but by 10 PM the effort had to be stopped until daybreak.

The Troop Executive Officer, LT Tom Brandon, took me to the Officers Club/Mess to spend some time with the few officers in the basecamp and to bring me up to date with what was going on in the Division AO. Tom was approaching the end of his tour in Vietnam. I had only seen him in Quan Loi on paydays when he flew up to pay the troops. He was a fine officer and did a great job as the Troop XO. I never knew him while he was a Platoon Leader, but he had a reputation to be proud of. The rest of the Squadron's combat elements were in field positions and our Platoon was going to move out to join the "B" Troop headquarters and at least one other platoon the next day. We would be leaving Phu Loi at noon.

Ahh! The bunk felt great. Clean sheets and reasonably safe quarters. We felt like the Cavalry of old who finally were safely tucked into the fort with the hostiles left outside the walls. Sure, we were susceptible to mortar rounds or sapper attacks, but we all felt safe and comfortable.

It could have lasted forever. Tranquility and peace at last. And with no artillery being fired over our heads while we slept.

Suddenly, there was knocking on my door and I was being summoned to the Squadron TOC (Tactical Operations Center). Dressing quickly and tripping through the darkness I found myself in the sandbagged bunker within about ten minutes. It was around 1:30 AM. The communications coming in over the radio were shocking. The second platoon of "A" Troop was under attack at Quan Loi and appeared to be in the process of being overrun. Everything was terribly chaotic.

I listened to the reports coming in from Quan Loi as the "A" Troopers fought for their lives. The battle had started with small arms automatic and RPG fire coming from the perimeter and from the roofs of buildings in the center of the base camp. The entire base camp was being attacked. The perimeter's barbed wire was breached with explosives at the same time and Charley swarmed throughout the base camp. The initial firing was immediately followed by a satchel charge being thrown over the privacy fence into the A-26 ACAV. Until recently I didn't know all the details.

While listening on the radio, I couldn't help but feel that Charley was trying to get even with me and my platoon. I asked to be flown into Quan Loi to help pull the "A" Troop platoon together and to bring some of my troopers along to help. I believed this attack to be retaliation for the dirty swimming pool incident and the major rice raid. My request was denied. So, guilt was to be my companion forever. Imbedded guilt for a failure to get even and for what happened to Gordon Smith became a part of me from that moment on. There was no sleep that night. I listened on the radio in shock. This was awful. Just awful. I prayed. And I wished to get back to deal with those caretakers, and their friends, bastards. I had told LT Smith of the departure of the Frenchman's daughter, but this method of attack could not have been anticipated. I was pissed and had strange, weird thoughts. Was this hate? Maybe, or just harsh sadness.

In time I was advised that the Quan Loi Base Camp was the upstairs to a major tunnel complex of Charley's, which even included a hospital. While we were diligently hunting him, Charley was under the earth we protected at night. It didn't surprise me to also be told that one end of the VC tunnel system led directly into the Frenchman's home. Was it true? I'll never know. I was also told that the enemy infiltrated the Frenchman's property through the swimming pool's drainage system. There were too many coincidences to believe there wasn't some cooperation going on between the plantation owners or their workers and Charley. I learned a lot about their appearance of friendship and what they would or would not do to appease or assist Charley.

I was bitter for many years. Eventually I concluded that the plantation owners walked a very fine line to insure their own survival and protect their business interests. And screw us. We were temporary.

At an annual reunion a few years ago, I met LT Smith and his ACAV Driver, SP4 Sie Moore. Sie related the following details.

> *I served in Vietnam from January 4, 1967 to January 3, 1968. On the night of July 10/11, 1968, I was the Driver of A-26 which was the Platoon Leader's ACAV (M-113 Armored Cavalry Assault Vehicle) of the 2nd Platoon of Alpha Troop, 1st Squadron, 4th Cavalry, 1st Infantry Division, when the Quan Loi basecamp was attacked by the Viet Cong. We had replaced a platoon from Bravo Troop on July 10, 1967 and this was our first night at Quan Loi.*

> *Our ACAV was positioned facing the perimeter with the wooden privacy fence of the French Plantation Owner's residence a few feet to our rear. At a little after 0100 hours Quan Loi was attacked by the Viet Cong. The initial attack included machine gun fire and satchel charges and grenades being thrown over the privacy fence, while the enemy breached the perimeter wire attacking from both the front and the rear of our positions.*

Immediately when the attack started the Track Commander of my track, Sergeant Charley Brown, was shot in the head and killed. Then a satchel charge was thrown into our track. I could not reach it from my driver's compartment, but I could see it laying on the floor and smoking. My entire life flashed before me and I knew I was about to die.

My Platoon Leader, Lieutenant Gordon E. Smith, who was firing the M-60 machine gun, must have seen it at the same time I did. He stopped firing the M-60 and grabbed the satchel charge to throw it out of the track. Just as he got it over the top of the ACAV it exploded causing severe damage to the right side of his face, his right arm (which had to be removed) and the entire right side of his body.

Lieutenant Smith risked his life to save mine and that of the medic Stokes, who was also in the rear of the track, even though he could have run out the back of the track which was open.

I am alive today because of the sacrifice that was made by LT Smith in total disregard for his own safety. I am eternally grateful for the heroic action and sacrifice he made for me and Stokes. In the face of serious injury or death he chose to go beyond the call of duty for his troops.

For his bravery Lieutenant Gordon E. Smith should receive the Medal of Honor.

SP4 Sie Moore's Troop Commander, CPT Charles B. Fegan (retired Colonel Fegan), had the following to say concerning LT Gordon Smith and the events that occurred.

The undersigned was the commanding officer of Troop A, 1st Squadron, 4th Cavalry, 1st Infantry Division from May 1966 until October 1967 in the Republic of Vietnam. 1st Lieutenant Gordon E. Smith was the commander of our second platoon.

On 10 July 1967 I was ordered to detach one platoon to support an infantry battalion at Quan Loi. I selected the second platoon (commanded by LT Smith) for this mission. I considered LT Smith to be my best platoon leader and well qualified for this assignment. LT Smith went to Quan Loi for this mission and I took the rest of the troop south to Lai Khe while the Division closed the road between Quan Loi and Lai Khe.

On the morning of 11 July, I received a report that our forces in Quan Loi had been attacked, LT Smith had been wounded and evacuated and the platoon had suffered additional killed and wounded. I acquired a helicopter and with my First Sergeant (SFC Nix) proceeded to Quan Loi.

After questioning my troopers on the ground and infantry soldiers in the vicinity I gained a picture of what had happened. Apparently, the Viet Cong had planned and prepared this attack over a long period of time. Prior to the attack it appeared that Viet Cong infantry had infiltrated the defensive perimeter using the drainage system for a swimming pool adjacent to the French plantation manager's home. These enemy soldiers had positioned themselves on the tile roofs of buildings in the vicinity where they could fire down into a quad .50 machine gun tub located adjacent to a friendly artillery battery's positions and into LT Smith's vehicles. These enemy soldiers waited for their main attack to begin before they opened fire.

Sometime after 1 AM on the 11th of July the enemy initiated their main attack by exploding a Bangalore Torpedo under the barbed wire which was immediately forward from LT Smith's position. There was an immediate assault through the breached wire by assorted enemy soldiers who attempted to destroy the quad .50 machine gun position and to disable/destroy LT Smith's vehicles. The enemy snipers on the tiled roofs opened fire.

LT Smith ordered his platoon to place heavy machine gun and tank canister fire on the roofs from which the enemy snipers were engaging his platoon. This friendly fire and the shards of shattered tile which it induced silenced the snipers.

LT Smith then directed a tank commanded by SFC Ausbach to move directly forward into the breached wire and stop the enemy attack. This was successful.

During this melee an enemy soldier attempted to destroy LT Smith's vehicle by throwing a satchel charge filled with explosives into it. LT Smith disregarded his chance to jump to immediate safety and elected to go down into the vehicle and throw out the satchel charge. He was successful in doing this however the charge exploded as it left the vehicle severely wounding him.

LT Smith's personal actions were in the very highest tradition of the United States Army and were directly responsible for saving the lives of his fellow crew members and in preventing the friendly forces defending Quan Loi from being overrun and killed.

At the time I recommended that LT Smith be awarded the Medal of Honor. I subsequently was informed that the recommendation had been downgraded to a

Distinguished Service Cross.

I now know that he was awarded the Silver Star. I respectfully request reconsideration of this Silver Star award with the aim of upgrading it to the Medal of Honor.

Unfortunately, when I sought out a senior officer endorser of this recommendation who was there at that time, I was advised that the lack of enough eye witness statements made submission of a request for elevating Gordon's award to a Distinguished Service Cross or a Medal of Honor impractical. And now I have been advised that he has passed away.

May God show him every kindness.

Chapter 34

Working with the Troop

The new ACAVs were prepared for moving by 10AM and the platoon headed back up Highway 1A at noon. With all that had happened overnight I didn't even say goodbye to SFC Coker. I deeply regretted this, and still do. Sergeant Coker, if you are still out there, look me up. I had to shake a heavy heart. We were moving into new territory and it required focus and staying extra alert. But blocking Quan Loi out just wasn't possible. When we arrived at the "B" Troop's field position about a kilometer south of an ARVN fortress, the news of Quan Loi had preceded us.

The new ACAVs were great. They were powerful and had a fresh feel to them. Like new toys. We met the current "B" Troop Commander (CPT Murphy) at last.

During the next couple weeks, the platoon was sent on search and destroy missions in a roughly five-kilometer radius from the Headquarters elements and returned every evening. It became obvious one day that trouble was coming when we passed the ARVN fortress. It had previously been fully populated by ARVN soldiers and their families, but now it was empty. We entered the compound and it was quiet as a tomb. Not a soul to be seen anywhere and their belongings all went with them. And they hadn't advised us of any problems.

As we moved back to the NDP and into our defensive positions, what appeared to be a vendor walked toward my ACAV. He looked like an ARVN soldier trying to make a little money selling Pepsi Cola in bottles from a wooden case tied to his belt at waste level with a strap around his neck from the forward part of the case. He was barefoot and wore ARVN fatigues, but the trouser legs were short, and you could

Pepsi toting VC scout

see heavy white fungus all over his feet and ankles. It was just like the Montagnard's, but he was no Montagnard, and he had never worn boots. Boots would have made this fungal condition itch unbearably. A Pepsi would have been refreshing about then, but something was amiss. His feet gave him away.

I jumped off my track and pulled my 45-caliber pistol from its holster. The Troop interpreter came over and interrogated the vendor.

He had been walking through the NDP all afternoon pacing off the positions of each track. He had to wait until our platoon returned to be sure of the exact locations of all the defensive positions. Rubbing a little Pepsi between my fingers made it clear that he had more sinister tricks up his sleeves. The Pepsi had ground glass in it.

The Troop Headquarters called for the POW's evacuation to a more professional interrogation site. Just before dark we were notified that we were supposed to be attacked by a Chinese-Vietnamese VC Regiment that night.

LTs Tom Brannon and John Conley as John becomes Bravo 5

We were on pins and needles all night. No one slept. We waited, and waited, and nothing happened. Without the advantages of what their Pepsi toting scout was obtaining for them, tackling a Cavalry unit was more than Charley wanted to do - - yet.

My Platoon Leader days were ending. I would never be so close to my troops again. It was a sad day, but time moved on. Tom Brandon's tour was ending and a new Lieutenant, Bob Bertin, had arrived to replace me. I returned to Phu Loi to become the Troop Executive Officer (Bravo-5).

Chapter 35

Life as an Executive Officer

Becoming the Bravo Troop Executive Officer (XO) was like being born again into a different world. Commanding a platoon was the greatest experience an officer could ever have. But becoming the XO had an empty feeling after all the adventures I'd been through with these awesome troopers. Now, overseeing the Troop's basecamp elements including the supply and the company clerk (administration) seemed boring by comparison at first. Keeping the Troop's administration and supply off the back of the Troop Commander was important work. Making sure that the combat elements had everything they needed to do their job was essential work for sure. Keeping a steady flow of bullets, beans, clean clothing, etcetera, to the field were important jobs. And running the Troop basecamp turned out to be a very responsible one.

There was a steady flow of troopers coming in and out of the country. When they first arrived in Vietnam, they would be assigned to a jungle familiarization course. There were uncertain troopers being assigned to their first combat unit and wildly happy one's going home. There were those returning from R&R (Rest and Recuperation) and those heading out for that much needed break from the war. There were sick and wounded men in the rear as well. From these transient troopers there was a requirement to provide men for guarding the basecamp perimeter and coordinating rapid maintenance on various vehicles that had to be left behind when the Troop passed through the basecamp. And on occasion there was the opportunity to replace the Troop Commander when he went on R&R. We had a great Troop Clerk and he kept a tight grip on all the administrative issues. And apparently, I was doing a good job as Major Barney Forbes, the Squadron XO, found me acceptable.

Major Forbes and I got along just fine from our first meeting a few days after I became the Troop Executive Officer. I was on top of the issues that mattered and that was what the Major wanted. As the Squadron Executive Officer, he commanded the Squadron basecamp and the new trooper's training school, and he ran a tight ship. He was tough and a good officer, and you got along marvelously with him if you did your job.

LTC Barney Forbes, Retired
(photo taken 2017)

One of the most memorable events was when Major Forbes was touring the Troop area and he entered a barracks where several troopers were resting between guard duty sessions. They jumped to attention when we entered, and the Major asked each of them a few questions. He asked one trooper what he thought about the mess hall food in the basecamp. The trooper responded that *"the food was pretty good sir except that there was a large cockroach in my soup."* Major Forbes, in his gruff manner, leaned forward to the trooper and advised him, just loud enough for everyone to hear - - *"Don't tell anyone son, everybody's going to want one."*

That's the side I enjoyed of the Major. We got along splendid and spent a lot of time chatting about home. I vividly remember how he went on about his wife and Mary's string bean casserole with almonds recipe. It would make my mouth water to hear such a detailed description. And it was also clear that he loved Mary, far more than that string bean recipe. Her picture was on his desk, but there was never a picture of that casserole in such a high place of honor.

Major Forbes was one of the most loyal and dependable Officers I ever got to know. He became a friend and was like the big brother I never had. If I knew that he, like I, had no brother, I would likely have suggested that we become blood brothers, Indian style.

CMMI

While XO, someone decided it was time to have a CMMI (Command Maintenance Management Inspection) of the Cavalry combat units. This was the first time it was done in Vietnam and we took it seriously. Careers rose and fell on the scores attained by these inspections in non-combat zones. We had no reason to think it would be any different here.

Nothing was ready for such a detailed inspection. The vehicles ran well, the guns fired well, but the log books were not up to date or even used in most cases. Our maintenance tools were not always there and often shared between vehicles in the platoons, and not everything was in good repair such as damaged headlights from pushing through the jungle.

The trick was to assemble several talented Non-Commissioned Officers (NCOs), who were experienced in these inspections, and fast on their feet. We had plenty of talented volunteers. Two platoons were kept inaccessible, supposedly on search

1st SGT Robert Moore and the NCO Cadre were essential in organizing the CMMI effort.

and destroy missions. One platoon was being cannibalized to get another platoon ready for the inspection. We got one platoon ready to start with and rotated the platoons between the inspectors. The Headquarters' Platoon's vehicles were in pretty good shape and were inspected while the platoons were being swapped out for inspection preparation. The inspectors were told that they must accommodate the combat mission, which gave us a way to pull it off.

Everyone enjoyed the diversion and we received over a 90% rating on all mission essential areas of the inspection. That was great, and we saw it as a very serious joke. We also did get a huge list of parts to order, which eventually paid off. And that was no joke.

At the beginning of November 1967, the Troop had a Change of Command. The new commander of "B" Troop, Captain Edward B. Bryson was a strong, domineering, hulk of a man. He was intelligent, and I felt he enjoyed his job. Soon after taking command a crisis surfaced.

The Laundry

A new laundry set up business down the road from the Troop Area, and started to compete with Mr. Chin, who owned the big laundry, steam bath and barber shop, across the parade field from the Squadron Headquarters. The proprietor, Ms. Yim was a nice-looking lady who spoke fairly good English. She was undercutting the prices we had been paying Mr. Chin, and she showed me ditches where Mr. Chin was allegedly doing our laundry. Gradually "B" Troop's laundry work was shifted to this new laundry. And then the troopers started coming down with serious rashes. I started an investigation.

The new proprietor said that she was the partner of a Vietnamese Colonel, the head engineer in Phu Cuong. I headed for his compound to question him and was assured that the Troop's laundry was done in a commercial laundry in Saigon. Insisting on an inspection, the next day Ms. Yim joined me for a ride to Saigon so I could inspect the laundry. Sure enough, she was able to take me to a huge laundry facility where they just happened to be doing some laundry with my own name tag sewed on it. Flags went up, but I kept quiet.

The next day I went to see Mr. Chin and we went away for a serious private discussion. He was afraid to talk about the laundry problem, and I recognized the symptoms of deadly serious intimidation. Mr. Chin gradually slipped when asked all the places where laundry was washed in the area, and who did it in each place. Mr. Chin claimed his was done in a commercial laundry, so I immediately put him in a jeep and left Phu Loi to give him a chance to prove it. And he did, without any foreknowledge where he could phony it up. That left a process of elimination to start inspecting the streams around Phu Cuong. After searching clothes lines next to two streams I got lucky. The stream on the grounds of the Engineer Compound had the Troop's clothing hanging on lines and there were women in the stream about 50 feet from the lines where more of the troopers' clothing was being scrubbed. To gain access to inspect the clothes, I had to threaten the workers with my M-16 rifle.

After a written report to the Squadron Commander, Yim's laundry was closed and kicked off the Phu Loi basecamp. I never did give Ms. Yim back the black molded statue head she gave me on our first meeting. The result was the returning of the Troop's business to Mr. Chin, and the rashes stopped for good. That made everyone happy, most of all Mr. Chin. She had undercut 1/4th of his laundry business.

Chapter 36

THE STEAM BATH

As I said, Mr. Chin had a steam bath and massage parlor. As XO I had a chance to enjoy the basecamp facilities on occasion, and that was one place that was enjoyable after a hot day of hard work.

One day I was mixing napalm to make foo-gas bombs to be used as booby traps in the basecamp's perimeter wire. I had a history with napalm and this was fun.

My first assignment in the 5th Marines when I was 17 years old was as a flame thrower operator. In a short period of time I had become the leader of a 22-man flame thrower section. I received a meritorious promotion to Corporal and became what many claimed was the youngest NCO in the Marines.

John's first real military job was a flame thrower operator in the 5th Marines at Camp Pendleton, CA

Now, in Vietnam I was using an air hose from a compressor on a 5 Ton truck to mix the napalm in a 55-gallon drum. In a moment of non-attentiveness, the hose became unsecured and spun the napalm mixture into my eyes. I was in awful pain and blinded. While twisting and turning in pain, I suddenly felt hands touch my shoulders and start guiding me back to my hooch. When I got there, water was poured into a pan and a kind lady rinsed my eyes out repeatedly.

Although I couldn't see, these were the tenderest, and gentlest hands I had felt in a long, long time, and I appreciated the help very much. This was a Chinese-Vietnamese girl from Mr. Chin's steam bath and massage parlor, who had been taking a walk after lunch with a couple other girls, when this all occurred. She (Huin) had never given me a massage before, but she became my favorite from then on. Her quick actions kept me from losing my eye sight, and I couldn't have had a more quickly reacting and caring nurse.

Huin looked in on me for the next several days to be sure I was okay. It apparently was hard to not be concerned for someone that she helped. Huin was in her early twenties and spoke some English. She was very nice and became a good friend.

Chapter 37

MISSING THE FIELD

I missed the field a lot and looked forward to the end of each month when I would pay the troopers in the far reaches of the AO. I would catch a ride on a helicopter to one platoon, then perhaps catch a convoy or a helicopter to the next platoon, etcetera, until everyone was paid. Often the platoons were spread down the roads to prevent attacks on convoys. Those were the times I would enlist a Lambreta three wheeled taxi to take me from track to track.

1LT Bertin, B-26
My former Home Sweet Home

There is a special recollection of SSG Bates' tank being parked under a huge cashew tree. I never saw such a beautiful domineering high and wide tree that made his 52-ton tank look half its size. The tree had hanging fruit that resembled light green bell peppers spread throughout the branches. Under each of these bells, which I was told was poison fruit, there was a single cashew nut. And this nut was also poison until it was baked. It seems like there was something new to learn every time I went to the field.

The visit to the 2nd Platoon was always a special treat. LT Bertin was a fine officer, and in full, professional command of his platoon. The visit was always too quick, as it was important to pay the troops in a hurry and get back to Phu Loi.

Chapter 38

GREAT TROOPERS IN THE REAR

One of the secrets to doing a good job as an Executive Officer was having a great Troop Clerk and Supply Sergeant. "B" Troop had just that. SP4 Taylor was a detail man and I never had to look backward at the paper trail. He knew what reports were most important and they were always fresh, allowing me to have a full grasp of the Troop's administrative business affairs all the time. SP4 Taylor was an excellent trooper and he also kept the Troop jeep in a good state of repair as one of his duties.

It was unfortunate when he rolled the jeep over while speeding down a road in the basecamp, returning from the Artillery EM Club, and likely had a few beers too many. Fortunately, he only broke an arm. One careless mistake did not seem to merit the punishment that he was eligible for, and it was a major exercise to protect him from the loss of his rank or worse. I spoke with Major Forbes about this and he added his protection. This was greatly appreciated.

The Supply Sergeant, SSG Turner, was always busy as the demands from the field were quite extensive. The field Troop was the sole priority, and although the supply system was excellent, it was necessary for the Supply Sergeant to be somewhat of a scrounger to make certain that every need was fulfilled with no delays. There was a great deal of pride in being organized to the point where the supply sergeant could get his hands on anything that was needed in the field at a moment's notice. The Troop Supply was complemented by an excellent Squadron S-4 supply operation headed by CPT Raymond Rosenberg, who proved to be able to move the supply system to acquire major equipment replacements wherever and whenever the need arose.

Chapter 39

ACTING TROOP COMMANDER

I had the opportunity to be the Acting Troop Commander in the Iron Triangle in November 1967 right after the 2nd Battalion, 28th Infantry Regiment (Black Lions) was mauled by the Phu Loi Battalion, while the "B" Troop Commander, Captain Bryson, was on R&R. Our Search and Destroy missions were in high, very thick brush and single canopy jungle. The weather was blistering hot. We were on search and destroy missions and we were wandering through the jungle, single file, just begging for Charley to pull off an ambush. This gave me a chance to meet more of our troopers, who I only knew from when they passed through the basecamp or on pay days.

This is where I met an NCO (that I will not name), who claimed to have received a Silver Star from a previous tour in the Squadron and made it a point to brag about a special relationship he had with General Westmoreland, who presented the medal. He was a Platoon Sergeant, and his run-in with me was memorable when he caught a trooper allegedly sleeping on guard duty. He snuck up onto the ACAV and physically attacked the trooper from behind. He also had a bad habit of putting cold steel up against a man's throat after sneaking up on him. And these men weren't always sleeping. The comments about fragging him were troubling. Fragging is a term used for tossing a fragmentation grenade into a place where it would kill an exceptionally bad leader. The term also included such actions as shooting the NCO or officer in the back during a battle. I had several heated discussions with this NCO on his leadership style. He did not take my comments well. Three months after that incident he was killed in the 1st Tet Offensive. I've often wondered if there was a connection. And research indicates he never was awarded the Silver Star he boasted of.

It was great having the experience of leading the Troop in the Iron Triangle. I learned a lot about how to deal with enemy attacks when your unit is submerged in extremely dense vegetation. The box formation could have been employed, but it could not be used the way the Squadron was deployed.

I was glad when CPT Bryson returned from R&R.

Chapter 40

RATS, RATS EVERYWHERE

Perhaps the most memorable basecamp experience was to fight the rat war. The men who were returning from R&R and pulling guard duty while waiting for transportation to the field would sit around in the evening drinking beer and eating barbeque chips, while relating their R&R adventures during their brief vacations away from Vietnam.

When they would fall asleep the barracks would be visited by alert, invaders. Huge, furry, hungry rats (some the size of adult cats) would creep up to their fingers covered with barbeque chip residuals, and lick, and lick, and lick. Then as they enjoyed their host they would nibble, nibble, nibble, nibble while the men dreamed of their vacations and perhaps encounters with beautiful maidens in more peaceful environments.

Eventually a nerve would be struck by the filthy ivories and the men would return from their slumber, startled, fearful, painful and screaming. They would be taken to medical care, and eight days of painful rabies shots had to be administered to their stomach muscles in a sectional pattern before they could be allowed to return to the field. And then they may need some additional recuperation after the shots before they could go to the field, as they would be combat ineffective for a while.

In the several days it took to fully understand what the reason was for the rats' actions, more and more rodents were attracted to the Troop area, where they would be as invisible during the day as the Viet Cong, and they would come out for the fiesta deep into the night. I learned that once this started many of the rats didn't really care if the men washed their hands before sleeping. They would delightfully chew finger and toe nails until they turned once again to eating flesh. This caused an overpopulation of troopers in the basecamp.

I went to the engineers for assistance and set perimeters of baited traps around the barracks. The first night resulted in four prisoners. More and more were captured each night until the war was won. Over sixty furry POWs in three weeks. Some troopers commented that the XO should have been saving pelts for a fine fur hat or a coat to sport around with when back in the States, as recognition for winning the rat war. That surely would have been a quick ticket to a psych ward.

Chapter 41

THE JANUARY 1968 PAYROLL

Christmas and New Years passed and January 1968 slipped slowly toward the end of my tour in Vietnam. The magic day was February 7, 1968. On January 31st I picked up the payroll and caught a chopper up to the road between Phuc Vinh and Ben Cat where the Second Platoon was out-posting the road. This appeared to be my final duty in Vietnam. After paying one platoon I hitched a ride into Lai Khe with the rest of the payroll and paid the "C" Troop Maintenance Section located in the parking area adjacent to the helipad. After paying the "C" Troop's Maintenance troopers I tried to call for a chopper to move to another platoon's location.

After several attempts I was abruptly told to *"get the Hell off the radio"* and complied. Not knowing the reason, I decided to place my briefcase with over $60,000 on the ground in the shade beside C-8, the "C" Troop's Maintenance Section's ACAV, using it as a pillow for my nap.

Dosing for a while, I awoke suddenly, engulfed in a thunderous explosion, flying thru the air with gravel and dirt filling every orifice of my head and embedding in my clothing down to my hide. As I crashed, rolling across the ground, ears ringing, with tremendous pressure and hollowness in my head, I was dazed and trying to understand where I was, and what was happening.

As I looked back about 50 feet toward the ACAV I saw flames roaring out of the top of C-8. The fording shield on the front was broken and hanging sideways. Small arms and 50 caliber ammunition were firing like strings of firecrackers and multi-color smoke grenades were exploding and mixing with the flames over the track.

I ran around the back of the vehicle and looked inside at a furnace with screaming crew members struggling to escape, while engulfed in flames, and red and white hot, melting metal. The ACAV's back ramp was down, and it was like looking into a furnace. A crowd was forming, but no one was yet attempting to help the crew members. I charged into the back of the track and guided one trooper to the back ramp, and others led him out, as I returned into the searing heat to find a way to the Track Commander, Donald William Allen, Jr., who was shirtless and surrounded by molten magnesium-aluminum alloy, blinded and screaming in agony. I had to go up to

Donald Allen, Jr.

the engine compartment and turn right and right again around the hanging melting metal to get to him. The heat was suffocating. I grabbed him in a bear hug from the front and told him to grab both arms around me. We back tracked out of the ACAV following the same path I took to reach him. I was able to drag him safely out of the track, while ammunition was exploding in all directions in the awful heat.

There was considerable yelling, and someone brought a 3/4-ton truck by C-8. The men quickly lifted the two troopers into the back of the truck and in his awful pain the ACAV commander had a terrible time turning me loose to be put into the vehicle. I was told a couple years ago that the driver was still in the driver's compartment. If I had known, I would have gone back after him. He made no sounds, so he must have been unconscious or dead. For some reason known only to the Lord I wasn't hardly singed in the inferno. Nevertheless, I continued to hurt over the driver's death. Recently, I was advised that there was no driver in that ACAV at the time. Thank God.

As I was about to climb into the truck a trooper tried to hand me my briefcase full of money. I instructed him to take the money to the Finance Office at Phu Loi. I must have been in shock as I have no idea who he was, but I would sure like to know.

I went with the injured men to the field hospital at the northwest end of the Lai Khe basecamp. After delivering the troopers to the field hospital, I returned to the burning track which was still significantly melting where it stood next to the tree line.

I listened to what occurred leading up to the attack. Troopers recalled that an odd-looking Vietnamese man in an ARVN uniform was seen walking up and down the road about 2 to 3 hours prior to the attack and writing onto something. The weapon had been determined to be a 104 mm Rocket. Later I was told that it was either a 122mm or 128mm Rocket. A single shot, and a perfect hit. So, so sad. The ACAV Commander was too burned to save. I never heard what happened to the other man.

Within minutes after my arrival I was informed that a radio message was received instructing me to get on a convoy that was just departing on a southbound trip to Phu Loi.

The excitement was just starting.

Chapter 42

THE 1ST TET OFFENSIVE BEGINS

Not having any information as to what was occurring was unnerving. I quickly jumped on a "B" Troop, 2nd Platoon ACAV in a convoy heading south. About fifteen minutes passed when the convoy started being closely overflown by a Huey helicopter gunship. As the chopper made its way along the column, it became obvious that the pilots were looking for someone, and the Quarterhorse insignia on the front made me believe that it might have been dispatched to pick me up. The track stopped and the chopper immediately landed. As I jumped aboard and put on the radio headset, I received the bad news.

"B" and "C" Troops were attacking into An My from the south. This village immediately to the north of the Phu Loi basecamp was crawling with North Vietnamese regulars. And Captain Bryson received five shots across his chest from an AK-47. The enemy also raked and killed the command track's crew members. The chopper whizzed cross country just above the treetops toward the battle at An My. I was now the Troops acting commander, and I had no idea what I was going to be dropped into.

The trip was fast and uneventful. A mental picture of the battlefield was described by the pilot. "C" Troop was on the west of the north-south road and "B" Troop was on the right side, and the fighting was from south to north. Both "B" and "C" Troops were short one platoon and some infantry were also on the ground, but they were being removed to free up the firing capabilities of the Cavalry and to assemble a blocking force at the northwest end of the village. As the Huey landed outside of the berm at the south edge of the village, I saw an ACAV coming my way quickly on the opposite side of the berm. I scrambled onto the ground, and at a dead run leaped over the berm and entered the back door of the command track, which had a fresh crew. I said a quick prayer as I pulled on my CVC helmet.

The driver sped the ACAV back into the attacking formation where, I received a quick SitRep (Situation Report) and learned that as the Troop entered the village on line, accompanied by a platoon of infantrymen, with two of its Cavalry platoons on line up front and the headquarters platoon directly behind, an NVA (North Vietnamese Army) Officer and senior Non-Com had jumped up to the left of the command track. The Officer held a white rag and the NCO still had his AK-47 in his hands. CPT Bryson thought he saw an opportunity to take an important prisoner and jumped off the ACAV only to be greeted by a sweep from the AK-47 across his chest from the lower left to the right shoulder and the NVA Soldier fired across the command track continuing the carnage. CPT Bryson and the crew were evacuated, and that is when I was brought in to take command.

Everyone was excited by what was happening and Sgt Cunningham, the Commo (Communications) NCO, had been fighting the troop for the past 45 minutes or so. He knew where every track was and understood the mission we were on, which allowed me to instantaneously grab control of the Troop. I was not an alien to these troopers and they never flinched at the abrupt change of command.

I jumped up onto the jeep seat mounted on the command track and advised the Platoon Leaders and the Headquarters elements that I was in command. Then I entered the Squadron command net to announce that I was in control, and to see if there was any intelligence as to what the Hell we were facing. There were no changes of orders or intelligence that wasn't obvious. I was advised that we were fighting North Vietnamese Army regulars. *No shit shineola.* They were jumping out from behind anything and everything. The troopers had to have eyes in the back of their heads to stay alive and watch every direction at once. Having the infantry moved off the battlefield was giving us the ability to shoot at whatever we saw move, even out of the corner of the eye, without needing to stop to refocus on each ground movement before shooting, a delay which could be fatal.

Lieutenant Colonel (LTC) John Siegel was cool headed, and a very intelligent Squadron Commander. He didn't micro-manage the ground commanders and it was appreciated. As the North Vietnamese started to withdraw to the northwest toward the blocking force, the "C" Troop Commander was receiving significant pressure over the command net. The enemy was leaving the village to the west in front of the "C" Troop's sector. "B" Troop had to hold back a little, as the combat pressure was reduced, in order to stay on line. The ground commanders were doing their level best to manage the plethora of details required to both handle the mission and keep their men alive.

Village fighting was new to us. The enemy had many advantages, and we feared that they would start using the villagers as decoys or shields. That made us push harder hoping that they would be too busy staying alive to use such tactics. I knew how vicious these dogs could get, so speed was essential. But we couldn't get ahead of "C" Troop.

It was hard work trying not to destroy the villager's homes while passing through a village. As the tanks and ACAVs moved forward, NVA soldiers would jump out from behind straw piles and homes to spray the troopers with AK-47s or shoot at the tracks with RPGs. The trek through the village was close to two kilometers, and it took several hours to fight through it. Our hope was that the villagers would stay in the holes they had built under their homes for protection. That was the standard operating procedure, but we were all very concerned, as we fought forward, that they might not be properly educated in these matters. Fortunately, when we came out at the north end of the village, no one felt as though any noncombatants were killed, at least not by us.

Once we were out of An My we swung to the east side of the village into the extensive dry rice paddies and headed back toward Phu Loi negotiating one paddy berm after another while the sun set. This was a slow process, but no roads could be trusted. It was too late to start sweeping for mines. The night was clear and beautiful, and no lights were needed to find our way south to the basecamp and to the area where we were to park our tracks overnight.

We weren't going to park in the normal troop areas for fear they were targeted by indirect fire. But we learned in a couple hours that everything was targeted, and it didn't take long before the mortar barrages began. Fortunately, the fuel and ammo trucks were already there so there was no delay getting ready to fight again. And the troopers had a hot meal before Charlie started lobbing mortars into the Phu Loi basecamp.

I have given it considerable thought and have determined that this is where I met CPT Eugene Daniels. Things had been moving very fast, but I refreshed my recollection as best I could. Gene was assigned as the new "B" Troop Commander, but I don't recall him being in the field for the first couple days of TET. I may be wrong about that. But, with his concurrence I continued to command the unit until he could become familiar with the Troop and the tactics we were using. He knew I would be going home on February 7th, so I needed a couple days to get my shit together before I departed. I believe also that he may have been with me when I welcomed the new troopers to replace our killed and wounded the first night of the TET Offensive, and was on the Command Track that evening.

We went to the airstrip and received seventeen replacement troopers straight off the plane. (This is also where I met 1st SGT Natividad Escobedo). None of the new troopers had any armor training and most were administrative personnel. The track commanders trained the new troopers throughout the night with the hatches buttoned up, because of the enemy mortars and rockets. The new men payed very close attention to their instructors. Those mortars and rockets were a Hell of a motivator. Fortunately, there were no direct hits on our tracks.

While the training progressed, the Troop Commanders were summoned to the Squadron Command Bunker. There was tremendous activity in this small semi-dark room surrounded and covered in multi-layers of sandbags and corrugated metal. This was the busiest S-2

Intelligence briefing I ever experienced, and it looked like the whole damned country was being over-run.

"A" Troop with CPT Fred Shirley at the helm had moved through the northern outskirts of Saigon when the attack started, to become

Captain Fred Shirley

attached to the 25th Infantry Division. He linked up with the 3rd Squadron, 4th Cavalry at the Ton Son Nhut Air Force Base and the fighting there was intense while we were being briefed at Phu Loi. It was clearly a mess everywhere you looked.

This was a major North Vietnamese invasion and it became abundantly clear that our mission was to turn this tide, repel these bastards, and hunt down the remnants when we got the upper hand. The risks had increased phenomenally as we were no longer fighting VC units. These were the best North Vietnam had to offer. They were fresh, well equipped and determined to destroy us all. And they had the skill and equipment to give it a try. It was without question - - Kick-Ass time again.

Chapter 43

TET 1968 CONTINUED

We were poised to depart Phu Loi at 0600 and be in position at the south end of An My by 0630, ready to attack through that village again, and then to continue the attack through Dog Leg Village a couple kilometers up the road from An My. Dog Leg was a much larger village (often referred to as Dog Leg 1 & 2 because of a small break in the middle of the village) and the NVA had to be cleared from this whole area. Hell was about to open its jaws again. We were determined to send these NVA home to Hades, where they belonged. This all was very serious business.

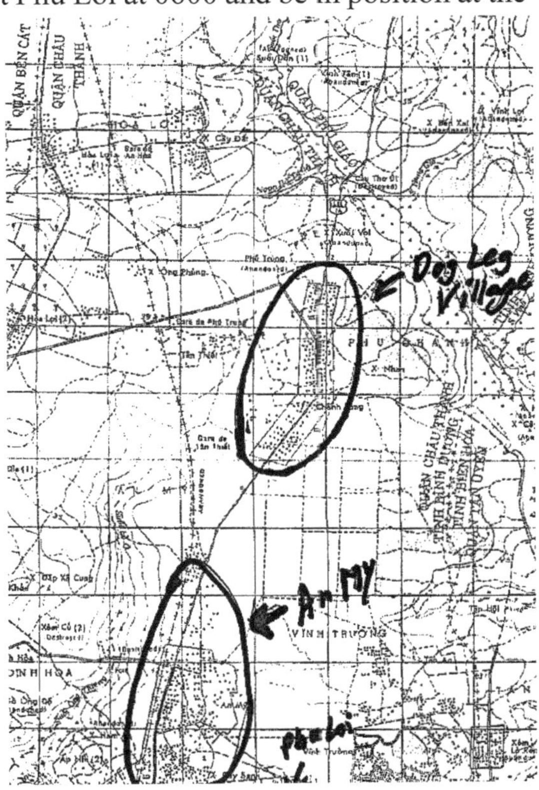

I called the "B" Troop Officers and senior NCOs together to explain the battle plan. I believe CPT Daniels stayed out of the field to in-process, but I'm not certain of that. I know I commanded the Troop at this point. All were very nervous. I had pulled out my new "Box" tactic and reviewed the old formations as well. Because of the size of the towns on our side of the road, we were going to push through with all Tanks and about half of the ACAVs in each platoon on line. The remaining ACAVs and the Troop Headquarters would spread out behind this line. Even the VTR (Vehicle Tank Retriever) would be in the second row. A few of the ACAVs were likely to be pulled back behind the second line where possible to provide some depth to the formation, because of the many obstacles we would have to go around or through. If we had a formidable defense to over-come, we would pull into a tight box formation until the obstacle was destroyed. That would be unlikely in these villages, but I preferred to brush-up on all formations so there would not be any confusion.

The Box Formation had been developed for jungle fighting, essentially putting two platoons next to each other in a box with three tanks up front bumper to bumper in each platoon and the ACAVs in rows behind the Tanks and with the Command tracks (platoon or troop formation) behind the row of tanks. This could be employed with one, two, or three platoons, side by side, making a front of all nine tanks. As I said, it was unlikely that a tight Box formation would be used in An My or the Dog Leg Village, but this was a good time to put it out there and briefly review its use. The new Troop Commander would need to see it in operation, and I didn't want any confusion when I showed it to him. A tight Box was not used on the 1st of February.

Five A.M. came quickly and some never caught a wink at all. Somehow the mess hall troopers managed to make the men a hot meal. That's what I liked about the mess hall troopers. They did what they could to help - always. They brought Mermite Cans (5-gallon insulated containers) of hot food to where we were parked and served it with hot coffee, milk, juice - the works. Then they took the equipment back to the mess hall and joined in the efforts to provide supplies to the field and prepare a hot meal if we came back that night. What great guys!

Everything was feverishly checked and rechecked. Intelligence had the villages full of NVA again. They had erected barricades throughout the towns, and they were ready for an armor assault. At 0600 we went out the north east gate of Phu Loi. The engineers had already swept a path for our exit, so we weren't likely to have any surprises by land mines. We went about fifty feet or so beyond the perimeter wire and headed north. At a point about 100 yards from the village berm I stopped the Troop and had the Platoon Leaders move the tracks into positions where everyone could see the berm and put all radios on the Troop frequency. I had a pep talk for the men in hopes that they could be cranked up to overcome their fear and to build confidence before the attack. I was especially concerned for the new troopers who had never been in combat. This was a Hell of an initiation.

When everyone was on the Command Net (command radio frequency) I gave what was to be referred to for forty years to come as the *"kill everything that moves"* speech. (When I say *"40 years to come"*, I'm referring to one of our medics who became an Officer and later a man of the Cloth (Medic (Reverend) Dennis Skiles), who attended my mother's funeral and was corralled by several of my adult nephews who had never met anyone that was with uncle John in Vietnam.) They were together in a huddle for ten minutes or so where he related this story to them.

'It started when your uncle climbed behind the 50 Caliber Machine Gun on the Command Track and told everyone to watch the water buffalo grazing outside of the Village berm. He fired one round straight between its eyes and began his speech with everyone's complete attention. All the new guys were about to receive their final training. This was all they would get. It went something like this.'

'Men, why did I kill that water buffalo? ---- Because it moved its friggin ears. When you enter these villages, if you want to live through the day you will need to live by your instincts. Believe, hope, and pray that all non-combatants are in holes under their homes and won't lift their heads until this is over. If you see a non-combatant, pull back if you can, but the risk is too great to pussy foot around. Believe that whenever your peripheral

vision sees movement, if it's not an armored vehicle, it's an enemy soldier pointing a weapon at you, and you are about to meet your Maker. What moved might only be a chicken, but it might be the last breath you take if you react slowly. Key up your instincts now and get ready for the fight of your life. Don't let your buddies down by slow reactions. The enemy you see move may be aiming at a friend. It's time for everyone to pull all your training and instincts together. This is not a test. In this game the devil is the umpire and we're playing for keeps. Now change back to your normal frequencies, say a prayer and get ready to fight.'

All was quiet. The troop moved into the attack positions. The first problem was to get past the village berm. The existing gaps would be mined. The VTR (Vehicle Track Retriever) was brought up on line. It had a bulldozer blade that could make holes in that berm. At exactly 0630 a burst of fire was made by all six tank machine guns these tanks and the VTR pulled right up to the berm. The tanks fired 50 Caliber over the berm while the VTR busted the first hole through the berm in front of our left platoon and another about 30 meters to the right. The platoons poured through the berm and regained their line, while the tracks slowly moved forward. By 0645 the entire troop was in its pre-established formation and making progress.

The enemy had fired a couple RPGs over the berm at the advancing tanks, but they were quickly overcome by the firing of the 50 Caliber machine guns and nothing was slowed by that initial resistance. As the Troop moved forward there were pockets of attacks on the armor vehicles. There were also cases where the enemy jumped up behind the front line to try to shoot the Cavalrymen in their backs. The double line prevented this trick from being effective. Progress was steady, but we were slowed so we wouldn't get ahead of "C" Troop on the west of the road. Again, the greatest enemy strength appeared to move in front of "C" Troop. That was their only possible escape route. "C" Troop was reinforced by attachments from Dreadnaught Bravo's (2/34 Armor Battalion) two M2A1s (40mm dual automatic guns). I am not certain of the number and types of weapons tracks that were attached, but it evened up the strength needed on both sides of the road.

After about two hours the NVA again were retreating to the northwest. But they were met by "D" Troop's Long-Range Reconnaissance Patrol (LRRP) and helicopter gunships from "D" Troop. When we left the north end of An My we had one wounded soldier med-evacted. So far so good. The wound was a small piece of shrapnel from an RPG round. As the tracks cleared the village, we went into a double column and moved on to Chanh Long Village, also known as the Dog Leg Village. The mortars started hitting around the tracks when we were about half way there. There were no direct hits and the "D" Troop gunship pilots managed to spot the flashes in the wooded area west of the dry rice paddies and west of the Dog Leg Village and responded with deadly accurate rocket fire. Artillery was adjusted into that wooded area and nothing was slowed.

We proceeded as we did at An My. There was a lot more fire over the berm and "D" Troop raked the area with their helicopter Gatling guns and rockets. The fighting was more intense than at An My and the NVA seemed to be far more concentrated and inventive. This was likely because we didn't go there the day before. We were almost hurt bad when several NVA soldiers came out of a well and animal feed stack behind us. Typical of the constant awareness of our troopers, an observant M-60 machine gunner saw the enemy soldiers with AK-47s and RPGs surface and take up positions to back-shoot our tracks. His fast reaction got the attention of other M-60 gunners, and no one was hurt except Charley. The NVA jumping up behind the front row of the formation caused us to drop grenades down wells and run over suspect personal property we would have preferred to avoid. On several occasions, enemy were squashed by the twisting tracks of tanks on food storage stacks and other piles of farm products.

During lulls in the fighting we hastily ate as we moved forward. It can be tough grabbing a bite on the move while having one's eyes scanning the area you are assigned to. C-Rations were gulped down cold. Beans and Franks were okay cold, but much of the rest tasted like crap to many of us. But it didn't really matter. Filling our cake holes was all that counted. No one was really thinking much about taste. Water was the most important nourishment. Every track had a couple 5-gallon cans of water.

And there was Pepsi Cola. Every track carried a couple cases plus small coolers. Huge blocks of ice about 3 to 4 feet long were broken into the coolers, and this was an essential item during the heat of battle. This was all the reason anyone needed to not be in the infantry. They couldn't carry the comfort items that the vehicles made possible. There was a considerable amount of jealousy in this regard, however most cavalrymen made it a point to be generous to the infantrymen. This also was an excellent attention getter when a trooper started to show an attitude problem. A good butt chewing coupled with the threat of being transferred to the infantry was an effective motivator in the Troop Commander's discipline quiver. Though available, it didn't have to be used very often. Seeing the Grunts (Infantrymen) struggling on foot was effective without reminding anyone that they lacked some of the comforts of home that we were blessed with. The morale was normally very high for the cavalrymen, especially when the fighting was regular.

Going through the Dog Leg Village was scary. It was hot and hard-fighting and the new men became seasoned cavalrymen that day and their morale was high when we cleared the north east corner of the village just before dusk. The plan was to return to Phu Loi, so I moved the Troop far enough to the east of the villages to avoid any RPG rounds that could be fired at us if the North Vietnamese managed to move back into the villages at dusk. We were not without losses, but the kick-ass attitude prevailed against the best the NVA had to offer. None of the new troopers were injured. I believe we had four injuries requiring dust-off and one KIA. I have no idea of the extent of enemy casualties, but it was extensive.

All but one trooper returned to duty in the next couple days. Although everyone was exhausted during this day of digging the enemy out of these villages, it was a real pump-up for all the troopers and the Troop was showered with compliments. The confidence level had grown from the uncertainty of the first day to knowledge that if we were aggressive and alert, it was only a matter of time before this North Vietnamese invasion would be smashed. And smash we did.

We exercised the Box formation every chance that came along. The normal formations were also used, single and double columns, lines, wedges and echelons right and left, but when it came time to engage the enemy in the jungle, the Troop learned to go from any formation into a Box and attack without hesitation into any threat. It became easier and easier with practice. The formation was unknown to the enemy and the ability to quickly attack with six tanks on line and the ACAVs in rows to their rear, either spread apart, or bumper to bumper as we entered the jungle, reversed any surprise the enemy may have had by getting off the first shot. I prayed a lot about that first shot.

After contact was made, there was no question who controlled the battle as we charged headlong onto a formerly confident enemy, destroying his bunkers and applying devastating fire to make his above ground escape nearly impossible. And the crushing machinery and grenades thrown into his spider holes and bunkers, as they became disclosed, made his underground exit or his notion to assault the Cavalrymen extraordinarily difficult. Don't get me wrong. Charley fought hard. We just fought better.

Remember that briefcase of money - the payroll? After a couple days of intensive fighting, the thought entered my mind as to what might have happened to the money. When the Squadron Commander, LTC John Seigle flew to our field position to say goodbye, as he was heading home, I informed him of the payroll I gave away in Lai Khe. LTC Seigle became quite alarmed and said he would check on it. Several hours passed and he flew back to our field position to tell me that every penny made it safely to the Finance Office. What a relief. What a lifting of pressure. What appreciation of a loyal Cavalryman, a man whom I didn't even know his name. Trooper, if you read this, please contact me. Your loyalty and honesty should be recognized.

Time to go home

My cup was overflowing from my adventures in Vietnam that were coming rapidly to a close. I had stayed in the field to assist where possible until CPT Eugene Daniels was familiar with the Squadron and Troop personnel, procedures and tactics. There is some disagreement on when Gene took substantial control of the troop, although the records show that he was assigned as Troop Commander from the 1st day of the TET Offensive. It doesn't matter. From my recollection he quickly took control of the Troop and

CPT Gene Daniels (lft)
and 1LT John Conley

did a fine job as the "B" Troop Commander. One afternoon, perhaps on February 4th or 5th, CPT Daniels and I had a picture taken with the Troop guidon and I made a mad dash to get processed out and head home.

I remember standing by the road in Phu Loi while the troop passed by, as I stood in the dust saluting the "B" Troopers with a heavy heart. After the troop departed Phu Loi I tossed my duffle bag into the jeep and headed for Bien Hoa Air Force Base for my meeting with the freedom bird. It hurt to leave, but I also felt totally fulfilled and appreciative of having survived my tour of duty with such honorable men. Little did I know as the plane lifted off that I was destined to return shortly.

END OF PART I

THE CAVALRYMAN'S

RITE OF PASSAGE

PART 2

RETURN TO HELL

Chapter 44

HOME AND AWAY

The trip home from Vietnam on February 7, 1968 was filled with the mixed emotions of tremendous happiness and deep, grueling, gut-wrenching remorse. Others may have felt different, but for me arriving home was a mix of pleasure, confusion, bewilderment, excitement, loneliness for my cavalry unit in Nam, fear for their welfare, and nervous of a nonexistent enemy that might be right around the corner, sneaking up on me every night. I didn't know quite how to take it. My body was in Michigan and my heart was on the other side of the world.

I now had families on both sides of the globe and the loyalties were deep to the family I just left, despite the gratification of having returned home to the safety of my biological family and friends. My moods flashed between deep depression, guilt that I had prematurely left my Cavalry family, while they were still in mortal danger, and being excited and high on enjoying my wife and my girls, now three-year-old Irene and a ten-month-old bubbly baby Maria and reuniting with a formerly very worried Mother and Father. Parties were had where my sisters, Virginia and Eunice, and their husbands and children, and close friends and relatives assembled. These events were intended to welcome me home, but down deep inside I felt like staying away from normal people. I felt very weird and I knew it would take some time to transition back from the war.

I didn't understand how much I had changed, and experienced a deep depression while sleeping in safety, waking in a quiet room without artillery booming all night long, and walking around a peaceful yard.

It all seemed alien. I was startled from sudden noises, and dreams were starting again, with nightmares that had no meaning except to rip me away from the peace I knew I should be feeling. I found myself studying the terrain around me for the enemy, especially at night. A good night's sleep was impossible, but I hoped all of this would soon pass. It was uncomfortable, very uncomfortable. And then there were the protests against the war. For the most part I ignored this, as the rants of cowards and idiots. What the Hell was there to fear in Nam that was so unusual? Real men shouldn't act that way! Wasn't war still a necessary rite of passage into manhood?

Less than two weeks at home and I was looking forward to my next assignment at Fort Hood, Texas. There was preparation for the move to be done. My wife and I headed for the closest transportation office which was at Selfridge Air Force Base, just 19 miles north in Mount Clements, Michigan.

There was a nice commissary and base exchange at Selfridge, and I really enjoyed my visit to the base exchange. When we arrived, I felt like I was on R&R again. The selections were so great I felt like a kid in a toy store. After having my fill of shopping, I spotted a rack of military newspapers near the checkout stand. On the Pacific Stars and Stripes a headline on the left column said in glaring bold type, **"1ˢᵗ Squadron, 4ᵗʰ Cavalry Troopers Missing in Action"**. I froze! They cited 2 bodies but didn't say anything about one. Everything they said was sketchy.

It was an awful shock. The identified missing trooper was the "B" Troop senior Medic. He was SP5 Julius Nicholas Szahlender and he was supposed to go home shortly after I did. This was family. It was awful. The Quarterhorse would never let this happen. Never! Unless there was a dangerous deficit in leadership, I couldn't believe this could ever happen in the Quarterhorse. This was unimaginable, and it was all I could think of. My mind was spinning, and I couldn't shake it and have any rest from that point forward.

It all became crystal clear during the drive home from Selfridge AFB.

I couldn't abandon my family in Nam in this crisis. I had to go back and do it quickly. I would take my family on a trip to Washington D.C. and visit the Officer Assignment Branch. I would not allow them to refuse me a trip back to my unit.

Since troopers that extended their time in Vietnam had a greater chance of getting killed, I was pushing my luck. Would I be required to give my life on this trip? I would try to get orders for my wife and my children to travel to her home on Okinawa as well. I knew that the folks at Officer Assignment Branch would not likely be able to tell me the extent of the problems in Nam, but if they did what I was asking, I could be relatively sure that the need for combat experience was significant. And my family would be with my wife's family to provide support if or when the bad news came. I never saw this as odd thinking or possibly a rationalization to leave the uncomfortable place I was in. This couldn't have been a more correct action to take. This was the state of my mind.

After bringing in the groceries, and supper was over, and everyone was relaxed together for the evening, I broke the news. I placed the Stars and Stripes on the kitchen table where my father was doing a crossword puzzle and stated my plans. There was silence. Silence so loud that it roared. There was shock and a tear came to my mother's eye. She and my father tried to understand, and she said, *"Johnny, surely the Army wouldn't allow this to happen. You've done your part son."* I can still see the hurt on her face, even today. My father and I took a walk through the orchard as we had done so many times before when man to man discussions were needed. He tried hard to understand what was incomprehensible, and he assured me that he would support whatever I felt was necessary. On returning to the house I started to prepare for the trip, and we left in the morning amid a deafening silence.

Although it was only going to be a quick trip, we planned to make the most of it. The motel in Arlington, Virginia had maps with all the sights to see, and the desk clerks were helpful in planning what was feasible for a small family with young children to see on a short stay. We drove through Washington DC and observed the White House, the Capitol and other government buildings. We also took a ride to the Jefferson Memorial at night when it was beautifully lit up.

A visit to the Pentagon the next morning resulted in getting directions to the old WWII barracks across the Potomac River that housed the Officer Assignment Branch. I confidently entered the old building and went to a reception desk at the head of the stairs on the second floor with my family in tow. I wasn't kept waiting, and a Captain and Major came out to greet me.

They were visibly excited to meet a combat officer straight from the TET Offensive, which was the hot news at that time. I stood out from my surroundings with my dark red laterite stained skin dominating my appearance and making my khaki uniform shockingly bold and commanding. My request and the reasons for wanting to return to the combat arena were apparently not something they had previously experienced, and they seemed to not quite believe what I was asking for. What sane person would want to go back there. But there was no good reason to disapprove my request, and I was fully confident of its approval.

The Assignment Officers went into the adjacent office returning with a hefty looking full Colonel who would be deciding my request. His appearance told me he never saw a combat zone. But he was the key. He wanted to meet the Officer that was so interested in returning to the fight so quickly. He granted my requests. Everything I wanted was approved, and in about 20 minutes I left with the Orders in my hand for myself and my family.

I needed to return to Michigan and prepare my family for the move. They needed inoculations to make this trip. And they had to store a small amount of household goods. The bulk of our household goods had already been in storage for the past year. We would drive across America to visit my sister Clara and her family in Anaheim, California. Tickets would be awaiting us at the Los Angeles International Airport. We would fly to Hawaii for a few day's layover, and then on to Okinawa. After a few more days I would continue to Saigon.

Chapter 45

RETURN TO THE FAR EAST

By the time we reached Michigan, anticipation could be cut with a knife. Mother knew the request was approved by the look on our faces as we entered the kitchen door. Tears fell from her sweet eyes, but I only could respond with a hug and assure her that this was necessary, and not to worry too much. I was not so sure down inside as to the validity of those assurances, as I sensed big trouble back in the war zone. A missing cavalryman was unheard of in my Cavalry Squadron, and I had a nagging feeling inside that this was my final adventure, and that I was being bated by Fate. But we all have a time to live and a time to die, and I wasn't going to hide from my duty. It was awfully hard to keep focused when those feelings of dying welled up. But that was doubt and it had to be overcome before arriving back in Vietnam.

The first time I went to Nam, my brother-in-law, Larry Summerfield, assured me of survival, if I made it through the initial attempt to kill me (see Chapter 7). That proved to be true, but this time there were no special words of wisdom. No one fully understood why I was doing this, except myself. Being a warrior was reason enough. Though everyone wanted to be supportive and tried their level best to give encouragement, I knew it wasn't easy for them. I appreciated their stiff upper lips and no negative comments.

In Hawaii, I had the opportunity to visit with my good friend Happy, Patrick C. Marciel, one of the finest Marines I had the good fortune to serve with. He and his beautiful wife, Vee, were former doubles surfing champions at Malabo. I was with Happy at the Marine Corps

Recruit Depot in San Diego, training recruits in swimming and water survival skills. Happy had patiently helped me hone my swimming skills, and when he started training the Penguins and Dolphins at Sea World in the evenings and weekends, my services were requested to train the first Sea Maids in SCUBA Diving and safety precautions when working with the sea life; and methods of avoiding injury during underwater ballet among the sea creatures. They were all beautiful, shapely college girls, but I did behave myself. It wasn't easy.

We had a great time getting these important Sea World shows ready for the grand opening and built a very close and enduring friendship during this period. I even created a Diving School so that as a military diving instructor, I could devise a way to qualify Happy as a diving instructor while he assisted in training the Sea Maids. Happy and I even studied for and took our GEDs together. That was the level of my education during the Vietnam period of my life as well, although my High School did Graduate me because of my GED Scores. College was not to come until my fighting days were over.

Happy was the first to plant the idea in my head to become an Officer by making a comment after a full-dress parade that he saw me as "Officer material." I would have gone to the Marine Corps Officer's School, but that would require me to first get a four-year college degree. I tossed that notion out the window courtesy of the U.S. Army allowing me to defer the college education until after Vietnam.

My family didn't get much of a chance to see the attractions in Hawaii as my eldest, Irene, came down with a bad cold and had to be heavily medicated. Happy kindly let me use his black and white T-bird while we were there. This was when Thunderbirds were small sports cars. It gave us an opportunity to see the flamingo show at Paradise Park, drive up to the Pali, meander through the beautiful tropical countryside and enjoy the gorgeous weather a little. We also went to a luau and a nice hula show. But Irene was ill, and it was necessary that she spend most of the time resting up for the next leg of our journey.

Happy picked me up one day and took me to the Don Ho Show, and following that, at a stage opposite where Don Ho performed, a great Tahitian hula show commenced. Happy had prearranged to have me drug up onto the stage with several other poor saps to learn the hula from a bunch of lovely dancers, and in front of a packed house. There was a huge, obese gentleman that was also selected from the audience. It looked as though the fat guy was going to have a heart attack. That night could have been a very long butt wigging experience, but thanks to the chubby fellow the act was ended early for the sake of his health.

The next morning Happy and I took a ride to talk about old times. He had been discharged from the Marines for medical reasons as he was carrying some significant injuries from a Viet Cong bullet lodged in his leg. I learned that another friend, Joel had returned home from Nam to find his children calling another man Daddy. He killed himself. Then there was another Hawaiian friend that we served with in San Diego who was killed in Vietnam.

We went to the National Cemetery. It was enormous. As we were driving down a road through the center of the thousands and thousands of white grave markers, I felt something inside and asked Happy to stop the car. I walked across the road to the left of the car about ten rows from the road and directly to Sergeant Quarantas' (sp) grave. We said a prayer for our friend, and left, a bit dazzled by the experience. Did he call to me? How did I know he was there among all those graves?

Before departing Hawaii, Happy gave the girls beautiful Leis (flowered necklaces). That's the last time I would see my friend.

The trip to Okinawa was long but uneventful. My brother-in-law, Sakae Higa, met us at the airport. It was a wonderful visit. The family was thrilled at having their daughter and her children home again. They seemed to understand the mission I had chosen for myself to go back into the war. My Mother-in-Law was so very happy to see her daughter and I enjoyed the treatment my wife received as a world traveler. They all catered to her while she spun her stories of grand adventures on the other side of the globe. It was terrific.

I particularly enjoyed my visit to Hama Higa Shima, a nearby island, where less than a decade ago I regularly brought my diving club, the Hanson Hydronauts, for weekend diving excursions around the offshore islands. My bond with the inhabitants of Hama was very close and endearing and we enjoyed our visit with Shinsho Morene, his wife Masako and their two little boys who were the same ages as my girls.

Shinsho owned a boat taxi service and had two boats about 50 feet long to take people to and from the main island, about a 40-minute trip one way. I frequently hired one of his boats for weekend diving expeditions in the early 1960s. Shinsho and I had become very close friends. The islanders had a huge party to celebrate our visit and we had a chance to walk up the mountain behind the village to the plateau where Hama and Higa, villages, from opposite sides of the island, farmed their crops.

Between the plateau and the village of Hama Higa, while sitting on a large flat, gray rock, my wife and I reviewed our history on these off-shore islands, while enjoying a gorgeous view of the Pacific islands around Hama Higa. We lingered there most of the afternoon.

It was very sad to leave Hama Higa and I recognized a growing emotional instability on the way back to the main island. I couldn't help but stare back at the island as it disappeared, while we traveled toward the Yakena Harbor on Okinawa. I hurt deeply, and my eyes were tearing uncontrollably. I loved these people and this spot on the earth.

The time spent on Okinawa was far too brief. At the going away party something quite strange occurred. I saw a jukebox and pressed the V-7 buttons. I couldn't read the names of the songs because they were in Japanese, but V-7 was what I remembered from long ago in a small cafe a way down the road. That was where my wife and I had dinner, after being married at the U.S. Consulate, with our good friends, Peeter and Kyoko Hansen, who witnessed our nuptials in 1963. It was a shock when the music started as it played the same love song, *Urudamachi*

Gitah, that was played on the other jukebox five years earlier on this specific V-7 selection. What a nice surprise, and how spooky and delightful. I confess that this was the only Japanese song I really liked other than the one my daughter sang.

Chapter 46

TO VIETNAM . . . AGAIN

The flight to Vietnam was spent calming the nerves of perhaps twenty or more nurses en-route to their first assignment overseas. Mostly they were headed for the Tuiwa Hospital. They were flustered and wanted to talk to anyone who had seen combat. And I was the only combat officer on the flight. This was a night arrival, and all went smoothly until the approach to Saigon, where the nurses could watch the green tracers coming up toward the plane. There was a bit of screaming, but they gained control after they knew nothing could be done about it.

In mid-March 1968 I arrived in Vietnam. It felt good to land safely. And there had been no uncertainty on this flight. I knew exactly where I was going, and transportation was my only concern. I quickly obtained the combat uniforms and equipment issued to all incoming personnel. Then I got lucky and caught a chopper making a delivery to Phu Loi. I walked to the Headquarters, dropped my bag at the TOC and took a nap until morning, which was only a couple hours away. I felt right at home at last. It's still hard to comprehend, but I didn't feel this comfortable when I got home in Michigan.

At first light I went to the Officer's Mess and ate breakfast. I had not quite left my table when I was greeted by Major Barney Forbes. We went to his office and had a long discussion. His first question was to find out if I had ever left Vietnam. The second was why I returned. I told him I wanted to know about the "B" Troop head medic. I listened, but I couldn't comprehend the logic of leaving deceased troopers out over-night. I didn't feel I was getting the complete story and that bothered me a lot

.

Soon I found that I would be assigned as the Adjutant and I had a very capable Lieutenant Eckman (sp) and Staff Sergeant Barry Nester running the S-1 personnel operation. There were plenty jobs to do though, and I kept busy with personnel chores.

As I said previously, in addition to directly supervising the Squadron's Personnel and Supply operations, Major Forbes oversaw manning the perimeter towers in the Squadron's sector of responsibility. He supervised the troop rear echelon personnel, and he ran the Soldier's School for the incoming troopers. He was the commander of all the Squadron's rear echelon elements. Among a myriad of other tasks, he made very frequent visits to the field and to the hospital to visit our injured troopers.

Major Forbes became more than a boss. He and I spent a lot of time discussing tactics, home, and food, and every other conceivable thing that soldiers discussed, who wished they could be directly influencing the combat actions in the field, but couldn't.

He kept telling me to be careful, because he felt responsible for me. We had become close friends while I was the "B" Troop XO. In addition to being a strong, hard core soldier, Barney Forbes had a heart of gold under that tough veneer that not many knew about. His comment of concern for my welfare was the only time that anyone ever vocally expressed a concern for my safety, while I was in Vietnam.

I learned a lot about this fine officer that many others never had the opportunity to know. He was one of the most loyal and dependable soldiers I ever got to know. When the chips were down, and I became buried in combat again, he was always there to make certain that my Troop was fully supported. About a month after I became the Squadron Adjutant, when CPT Serio was killed after three days in command, I became the "A" Troop Commander. Through the intercession of Major Forbes, over the stanch objections of Major Tom Kelly, the Operations Officer, 1st Sergeant Natividad Escobedo was reassigned to be the "A"

Troop First Sergeant as well. This was a huge favor that I will never forget. There was a time when Major Forbes was like the big brother I never had. And he had my back.

Chapter 47

WHAT HAPPENED TO JULIUS SZAHLENDER?

About the time I left for home, the Squadron moved north in pursuit of a retreating enemy that had been whipped trying to get into Saigon by over-running the American and ARVN basecamps and the very powerful forces that stood in their way. The NVA continued their struggle as they withdrew, forcing the Division to fight hard for control of its area of operations.

It would take years for me to wrap my mind around what I believe happened to our former head medic. Over the years I received several different stories as to what occurred. To me it appears that the incident was a bad (dumb) mistake of war. In war shit happens fast and decisions are not always made with all the cards on the table.

On February 24, 1968 when the Squadron was moving back to Phu Loi. "B" Troop was stopped just north of An My to allow a unit of thin-skinned vehicles to get into Phu Loi ahead of them. The medic track was a couple vehicles behind the lead tanks. The head medic, SP5 Julius Szahlender, saw a body dressed in military fatigues with a 1st Infantry Division patch on his shoulder in a small gully about ten feet from the road. He jumped off the medic track and started down the steep bank to provide medical assistance. As he approached the body two or three claymore mines exploded. It was a booby-trap ambush.

Szahlender's body was left in the field overnight, which resulted in the Missing in Action report on the front page of a Stars and Stripes newspaper, motivating my immediate return to Vietnam.

I stubbornly pursued a complete answer for 47 years and was only able to discern that "B" Troop was ordered to "immediately" return to Phu Loi, as they had to go to the Di An basecamp early the next morning. I was also able to determine from a medic who went to retrieve his body the following morning, that there was no doubt that Szahlender had been killed instantly.

In my research I was reminded that there is no rule of war to preclude leaving bodies on the battlefield for later recovery. However, the adverse impact on unit morale made this a questionable practice to me in this instance. I was told that 97% of the time it would be unheard of to leave bodies behind, and this was one of the other 3%. Still I've never heard any details as to why this was such a rare circumstance.

Szahlender's body was removed the following morning using ropes and recovery equipment. This tripped more claymores that were apparently put in over-night. Charley knew the Americans would not leave bodies in the field for long, so they put in more booby-traps. It was only then when it was determined that the decoy body was not an American.

I've been asked, that as a result of these circumstances, did I have any remorse of my decision to return to Vietnam. The answer was and is an emphatic *"NO"*. I was able to make a difference during that period, so there are no regrets. And I recognize that mistakes do happen in war.

Chapter 48

LIFE AS THE ADJUTANT

As I said previously, I had a highly qualified Lieutenant and Staff Sergeant in place to conduct the daily business of the S-1, Squadron Personnel Office. I really didn't have a great amount to do except write some awards and prepare administrative reports, and then brief the Squadron Commander in the field every other day. This is when LTC Thomas Tyree and I would discuss personnel matters and casualty reports.

A prior Adjutant, who was relieved of his duties, had prepared many well written phony awards for himself. Major Forbes told me to throw them out. He recalls today that I said *"No sir. "Them's" good examples."* I probably said it just like that. Having a handicap of not being able to write well didn't make me unqualified to read and duplicate something that was well written.

I was probably being a royal pain in the ass in more ways than one. Warrant Officer (W-1) Franklin Vance Anderson from "D" Troop would fly me to the field to arrive at the Field TOC (Tactical Operations Center) at 1700 hours sharp. I would report to the Squadron Commander, who normally had his long skinny knife (a Russell

WO Franklin Anderson

Fighting Knife) out and would be pruning his fingernails on schedule when I arrived. I figured that they taught this skill at West Point. OCS officers used an inexpensive fingernail clipper.

WO Anderson, at 21 years old was an amiable and talented Cavalry pilot and we became good friends almost immediately. I felt a terrible loss when he was killed on May 17, 1968, along with SP5 Brent J. Bertsch, flying his OH-6A helicopter (Loach) at treetop level on a visual reconnaissance mission.

I quickly got to know LTC Tyree and became highly critical of the number of men who were being killed in the Hobo Woods and the Trapezoid areas west of the Thunder Road where contact was being made with the VC Phu Loi Battalion almost daily. The Phu Loi Battalion had been in this area for years and conventional tactics were bringing an unacceptable level of casualties.

LTC Tyree, a West Point graduate with a long family history of West Pointers, did not like what he was hearing from this OCS First Lieutenant. It seemed hard for him to accept the fact that a non-West Point officer might have something worth listening to. With each visit, I would try to give a little advice on the way I would attack the enemy, which had been successful in the past, but I got a deaf ear. I wasn't terribly surprised, and could have clammed up, but it was my duty to be candid and help if I could.

LTC Tyree promotes John to Captain

On one of these trips to the field I was promoted to Captain effective April 1, 1968, and that seemed to make a little difference, but not much. I would discuss the tactics being used and bemoan the losses after every trip to the field with Major Forbes, and though we would discuss these matters, we were helpless to contribute productively to the tactical actions in the field. But there was never-the-less some enjoyment being created in Phu Loi. And little did I expect what was soon to happen.

Chapter 49

THE PRE-NATAL CAPSULE CAPER

Mr. Chin, the owner of the laundry, steam-bath, and barber shop came to the Squadron S-1 Office to ask me for help. It appeared that Mrs. Chin, a young, vivacious, admirable young lady believed he was diddling with the girls in the steam bath, because he was coming home much too tired to perform his husbandly duties. He had read about a new pill, Vitamin E, and was hoping his American friends could help him get some. Mr. Chin swore he was not being unfaithful, but he was always very fatigued when he returned home from work. I told him that I would see how I might be able to help, and that he should come back the next day with Mrs. Chin. At least she could be told of his concern and perhaps knowing that he was ill would help them with their problem.

After he left, Major Forbes (who had been eavesdropping from his office across the hall) and I discussed the dilemma and the decision was to discuss this with the Squadron Surgeon. It was fortunate that the Surgeon, Captain Leon Cantor was returning to the basecamp from the field later that afternoon. Before dinner, I strolled over to the dispensary and presented the problem to the Surgeon. The gleam in Captain Cantor's eyes told me that he had a plan. In small boxes on the bottom of some metal shelves were bottles of blue and pink pre-natal capsules large enough to choke a horse. They had been shipped to the Cavalry in error, but now perhaps they would serve some useful purpose. The label was removed from a bottle of perhaps 100 blue pills and a capitol "E" was written on the bottle. I left well equipped to solve a problem.

Just like clockwork, at 10 am, Mr. and Mrs. Chin arrived at the Personnel Office. Major Forbes was in his office when they arrived. Mr. Chin was excited, and his lovely bride was nervous and quite embarrassed. This public airing of their sexual problems was not what an oriental lady was normally subjected to. I wasted no time in explaining to her that Mr. Chin had confided in me as to his problem, and assured Mrs. Chin that I believed her husband was faithful. I told them that in the plastic bottle I was holding, with the large black grease pencil "E" on the side, was the answer to their problems. Their eyes both lit brightly, cheeks narrowed, and their mouths dropped open in awe as the top was removed and a huge light blue capsule was lifted into view. The size was impressive, and on sight gave reasons for great expectations. I went on to instruct the couple to patiently have no sex for 10 days while Mr. Chin regained his strength. Mrs. Chin was to leave him alone for the entire time. And he was to report on his improving strength daily during this period.

They left smiling and giggling like children and were full of anticipation. Mr. Chin reported daily on schedule, coaxing after several days for a little leeway to perhaps try out his new-found strength earlier than the allotted time. Being sternly advised to follow the instructions, Mr. Chin was climbing the walls as the end of the strengthening period approached.

On the 10th day the couple went home early, very early. All the workers at the laundry were giggling uncontrollably when I came into view. This was a very important issue to ten or more people who worked for the Chins. So much for secrecy.

The next morning, while walking across the parade field, Mr. Chin came gleefully running to meet me. He seemed to be hovering a foot off the ground and there was a definite skip in his step. He was overly anxious to tell me that they had enjoyed themselves everywhere in their home over and over and over through the afternoon and night. Wow! Such Joy! Such Happiness!

As I passed the laundry, several young ladies were giggling shyly while unsuccessfully trying to hide their knowledge of Mr. Chin's miraculous recovery. And about halfway up on a huge pile of jungle fatigues that went all the way to the ceiling, that were awaiting shipment to the washing machines, there lay Mrs. Chin's disheveled body in obvious total fatigue. Her cloths, until now, had always been impeccable as was the rest of her appearance. Uncharacteristic of this normally poised, lovely lady, there she was with a gentle, slight smile, appearing like a half wilted rose after an awful thunderstorm, silently drained of all of life's energies.

In contrast, Mr. Chin strutted and crowed like a bantam rooster who just kicked a big leghorn out of the barn yard to restore himself to kingship over the hen house. He chattered non-stop, thanking and thanking me for the magical medicine. It was clear that I would be idolized by the Chin family and friends for a long time to come. Everyone in the rear echelon who knew of the experiment got a big kick out of the Pre-natal Capsule Caper.

Chapter 50

SUDDEN CHANGE IN COMMAND

On about April 12, 1968 I was informed that when Captain Fred Shirley departed country on the 14th of April, the S-3 Air Officer, Captain Robert Frank Serio would be taking command of the Hardcore Alpha Troop. Since he had no combat experience and because the Troop was to be moved from the water plant north of Saigon to deep jungle duty, I offered to ride with him for a few days. This was unacceptable to LTC Tyree, as CPT Serio was a *"West Point graduate, and well credentialed to assume command under any conditions without assistance."*

CPT Robert F. Serio

On April 14 I saw CPT Shirley off at the Phu Loi Squadron Headquarters as he was leaving to fly home. At that point I believed I would be the Adjutant until it was time to leave the country again. Little did I know that Charley would turn everything upside down in a hurry. The little bastards were like that.

The Squadron Headquarters moved with "B" Troop and an Artillery unit from the Trapezoid to the east of Thunder Road, along the Ben Cat to Phuoc Vinh road, to an NDP where LTL-16 was intersected. This spot, known as Claymore Corners, was on the northwest corner of a jungle area known as the Catcher's Mitt. Alpha Troop linked up with the Squadron Headquarters at this location in a cleared area about a hundred meters away from that intersection. On the 16th of April some enemy contact was made, and on the morning of April 17th there was more fighting.

Around 1500 I was called to the TOC at Phu Loi and told over the radio by Major Forbes to pack a bag for an extended stay, and a chopper was on the way to pick me up. Life was about to get exciting again. I had no idea what the Hell was going on, but Major Forbes had been at the field TOC all day, and when he talked there was deep concern in his voice. I had a premonition of heading straight into the hands of Fate. By the time the helicopter arrived at Phu Loi, I was on the airstrip ready to throw my bag aboard. Flying at treetop level northeast from Phu Loi, one of the pilots informed me of what had happened.

Captain Serio had been hit in his side by an RPG and the troopers were pretty shook up, as was the Squadron Commander. I was being made the new Alpha Troop Commander on arrival. I knew that "A" Troop had been working between Long Bien and Saigon since after the 1st Tet Offensive, and was of the opinion they had not been subjected to much deep jungle fighting, but they were disciplined and did know how to fight.

As the chopper was landing, the pilots hovered a little, so I could look the area over quickly to form a mental picture of just where the perimeter was located. It was bordered on the north by a shallow gully that went to the east, swung around the eastern side of the perimeter and into heavy, twisted secondary jungle about 20 feet high. There were clearings going back through the heavy jungle to the east that bordered the secondary growth and heavy jungle. And there was evidence that tracked vehicles had recently been maneuvering through these clearings to the east of the perimeter.

The east side of the perimeter was about 50 feet from the thick brush that led into the jungle and the shallow gully was not more than a few feet deep and was directly in front of "A" Troop's tracks. To the south there was a clear area between the north-south road (LTL-16) and the jungle which extended to a small village about 800 meters or so to the south. And beyond that village there was another larger village about a half mile or so further down the road. The north-south road was clearly unused, undoubtedly heavily mined as there wasn't any evidence of bicycle, vehicle or animal traffic.

Once on the ground I headed straight to the TOC, a grouping of three oversized headquarters tracks with green canvas hooked in between them. Before LTC Tyree and Major Forbes entered, I had a quick look at the situation map, and it was full of enemy units. Perhaps we were next to a major staging area for another attack on Saigon. When they did enter the TOC, I was made the "A" Troop Commander.

No one knew that this was the beginning of the 2nd Tet Offensive of 1968 ("Mini-Tet"), and that this was where COSVN Headquarters, the North Vietnamese Army's tactical headquarters in South Vietnam was located. The evening briefing was abbreviated somewhat so I could get to my troop as quickly as possible.

Before leaving I told the Squadron Commander that "A Troop would be trained that night in the Box formation I previously told him about and would use it if we had to attack into that thick jungle. LTC Tyree was visibly shaken at the time and wasn't in the mood to argue tactics. He merely acknowledged my remarks. I also alerted the "B" Troop Commander, Gene Daniels, that the Box would be used. It had not been used since I had left "B" Troop, but he remembered it.

As I was heading for my troop there was a short burst from a 50 Caliber machine gun along with some hollering to cease fire. "A" Troop was shooting up a "B" Troop ambush patrol. Good God, what's next!

Almost immediately a mob of "B" troopers were coming across the perimeter toward the "A" troop vehicles looking for a fight. I knew a lot of these troopers and this wasn't going to happen. I quickly inserted myself between the angry "B" troopers and the "A" troopers who were coming to meet the threat. The "B" troopers, where very angry and vocal as I would have expected them to be, bent on avenging the dead and wounded members of their patrol.

What a Hell of a position to be in, but I knew that good soldiers would follow orders, if I held my ground. It took a couple minutes, but the 20 or so troopers shouting loud, taunting statements were stopped and both groups headed back to their tracks without any further disruption.

I threw my bag on the A-66 ACAV and called for all the Officers and key NCOs to come to my track immediately. It was uncomfortable having all the troop leadership in a bunch, but time was pressing, and command was not fully assumed until this meeting was over. They all assembled within about 10 minutes. 1st Lieutenant Joseph Scates was the 1st Platoon Leader, A-16. His ears were still ringing from some close RPG explosion earlier that day. 1st Lieutenant Michael Bache was the 2nd Platoon Leader, A-26. The 3rd Platoon, A-36, commanded by 1st Lieutenant Ivan Prichard was detached and replaced by the third platoon of "C" Troop. C-36, 1st Lieutenant Joseph Birindelli, an Engineer Officer who filled out the Troop. Joe Birindelli, who was an experienced Cavalry Platoon Leader, had never served under his own Troop Commander, but had some very significant independent experiences with his fine platoon.

Chapter 51

PREPPING FOR A BRAWL

We were assembled in a bunch behind A-66 and I had a receptive audience of Platoon Leaders and Platoon Sergeants, plus a few of their NCOs. All were quiet and attentive.

I introduced myself and gave a brief summation of my philosophy of jungle fighting, assured everyone that I knew what I was doing, and expected nothing less than disciplined teamwork and quick responses to whatever the enemy had to offer. Then I got a stick out

Joseph Sikes

Michael Bache

and drew the formations we would use in a jungle fight. I went through every standard formation for moving the troop in and around the jungle and how to get from them into the Box Formation just as soon as fire was received, and of course how to get back into the standard formations.

The plan was to lead with A-16 with the A-66 track and the Zippo track close behind the platoon leader's track, followed by C-36, and A-26 would be in reserve along with the Alpha Headquarters combat trains vehicles. The order of march was determined by questions I had asked earlier at the TOC about the experience of the platoons. I needed the most experience up front as my analysis was that Charley knew they had killed CPT Serio and would believe they were dealing with a demoralized unit. I had no intention of giving the little bastards that edge.

Joseph Birindelli

Time was of the essence, and I wasn't in the mood for complicating matters with a long discussion of my own experiences. Joe Birindelli was quite concerned, based on the comments in his Manuscript "WRONG PLACE, WRONG TIME". He and several of his NCOs were concerned that this new formation was an invention of someone at the Headquarters and untried. I never told them that it was something I had created, and it had previously been successfully used. Being good Cavalry Officers and NCOs, my orders were faithfully carried out, and it was after midnight when the training was complete.

I knew a better sales job was needed, so I headed out through the platoon positions to meet the troopers after telling SP4 Hubbard to get the command track cleaned up. The men on A-66 were all killed or wounded, except for the driver, SP4 Hubbard. 1st Sergeant Bell, who was replaced to go home on April 18th, had shifted people around to re-man the vehicle.

SP4 Hubbard

SSG Tom Reed, the Track Commander, was blown down into the track, and he found himself outside A-66 on the ground in shock holding a shotgun with a broken off stock and firing into the jungle. Tom had an injury on his right arm. He was a former Marine Corps NCO and when he returned before we left in the morning, he was quite pleased to hear that I also was a former Jar-Head NCO.

I talked with Hubbard after I toured the platoons, which gave him time to reorganize the track that had everything thrown helter-skelter from the RPG blast. Captain Serio didn't suffer as the RPG round hit him in the rib cage. The temporary Forward Observer, filling in for LT Mark Darrow, who was on R&R, and the M-60 Machine Gunner were also killed instantly. Small body parts would have to be removed for the next couple months, whenever a trail of ants would be found going to and from the many crevices on the track. It was hurtful and demoralizing, but something we had to rise above.

SSG Tom Reed

Tom had taken one Hell of a mental hit and I had to consider whether I should send him back to the rear for a while. I decided that I needed him in the field, and he was insistent on staying, so I let him stay.

There was a lot of nervousness, and many of the troopers asked questions about this Box Formation. Apparently, the Lieutenants and NCOs really didn't know how to take this new way of meeting the enemy, and there was no way to sell all its advantages in that quick orientation or while walking through the platoons.

Some of the men saw how I handled the fight that was developing earlier with "B" troopers and were apparently ready to try something

CPT Conley
A-66 Snoopy ACAV

this new Troop Commander was pushing. Many had lost their confidence and needed some pumping up. I went to each track without the company of the platoon leaders and talked with the troopers. It was clear that this was needed. And I learned a lot about the status of maintenance and other issues at the same time. The Tanks and ACAVs were in good shape maintenance wise, but there was a problem with the 50s being reported.

It was necessary to keep the head space and timing properly adjusted on our 50 caliber machine guns or they would jam after a few rounds were fired. Ouch! Several of the ACAV Commanders related this as a problem. This would not do tomorrow or perhaps even tonight. C-36, Joe Birindelli, didn't seem to have this problem, but I was sure he would also like to test fire his 50 caliber machine guns before going into that jungle after the NVA in the morning.

I headed straight for the TOC and advised the Squadron Commander of this problem. He determined that "A" Troop would lead out in the morning, and we would take a detour to test fire the machine guns. I needed to solve this problem as quickly as possible. I returned to my track to get everything set up like I wanted it. The jeep seat, which was mounted on the top left rear corner of the ACAV, had been rinsed off, but the blood stains were clearly visible.

Before we left in the morning, SSG Reed returned from receiving medical treatment on his arm and briefly told me what had happened on 17 April. The Troop was moving south between the north-south dirt road, LTL-16, and the jungle. The Troop Commander's track was at the end of C-36's platoon as they moved south in a single column. They were to pick up some LRRP troopers that had been ambushed. Suddenly they were receiving heavy fire from the jungle. They returned fire and moved toward the jungle. LTC Tyree told them to continue on to pick up the LRRPs. They turned back to the right and shortly an RPG Gunner jumped up from a patch of brush and fired broadside at A-66. And the enemy continued the heavy machine gun fire from the tree line.

SSG Reed had an interesting family lineage which had soldiers going back to the civil war and beyond. His father had the misfortune of being part of the Bataan Death March and was one of the prisoners that LTC Musie's Rangers saved from the Capatchuan POW Camp in the Philippines just prior to their impending mass slaughter. (Read <u>Ghost Soldiers</u> by Hampton Sides).

The Command and Control chopper also caught its skids on the NDP's perimeter wire on the 17th and crashed. Fortunately, no one was hurt. LT Birindelli was awarded a Silver Star for assuming control of the Troop under fire, while his tracks and those of A-16 returned fire on the wood line. After a short time, a cease fire was called, and the Troop extracted the LRRP patrol and moved back to the NDP. Only two of the LRRP troopers were still alive. There are other versions of this story, but none were terribly important to me at the time, or now. It was a terrible loss.

I learned long ago that there were probably hot spots on earth, which were doors into Hell. It felt like we were within a stone's throw of one.

When the sun set on the 17th of April, the Artillery opened up with volleys of H&I (harassing and interdiction) fire. I was able to sleep amid such blasting noise and tied one end of my hammock to the corner of the ACAV and the other to a young tree about ten feet away. It felt good to settle into that hammock, say a couple quick prayers and drop into a deep slumber.

But Charley wouldn't allow such peace and was out to silence the artillery. Sometime after midnight you could hear the thump, thump, thump of mortars inside the perimeter. I awoke finding myself standing in the center of my hammock. It's a mystery how I got off that damned thing and into the ACAV safely. In any case we quickly buttoned up the track and prepared to make a response to this intrusion. A Headquarters mess hall vehicle was hit and there were several wounded C-36 troopers. In the heat almost everyone was sleeping outside which invited injuries from mortars.

Muzzle flashes of Charley's mortars were spotted south of the NDP, in the direction of the village. On orders from Squadron my track and A-

26's platoon moved out of the perimeter and headed toward the village while staying close to the road. There was no choice but to move toward the mortar site as the only other option, which was to fire toward the village, would have created undesired collateral damage. We marched artillery on pre-established checkpoints between ourselves and the jungle, just in case Charley had an ambush in mind. The mortar firing suddenly stopped as we neared the village, and when we arrived at the mortar site the enemy was gone.

We returned to the perimeter with sleep in mind. As we pulled A-66 into its position I saw that the sapling my hammock was tied to, sported a shredded one-half of my new hammock. The rest was hanging from the corner of my ACAV. After the adrenaline rush subsided, I tried to get some shut eye inside of the track on the ammo boxes. But most of the night I listened to the artillery H&I fires and the situation reports from the platoons and anticipated the upcoming day and the serious business at hand.

Chapter 52

THE JAWS OF HELL REOPEN
APRIL 18, 1968

I was up before 0600. I may have gotten an hour's sleep. The troop had a hot breakfast and was ready to move before 0730. The mess truck had been partly damaged by a mortar round, but that didn't affect the food that the Mess Sergeant was able to prepare. Scrambled eggs, flap jacks, bacon and sausage, bread, fruit, milk and coffee. Yum, Yum.

My Track Commander may need some time in Phu Loi to clear his head after what happened the day before, which unceremoniously blew him down into the ACAV. He could work with the supply Sergeant for a while and SSG George from the 1st Platoon would replace him.

1st Sgt Natividad Escobedo joined us the morning of April 18, 1968

But Sergeant Reed assured me that he was okay, so I kept him on A-66. When we were getting ready to depart the perimeter, it was time to say a prayer for divine assistance, which I felt sure we would need, and asked Jesus to ride with us so my troops could get through this day safely.

When it was time to move out, we hit the SP (start point) at 0845 sharp, right on the button. In a single column the lead Tanks of A-16 moved east through the shallow gully and around and through some heavy brush for several hundred meters. Then we moved into a clearing to the left and allowed "B" Troop to pass.

There were several 50 caliber machine guns that needed their head space and timing tweaked. The wrenches came out as soon as we stopped and in about twenty minutes all the 50s were ripping up the countryside. The problem wasn't as widespread as reported, but it was certainly better to be safe than sorry. This was potentially an extremely dangerous matter as the main battle weapon on each of the ACAV's was its 50-caliber machine gun. Thank goodness the problem was reported and corrected before we went further. If I was right, we would need all the weapons working perfectly before long.

"B" Troop had moved in a southerly arc and was about 200 meters ahead of "A" Troop when we started moving again, this time in a double column. C-36 was in a double column in front, A-16 was in a double column behind C-36. My ACAV was near the front of C-36's platoon, as was Zippo Reb and the Medic's Track. Then the Troop Combat Trains (1st Sgt's ACAV, the maintenance track, the VTR, and the Zippo refueling truck) followed with the 2nd Platoon, as the reserve platoon, at the end of the column.

Bravo Troop had reported finding Russian or Chinese CS (Tear gas) Canisters, but we missed that report while test firing and learned about it later. As Alpha Troop got underway it wasn't long before the S-3, Major Tom Kelly, flying in one of the Command and Control helicopters, informed me that a man was seen running in a small clearing near what looked like a hay rack to the left front of my advancing columns. Why would such a thing be in this jungle, I wondered?

As we moved toward this small clearing from the scattered heavy brush, an RPG was fired at a lead Tank and another at the first ACAV on the left of the formation. We lost two brave troopers and had another couple wounded. SSG Fredrick D. Wescott Jr, and SP5 Thomas J. Lawson were killed (no pictures available).

I ordered "A" Troop into its first Box Formation: *"Form a box to the left and turn left"*, and I watched each track jockey into position. The Box was formed within two minutes and moving forward firing 90mm canister rounds directly to the front and 50 caliber and 7.62mm M-60 machine gun fire to the front and flanks. It was obvious that the troopers had been thinking hard on this formation overnight and it came off like clockwork. One would have

Forming into the Box

thought this was something they had practiced many times before. This was a darned good sign as to the quality of these troopers and I was very proud at the awesome way my command was executed. But I was deeply saddened by our losses.

Zippo Reb

I was where I liked to be, behind the third Tank from the left. To my left was the 1st Platoon Leader, LT Sikes, and two tracks to my right could be found C-36, LT Birindelli. Behind the ACAV to my right was the Zippo (Flame Thrower) track fully charged and at the ready. As we pushed forward with the six Tanks nearly bumper to bumper and the ACAVs in rows behind the Tanks at an interval of about ten feet, everyone inside the box watched the ground carefully for spider holes and bunkers. There was no way that Charley could jump up in front of the Tanks with the jungle being pushed in his face, so the action would have to be after the Tanks passed, from the flanks or with mortars.

The bastards didn't know these tactics and would not know that the

ACAVs were behind the M-48 Tanks until they opened their spider-holes and jumped up to shoot the Tank Commanders in their backs.

Mark Darrow
Artillery Forward Observer

The trick was to pull ACAVs over the holes to keep the enemy in place and then back the ACAVs off one at a time to drop grenades into the holes. As base camps or other enemy positions were crossed this efficiently eliminated the enemy. The ACAV drivers became very important as they were normally the first ones to spot a hole. While we moved forward our Artillery forward observer (FO), LT Mark Darrow, a damned fine officer, called in artillery to our flanks and front and requested close air support. Almost immediately artillery started ripping up the jungle on either side and to the front of our formation, which was very comforting.

We pushed into the heavy jungle and keep the volume of fire steady as we assessed the enemy's strength. Within minutes it was clear that the enemy was going to accept the fight and not run. They had no idea what they were getting into.

Suddenly Tom Reed bent forward against the 50 Cal. I thought he was hit. It was difficult to control the fight and get him out of the cupola at the same time, and it was dangerous. Tom was unconscious, but otherwise not injured. I got his heavy 200+ pound body down onto the floor of the ACAV and put the M-60 Machine Gunner behind the 50 Cal until SSG George could jump aboard. The medics took Tom to the rear for dust-off. Including Tom, on first contact, there were 5 men in need of medical evacuation. The Dust-off Chopper was called.

The incoming RPG and machine gun fire was intensifying. I backed the Box up about thirty feet and increased the heavy Tank firing to the front, using the cannister ammunition to loosen up the jungle that was getting thicker as we moved forward. As fast as we had backed up and placed a barrage on the jungle, I ordered the attack to resume and called for high performance aircraft support. The NVA increased their fire and so did we. We had built a nice wide path into the jungle about 100 feet wide and 150 meters deep by this time and Charley was constantly engaged.

I had ordered another hard push, when suddenly the Squadron Commander, and General Westmoreland were talking helicopter to helicopter on our troop frequency. It's one thing to listen in on a ground commander's frequency, but it was bullshit for anyone to talk between helicopters flying overhead, as it made it impossible for the ground commander to control his unit. This overrode my ability to talk on my assigned frequency. Our commo was effectively jammed, and I couldn't control the battle. This was as bad as friendly fire. There is nothing friendly about it.

I was super pissed. It's a good thing I had competent platoon leaders on their own frequencies. After a couple minutes there was a slight break in the conversation. I jumped in and said some things that were a bit uncharacteristic for a young Captain. *"You fucking chicken hawks better get the Hell off my G.. damned frequency and stay off. I have a Med-Evac en-route, high performance aircraft on the way and a battle to run. If I hear you on this net again, I'll turn some guns upward and shoot you bastards out of the sky."* There was a moment of silence and then *"Roger"* (General Westmoreland), *"Roger"* (LTC Tyree).

The battle raged on and shortly an F-105 came up on our Command frequency. I informed him of the layout of the battlefield and that I would pull the Tanks back about 50 feet. The 250-pound bomb was to be placed just inside the wood line in front of the Tanks. Everyone was ready to receive the support. When the pilot informed that he had dropped the bomb, the six second count would start and on the count of five all Tank hatches would momentarily close. After the blast, the hatches would flip back open and we would immediately attack.

Suddenly I heard a familiar voice. *"John" "Where's John" "Right up there Sir."* As I spun around the F-105 pilot announced the drop. I yelled *"get up here, quick"* as I counted the bomb down and reached over the side of the track, I grabbed the tall Lieutenant Colonel by the shirt and jerked him over the side of the track to safety. As he cleared the top of the ACAV, there was a huge explosion and a jagged piece of steel from the bomb about a foot in diameter ripped through the air not six inches from his rump. From the blast, the fronts of the 52-ton tanks lifted about a foot and a half into the air. The blast was awesome. I couldn't help editorializing *"Perfect, just fuckin perfect"* followed by an excited *"Attack"*.

Then I turned to the Squadron Commander who was standing with his 45-caliber pistol in hand, looking over the edge of the ACAV, at the ready, prepared to fight, and I said, *"what the Hell are you doing here?"* He responded that he gave his command and control chopper to the wounded troopers to get them evacuated to the hospital. I guessed my nasty, course comments embarrassed him a little.

About that time, on the Squadron Command net (frequency), Major Tom Kelly was asking if anyone knew what happened to LTC Tyree's chopper. I quickly informed him of what happened. Apparently, he had not told anyone what he was going to do. Kelly didn't realize that I had a bitch box (external speaker) fastened to the auxiliary radio receiver. He said, *"that dumb shit, look out for him."* I responded quickly that I had an external speaker about two feet from Dragoon 6's head. There was an audible *"oopps"*. I told him to cancel the dust-off.

I turned to the Colonel and said: *"you're the senior officer on the ground, now, sir. Do you want to command the Troop?"* LTC Tyree said *"no, you're doing just fine,"* and the battle continued. The Colonel helped on the track by passing ammo and assisting where ever else he could. This was probably his first full appreciation of all the things a Troop Commander and the troopers had to do during a battle and what it took to control that awesome firepower in the attack.

LTC Tyree was a brave man and I rather enjoyed his going from one place to another with his 45 Caliber pistol at the ready, looking for a target. I wish an NVA would have jumped up out of a hole to give him a chance to use that 45. There was no question that he was a good trooper, and I was glad to show him what he could never appreciate from his C&C helicopter. In about half an hour the C&C (Command

and Control) chopper returned, and everyone was relieved to have the Squadron Commander in the air again. About that time the first gas attack occurred.

Chapter 53

THE GAS ATTACKS AND OUR RESPONSE

Charley suddenly countered with a gas attack. It seemed like we were attacked with gas from all directions at the same time. Putting on the gas masks happened quickly, and there was a sudden realization as to just how hot and humid it really was. The gas masks almost immediately steamed up. If Charley would have realized his advantage at that moment, we would have been in a Hell of a fix.

The gas was heavy, and my skin tingled and started to burn. Not being able to see through the fogged-up masks created an immense problem. There was no good choice. I cracked the side of my mask and took a small breath. It was as strong a tear gas mixture as I had ever experienced in training. I took a couple more breaths, hoping it was not laced with any other agent. But knowing that the steamed masks would incapacitate the entire troop, my next move was forced by the circumstances. I ripped off my mask and ordered the same for the Troop. The gas hung in the air. We all cried, and fought, and cried. Our lungs burned as did our sinuses, throats, faces and arms. We coughed, and we fought. I'm glad LTC Tyree was back in the air before Charley gassed us.

"A" Troop was hit seven times with that nasty tear gas, but the shock effect had soon worn off. The temperature was 130 degrees in the stillness of the jungle, and the gas hung in the air seemingly forever.

At some point after the gas attacks, "A" Troop was running low on ammunition, so we backed up and made room for "B" Troop to pass through in their Box. While Bravo Troop maintained contact and pushed the battle forward, "A" Troop resupplied with ammo and fuel

GIs Clash Twice With Reds, Kill 114 North of Saigon

4/18/68

By SPEC. 5 RAY BELFORD
585 Staff Correspondent

SAIGON—U.S. forces reported killing 114 Communists in two battles north of Saigon Thursday. In one of the actions the Americans reported the enemy hurled tear gas grenades into their positions.

In one battle, 30 miles northwest of Saigon, 57 enemy were killed during three hours of heavy fighting by cavalrymen from the U.S. 1st Inf. Div. Another 57 Reds were killed by infantrymen from the 199th Light Inf. Brigade, supported by helicopter gunships, air strikes and artillery fire, 31 miles northeast of the capital.

Ground fighting throughout the rest of the country was generally light and scattered.

In the 1st Inf. Div. action, a cavalry troop drove a large Communist force from bunkers and trenches in a base camp 11 miles east of Ben Cat during a savage three-hour battle which saw the Communists hurl tear gas grenades at the attacking U.S. troops.

The Communists also fired rocket-propelled grenades at the U.S. armored vehicles.

The "Big Red One" cavalrymen poured heavy tank fire into the base camp as they continued their advance and the enemy broke and ran in late afternoon.

The U.S. forces moved into the base camp and found 41 enemy dead. As they worked their way through the camp searching for small arms and ammunition, they killed another 16 enemy soldiers with grenades and tank fire as they blew up the numerous spiderholes and bunkers in the base complex.

Three U.S. cavalrymen were killed and three wounded in the fighting.

that was brought in on several Chinooks and other helicopters into the clearing that we had surgically cut into the jungle. While we were re-supplying everyone gulped down some C-rations and breathed deeply of the fresh air.

The "A" Troopers were soon biting at the bitt to get back into the action as they felt this was their fight, and they wanted to cross the basecamp themselves, and not have another Troop finish their job. I called Dragoon Six and announced our readiness to attack. "B" Troop was backed off a little and "A" Troop charged back through their formation and into the assault. "B" Troop was then moved to another location but kept close at hand.

Soon there was increasingly heavy resistance to the front, so I ordered the line of Tanks to move a little to the right and left to make a hole, and Zippo Reb was brought forward. The Track commander, SGT Charles Jones had 250 gallons of napalm to break up the NVA's defense. He sprayed a wet load of about 150 gallons into and around the fortified positions between 35 to 50 meters in front of the Tanks. Then he ignited the napalm and sprayed a hot load across the front. It was beautiful - all 3,500 degrees Fahrenheit of it, as it made a loud "poof" and it all ignited at once.

It was hot and very pretty. I found myself laughing almost hysterically as the machine guns mowed down the NVA that were running, trying to escape their burning clothes. Others were suffocated as the air was sucked from their bunkers. A look around told me that the sadism I was feeling was shared by many of the troopers. Maybe this laughter was a way to let our own fears out. Maybe it was something else that only a Shrink would understand. It was an excellent payback for the gas attacks. The Tank Commanders could taste a final push into Charley's basecamp, and we started steadily moving forward again, while Zippo Reb was sent back to the Troop Trains to reload.

Significant bunkers and holes were finally appearing as the Tanks moved over a line of fortified positions, twisting and crushing the NVA. But suddenly, heavy fighting started on our left flank and I realized that our six Tank front was not covering the entire enemy camp. That's when the Reserve, 2nd Platoon was brought up on the left flank to create a box with a nine Tank front, hopefully to later drop a platoon back into the reserve position. It was a calculated decision and took nearly ten minutes to effect.

The final push was then made and the ACAVs were pulling over holes all over the place. One after another the holes were exposed, and we dropped hand grenades into them. Slowly the Troop moved through the enemy basecamp which was about 15 to 20 meters deep and we secured the area. The officers and troopers on the ACAVs were dropping grenades into holes and bunkers and firing point blank at North Vietnamese soldiers trying to make their last stand or escape.

Through all the chaotic fighting Mark Darrow was calling in and controlling the Artillery on the front and flanks of our formation. It's a wonder that the NVA were able to stage any counter-attacks, but to their credit they tried.

Once the enemy basecamp was secured, troopers were dismounted to

Searching the Enemy Camp

check under the brush to make sure all the enemy had been killed. When that process was complete Dragoon Six landed close-by with a couple officers from the TOC to examine the destruction and carnage. Troopers poked around for any documents that the intelligence folks could use and nothing of significance was found. Several primitive gas masks were found which indicated that the enemy was ill equipped to use the tear gas and fight at the same time. They would have had the same problems of fogged vision that we suffered. And we gathered a lot of enemy weapons to ship back to our Arms Room. They were good trading items to obtain some of the creature comforts from the noncombatants when we passed through a base camp (steaks, beer, etc.).

I impulsively dove to the ground and listened carefully by a crushed defensive position. A faint sound of

Red Dog a few months later

crying could be heard beneath the ground. I took a risk by reaching deep into the hole and felt around carefully. After a couple minutes I was licked. I pulled my arm back out with a ball of red fur in my hand. I had a fluffy red puppy that was clearly pleased to be rescued from whatever she had experienced during our assault. I immediately named the little girl "Red Dog." She was either used as security by the NVA (which I doubt) or intended as food for later. A pet would also be doubtful for these savages. She was a pretty little thing, and with my attraction to animals, this gal would become the troop mascot for sure. As a matter of fact, if a password or call sign was forgotten by the troopers, a second choice would always be a password of *"Red"* - - and a response of *"Dog"*. And the little bitch was destined to be everyone's pal when they had a reason to go to the basecamp. She was put on the Command Track and finished the rest of the day in the field. A few months later, she mated with the ugliest mutt at Phu Loi and had a beautiful pup.

After the area was searched and a count was taken as to how many enemy dead were verifiable (essentially in the open), "A" Troop continued to move forward in the Box after reestablishing the reserve platoon. There was nearly 100 meters of jungle to navigate before we entered a clearing and except for a couple minor attempts by NVA soldiers to snipe at the cavalrymen, the progress was uneventful.

Red Dog's 1st Baby,
"Trooper", held by
CPT G. Gram Poole

Although there had only been about 60 to100 enemy dead reported, there were undoubtedly far more killed. In retrospect it was clear that this was one of the best NVA Battalions the Troop would meet and they had fought gallantly. And this was the first time a unit was gassed in Vietnam, as far as we knew. The gas was nasty, and I would have to find a way to use it in the future to the Troop's advantage, if I could.

The Troop suffered four casualties from the first contact and even with our losses everyone was feeling great as they moved through the brush bordering the heavy jungle and into the clearing. We had done enough damage for one day and when we reached a major clearing, we received a welcome order to move back to the NDP. This was good news. It was about 1530 hours. One quick look around and I had my bearings. The Troop moved into a double column until they were at least a quarter mile away from the battle area and we reconnoitered the edges of the clearings by fire and any other possible area where a sniper or RPG Gunner could get a shot off against a very happy bunch of warriors. On April 18 we lost two good troopers and several crew members suffered temporary flash blindness and hearing damage. That was terrible.

After we started our move toward the NDP, I gave the troopers their first real complement of the day. I told the Officers to inform the men that they were now true, seasoned jungle fighters and a Cavalry Troop that I was very proud to command. The Officers and the Troopers loved this new formation which was so superior to a column or a double column in the jungle, and I've received positive comments ever since.

Radio discipline got a little crazy on the way back to the NDP as the men knew they had just kicked some royal ass and were back on top of their game. They had done a superb job and knew that everyone agreed with that. They were rode very hard, but they were not going to be put away wet. These horse soldiers met the enemy and destroyed them in a manner that was by far as decisive as any Cavalry unit had done in the past. And with a minimum of casualties, although each casualty still hurts to this day. I listened as they blabbed and bragged, and I enjoyed it all. I switched to the Platoon frequencies from time to time and was convinced that the Troop's morale could not be better. After about fifteen minutes I tightened up the radio discipline so that any enemy soldiers that might be eavesdropping wouldn't get any misguided notions that there was a lack of discipline and control.

Many award recommendations were submitted, and some were approved. Unfortunately, we were unable to overcome the limited awards policy of the Division and Department of Defense. But most of all we accomplished what was heretofore considered impossible - - an attack into Hell and back.

Chapter 54

A SOFT LANDING

Pulling into the NDP and moving into the positions on the perimeter was comforting. I was coming off a lot of adrenaline and stunk of tear gas and perspiration. Everyone was the same. The Mess Sergeant had a hot meal waiting and the men were as hungry as horses. But with the awful smell of tear gas, he must have thought he was feeding a herd of skunks.

Feeding had to be done while maintenance was pulled, ammunition was resupplied, and the vehicles were re-fueled. Personal hygiene followed getting ready for the next fight. As the Command Track stopped in its defensive position, one of the troopers asked if he could clean off my map case. This was done by spraying mosquito repellant on the plastic case and wiping off all the grease pencil information. Then another trooper asked if he could clean my pistol. I consented, just to have another ask to clean my AR-15. I had clearly made some loyal friends that day. They were doing this out of appreciation and felt it to be an honor. This was treatment I never experienced before and was a little embarrassed by it. But it was very nice.

As soon as the map case was cleaned, I headed for the TOC, entered and passed through a bunch of happy and admiring Headquarters troopers. After accepting the brief congratulations from a few of the officers in the TOC, I settled down in front of the situation map and copied the reported enemy positions onto my map case. Looking at the map spread out on this huge situation board gave added perspective to the area and the aerial photos gave me as much interest. I asked some questions, but mostly I carefully studied the tree lines and open areas and tried to imagine how and why the enemy units would be moving around this area and how they might reinforce each other if they held and fought in various spots.

Some of this was daydreaming, and I was hungry and tired. My body had not endured such abuse nor had my mind been stressed so much for quite a while. I knew I would be back for a detailed briefing on the next day's mission in a couple hours, so I got up to leave. As I did the radio announced the arrival of General Westmoreland - *"Dragoon 6 this is Danger 77 coming into your location."*

All the headquarters personnel in their nice clean fatigues scrambled to the door and stood in two neat rows which blocked my exit. As I started pushing my way to the door, Major Kelly came to me and said in my ear, *"Okay Captain, here is where you get yours"* followed by some foul word like *"ass hole"* or *"you SOB." "The General wants to talk to you."*

I continued toward the exit and in about 10 steps found myself looking up at a very clean looking, tall, General Officer with his four stars shining on his uniform and hat. I was face to face with the most powerful man in this country. I regretted somewhat that I wasn't a little cleaner for this occasion, but what the Hell, I was probably on the way to prison for what I said anyway. I expected the worst. Surely nobody could get away with cursing at and threatening the Commander of all the troops in Vietnam. I snapped to attention in front of the General. He had time to know everything about me since the incident was at the start of the battle. It was quiet. Not a single sound. A tomb could not be quieter, and a pin dropped on the dirt floor would have sounded like a hammer on a tin roof.

"Were you the commander of "A" Troop in the battle today?" "Yes Sir" "How many of your men were WIA or KIA ("Wounded in Action or Killed in Action")" *"4 WIA, 2 KIA Sir." "And the Enemy?" "About 100+ KIA Sir."* Then quiet again. *"I want to know just one thing Captain?" "Yes Sir." "Would you have done it?" "Would you have shot me down?"* Delayed quiet again. *"Yes Sir.*

I had a Med-Evac en-route, an air strike on the way, and I had just commanded a push forward into the enemy's face. I was the ground commander, so I was responsible, and you and Dragoon 6 were keeping me from doing my job. Yes sir, I would have done it. But I'm glad I didn't have to. " It was quiet as death again and the General stood there thinking. I don't think anyone breathed.

I knew I was on my way to jail, but I had my say and felt justified.

"John, it is John isn't it." "Yes Sir." "Nobody has ever said anything like that to me before - - ever." "John, you were right, and I promise never to talk on your net again without first asking permission." "I like that new formation you used." "You and your men did a great job today and I want you to go back to your men and congratulate them for me." "Yes Sir."

I smartly saluted and departed. The General provided the Troop with a nice letter recognizing its accomplishment and another one later-on. They were hung in my Orderly Room in Phu Loi, but they disappeared into the hands of some souvenir collector or unknown archives.

I walked back to the Troop pleased with how that conversation with the General went, but mentally exhausted from it all. I felt like I was walking a foot off the ground. As I approached A-66 one of my troopers came forward quickly with an overfilled tray of food and another had a mermite can full of coffee. This was indeed the best day in my life. If I died tomorrow, I had accomplished more than most men in a 24-hour period, and I felt it. And I thought, *'Sampson must have felt like this after whopping those Philistines with that jawbone of an ass.'*

Before I ate, I had all radios switched to the Troop command frequency so I could pass on the complements of General Westmoreland and add a few more of my own. The men were relieved as well. They knew what had happened and most expected to lose their third Troop

Commander in a week when the General flew in. They were experiencing a high that few men ever get to know after having their morale smashed by the loss of a great commander, Captain Shirley, only to lose a new commander in just three days, Captain Serio; and then spending a day with yet another new commander with new tactics that jerked a knot in Charley's ass, and having their morale thrown back to the top of the charts. When I survived the visit with General Westmoreland their anxiety evaporated.

I gobbled my food down like a pig and was surprised that I was able to eat it all, especially since it had become cold by now. Before cleaning up, I walked from track to track thanking the men for doing such a splendid job and promising them more good fights to come. Then I cleaned up and prepared for the Squadron's evening meeting in the TOC.

That night I gave a lot of thanks to our Lord for his assistance. He had spared us and made us heroes. But I was humbled by our losses which I never would get used to.

Chapter 55

DAILY BATTLES WITH COSVN

This began a series of battles with the NVA. It also quickly became clear from the enemy's tactics that they were reverting to a hit and run routine. Trying to stand up to the Cavalry was fool hearty and they were quick learners. Unfortunately, we never knew when they might allow a major fight to commence, so we had to assume that every time we were shot at, they were ready for pitched battle.

Their hit and run tactics were not the same as the VC employed. It wasn't an RPG or two and then run away. These were pros and their initial engagement would take the appearance of a willingness to lock horns in a major battle. But once we would deploy into our Box and commence a drive 50 to 100 meters into the jungle they would disengage and disappear with their dead and wounded in tow.

In a couple days SSG George replaced SSG Reed as the Commander of A-66 as Tom Reed, a great NCO, needed to return to the basecamp to recuperate from the shock he experienced when the bodies of the A-66 crew exploded onto him. He worked for the Supply Sergeant for a while before becoming the NCO in charge of protecting the perimeter of the Di An basecamp.

1st Inf Div

Units of the 1st Infantry Division reported killing 69 enemy soldiers in operations near Lai Khe during one day of fighting.

A troop of the 1st Squadron, 4th Cavalry received sporadic enemy fire as it was moving on a reconnaissance-in-force miles east of Lai Khe. Continuing the mission, the unit saw what appeared to be a battalion size basecamp. As they approached the camp the armored unit received automatic weapons fire.

Artillery and light fire teams were called in as the unit continued to exchange fire with the enemy for an hour. The cavalrymen then entered the basecamp and counted 41 enemy dead.

While searching the basecamp small arms fire was received from hidden spiderholes. Grenades and tank fire were employed against the enemy and more VC were added to the total. The cavalrymen suffered two killed and two wounded who were evacuated.

In other scattered action throughout the day, 1st Division soldiers killed 12 VC and captured two rifles. A total of enemy basecamps were found

Many of the clearings were quite large and provided a good opportunity to practice our formations. As we searched for the NVA we would alternate the formations and get some practice quickly going from all of them into the Box, and out of the Box into the various combat formations. It wasn't long before everything ran smoothly.

One evening in the NDP I saw a tall man with a small Afro hairdo, with no weapon and no helmet on his head (which was the Standard Operating Procedure). He was playing music on a tape player and dancing with his friends. I called 1st Sergeant Escobedo and asked him what the Hell was going on by that track, and who was this trooper not carrying his weapon. He told me that this was SGT Cleophas Mims, my senior medic, who was a conscientious objector, and didn't carry a weapon.

I had formed an opinion in my enlisted years that conscientious objectors were worthless, sporting a wide yellow stripe down their back, and told the 1st Sergeant that I didn't want him in my unit. Calmly, the 1st Sergeant asked me to hold up on my judgement for a few days to observe this trooper as his opinion differed from my own. I agreed, as I really had more on my mind than to deal with this problem anyway. I normally deferred the discipline of the troopers to my NCOs and Platoon Leaders unless they brought a problem to me as being bigger than they could handle. It could wait, and I wasn't disappointed.

On the 20th of April I brought the Troop due east of our NDP about 2 kilometers. We were about 100 meters from the end of a large clearing when machine gun fire erupted from the jungle directly to our front. As the tracks were deploying into a Box an RPG was fired at the lead tank. It hit the turret just above the driver's hatch and SP5 Bainey's head. The explosion was just a little over a foot above his helmet. Bainey was SSG George's closest friend from Radcliff, Kentucky, just outside of Ft. Knox. Although there appeared to be no serious damage to the tank, Bainey was likely hanging onto life by a thread. SSG George asked if he could go to the crippled tank to help get his friend and the tank out of that position. We didn't know how bad Bainey was injured at the time but did know that the tank had to be moved off line until the damage could be evaluated. I called for a dust-off chopper as SSG George ran forward to the tank, while the other tanks moved forward and laid a heavy barrage of canister and machine gun fire onto the enemy positions along the tree line. He climbed into the driver's hatch and backed the tank off line.

SP4 Hubbard,
New A66 Commander

Bainey was dusted off to the hospital within 10 minutes, but when SSG George returned, he advised that his friend would not survive. Again, once we entered about 50 meters into the jungle the NVA cut and ran carrying away their dead as usual, so we had no idea how many of them we killed or wounded except for several blood trails. SSG George then became the Platoon Sergeant of the 1st Platoon, and SP4 Hubbard became the ACAV Commander of the command track, A-66.

On the 21st when we returned from our patrol the bad news was received that SP5 Bainey (no picture available) had died. I spoke with the Squadron Chaplain, Captain Doug Bol, about having a memorial service and he consented. Before I knew it, he had three M-16 rifles with their bayonets pushed into the ground, with a pair of boots in front of each and a helmet on the rifle butts. The service was for our KIAs from April 18 as well as for SP5 Bainey.

I had my driver, SP4 Hubbard, ready to play Taps on his harmonica, but Doug insisted on conducting a so called "Regulation" memorial service with no Taps. I felt frustrated and didn't think I liked this Chaplain. After he finished officiating the Memorial Service, I could see a lot of sadness in the troopers that attended, so as soon as he departed, I gave a little ending to the Service with a pep talk that we were going to get even for the loss of our brothers and kick some more ass. I don't know if my show of emotion helped my troopers, but I hoped so. It helped me.

I had my mind made up that I didn't like this Chaplain Doug Bol, but after hearing of the ride "D" Troop gave him in the gunner's position of a Cobra Helicopter when he arrived in Vietnam, I had to reconsider. While flying in the Cobra he had to fire on about 20 enemy soldiers crossing a stream and he didn't hesitate. Before long we became friends and I enjoyed his company whenever we found ourselves in the same location. He monitored the many battles we got into over the TOC radio and counseled me on many occasions to clean up my language during these fights, which I never did. He was a good man, a good soldier, a very good chaplain, and a loyal friend. He was the only Cavalryman that had an opportunity to tell my father about my wartime actions prior to Dad's death. (Unfortunately, Doug was taken from us a few years ago by cancer. This has happened to so many of our Troopers - all exposed to Agent Orange.)

Chaplain Doug Bol

We aggressively hit the enemy every time he held still to fight, but the battles were small now. Bravo Troop was experiencing the same inability to get Charley to commit himself to a major battle.

This period did give me a good opportunity to observe Medic Mims' heroism and to appreciate his willingness to run any place on the battle field to tend to injured soldiers. The issue of his not carrying a weapon was quickly closed just as the 1st Sergeant had advised.

On April 25, 1968 the Squadron Headquarters and "B" Troop left the NDP, turning over the responsibility of this area of operations to the 1st Battalion, 26th Infantry. "A" Troop became attached to this battalion and combat operations continued.

Chapter 56

MAY DAY PARTY CRASHING

Then came the first of May which was a big holiday for the Communists. Nothing happened on our search and destroy mission during the day. Shortly before sundown Alpha Troop loaded up an Infantry company commanded by Captain Cox, who attended Officer Candidate School with me at Fort Benning, Georgia. He was a strong leader and it felt good to move him and his Company to a jungle position near the village to the south of the NDP. We drove right down the edge of the jungle, so we could look directly into the foliage and see if anyone was watching.

When we were about 150 meters from the village, we dropped off the Infantry and continued toward the village, intent on doubling back to the NDP closer to the road. When the jungle ended on our left flank, we were looking over barren land down to a stream that ran all the way to and past the village. On the opposite side of the stream the ground rose at about a 35 to 40-degree angle. This was a garden plot for the village and the cleared area was nearly 100 meters wide and 40 meters to the top of the slope where the thick jungle resumed.

Suddenly an explosion of NVA soldiers came running out of the village, like hornets after someone hit their hive with a stick. The difference was that they were not heading for us. As they crossed the stream, many were trying to get their clothes on, and they spread out over the naked face of the slope as they ran for the safety of the jungle.

This created a lot of excitement and we couldn't start shooting fast enough. It was a turkey shoot although to my disappointment at least ten of the turkeys made it to the jungle at the top of the hill. I told C-36 to take a few ACAVs across the stream, and to go up that hill so he could spray his machine guns directly into their jungle escape route. Joe was finding it difficult to understand me, and since time was of the essence, I yelled at him to *"Follow Me"* and took two of my Headquarters ACAVs and went up the hill as fast as we could while instructing the ACAV Commanders to spread out and move forward a little at the top to allow room for C-36. That worked out just fine and we were soon shooting into the jungle.

But moving forward into the edge of the foliage was a big mistake. Who would have thought that as we pushed through the outer edge of the jungle, we would suddenly drop over an invisible cliff that went over 20 feet straight down. Now we had 3 ACAVs in a huge hole. Being on top of my track made me fall forward, past the driver, to the bottom. As I got my bearings and looked skyward, I could see the stars and realized that it was getting dark awfully fast. LT Birindelli appeared and yelled down to see if we were all right.

None of the tracks rolled forward onto their backs, but all three were nose down, and by the grace of God no one was injured, except for my pride. Joe was great with this recovery job. After all, he was an Engineer that had recently left a job with the Corps of Engineers. And he knew exactly what to do. He quickly hooked three of his tracks up to each of our ACAVs and pulled them all out of the hole within 10 or 15 minutes. I was happy to get the tracks back across that stream. Fortunately, Charley didn't anticipate this event and catch us with our pants down. It would have gotten very nasty for us if he had. Sometimes we learn the hard way.

With all this activity the ambush was called off, so we picked up Captain Cox's Company and returned to the NDP.

Chapter 57

TAN HIEP
MAY 4, 1968

On the third of May we pulled up stakes and headed south to Phu Loi. It felt great to be inside of our basecamp, and we took advantage of it to pull maintenance until nearly midnight. But peace wouldn't last very long. On the morning of May 4, 1968, the 1st Battalion, 18th Infantry was making a sweep from south to north to and through the village of Tan Hiep which was southeast of the intersection of the road that ran north out of the Di An basecamp and the east-west road that went to Phu Loi (Route 313). As they proceeded through the wet rice paddies south of the village, they came under heavy fire from dug in positions in the rice paddy dikes along the perimeter of the village's rice paddies.

Lt Joseph Scates with his 1st Platoon was dispatched to set up a blocking position north of the village. The remainder of "A" Troop with C-36 was ordered to the Di An basecamp. As we neared Tan Hiep we became attached to the Infantry and ordered to move inland into positions where we could support the Infantry who had become pinned down in the rice paddies with many injured and dead soldiers.

This was a mess. We had no choice but to position ourselves on the same muddy rice paddy dikes that Charley was using for his dug-in positions facing the rice paddies. I had a significant concern for the VC coming out of holes between the tracks causing friendly casualties. A-26, Lt Bache, wrapped his platoon around the south end of the wet ground and moved as close to the action as possible where they could support the Infantry, and C-36 spread his tracks along the west side of the rice paddies and moved forward to where they could provide support. The Headquarters tracks moved into positions on a rice paddy dike between the Platoons where I could best control the Cavalry fire. The medic track, A-63, chose a position to my right where they could see down the rice paddies to the north.

Charley was well dug in, but we could fire on his positions along the rice paddy dikes to help cover the Infantry. Since we were in an "L" position around the rice paddies between Charley's bunkers, we had to be careful not to fire on one another. Sgt Mims and another medic were sent forward on foot to help evacuate the wounded, and we called in a dust-off helicopter about 20 meters to the rear of A-66.

Heroic Medic Lets His Prayers, Skill Do All His Fighting

By SPEC. 5 JACK BENEDICT
S&S Staff Correspondent

DI AN, Vietnam—After eight months on line with a fighting unit in Vietnam, Cleophas C. Mims has yet to carry a weapon.

Spec. 5 Mims is a conscientious objector who fights to keep men alive. "I've also treated Viet Cong," he says. "The men needed help and I am a medic."

Mims explains: "I'm not better than anyone else for not carrying a weapon—it's a matter of a man's own conscience. I've never had the test to take a man's life. God has protected me."

Shy, but quick with a smile, Mims doesn't talk much about the actions he's seen with the 1st Sq., 4th Cav., part of the 1st Inf. Div. Mims, a Seventh Day Adventist from Chicago's South Side, has been decorated several times for his cool reactions in battle. He has won a Silver Star, a Bronze Star with "V" device, an Army Commendation Medal with "V" and a Purple Heart.

He won the Silver Star after a tank's .50-cal. machine gun mount was hit by an enemy rocket during heavy fighting. He dragged the wounded tank commander to the back deck of the tank and covered him with his own body as a rubber tree, blown in two by the firing crashed down upon them.

Both of Mims' eardrums were broken by the close explosion, but he spent the rest of the day helping the wounded. "Things happen very fast," he shrugged. "I guess it was just another day."

Mims is now working with Hq. Troop of the 1st Sq., 4th Cav. in a special platoon used to root out the local Viet Cong infrastructure.

He asks the men to look for sick or injured people in each village they visit. He has treated over 200 people individually during his housecalls, which he calls "mini-medcaps."

Before joining the service, Mims attended Oakwood College in Huntsville, Ala., studying for the ministry. He also joined the Special Medical Cadet Corps offered by the Seventh Day Adventist Church to train medics in case the men are drafted.

Much of what he learned helped him later while training as a medic in the Army school for conscientious objectors at Ft. Sam Houston.

Mims said he joined the Army because he was restless. "This was the experience I needed to know what phase of the ministry to go into," he said. He wants to finish his clerical training and re-enter the Army as a chaplain.

"Adventist men often have difficulty finding a place or the time to worship as they wish," he noted. "The 4th Cav. has been very good in getting me to church by shifting my duty times. I can attend the Adventist Church in Saigon as duty allows."

CLEOPHAS MIMS
Heroic Medic

Pacific Stars & Stripes **7**
Sunday, Jan. 12, 1969

the wounded, and we called in a dust-off helicopter about 20 meters to the rear of A-66.

SGT Mims ran like an Olympic sprinter and it was inspiring to see him charge forward and come running back with one wounded soldier over his shoulder after another, delivering them to the dust-off site. The second time he went forward I saw him step on an enemy soldier's hand that protruded from his position in the rice paddy dike to my left-front. A rifle muzzle quickly came out of the hole and I got a lucky burst from my AR-15 directly into the enemy's face. Mims ran forward at least six times and brought back a wounded Infantryman each time and they were treated and evacuated to the hospital. That evening I had a Silver Star recommendation for heroism

SGT Cleophas Mims with his well-deserved awards.

submitted for Mims. He was a brave trooper and it's these moments you never forget.

LTC George Tronsrue, Jr., the 1/18 Battalion Commander, was flying over the area and helped direct our fire. He was concerned not only with the Company in contact, but, as the enemy's fortunes changed, some of them were trying to move southeasterly through the trees along the river bank on the east side of the rice paddies to escape the overwhelming firepower that they were facing. (Years later he wrote an article praising CPT Fred Shirley for his leadership during this battle. He was embarrassed to learn that I was the A-6 he was talking to. I took that as a complement, since Fred was a terrific commander.)

Let me tell you a story about our forward Observer, Mark Darrow. A short while after he received shrapnel wounds in his face and neck (at least 35 fragments), on May 4, 1968 Mark was hit in the head by a bullet which entered just under his left eye and lodged in the back side of his maxillary sinus. As he had no vital signs, the "A" Troop medics dusted him off in a body bag and he was delivered to Graves Registration. He vaguely remembers coming partially awake in the bag. There was a large pile of bodies in body bags stacked up while they were being processed. Mark was fortunate to only have one body on top of him. He worked his way out of his bag and pushed the deceased soldier off to the side until he could get free. Mark was crawling across the floor when someone came into the room and said, ***"Where the Hell do you think you're going!?"*** Mark was evacuated to the hospital. When he awoke, he saw the smiling face of Major Barney Forbes. Despite having the bullet lodged in his head, LT Mark Darrow returned to duty in 3 to 4 weeks. Now that's the kind of American that made returning to Vietnam a necessity and an honor. He was an Artilleryman, but he had a Cavalryman's heart. He was a true Cavalryman.

It was nearly dark when the village of Tan Hiep was secured. Once this was accomplished, the Troop was moved into the Di An basecamp which was several kilometers to the south. The night of the 4th brought a surprise as I received my own 3rd Platoon back from their detachment. "B" Troop had to detach one of its platoons to replace my returning Platoon. So, LT Birindelli (C-36) became attached to "B" Troop. On the fifth of May we again found ourselves in quite a mess and the start of the most viscous and memorable battles.

Chapter 58

XOM MOI (2)
MAY 5, 1968

The day started with our 1st Platoon being reattached to the 1st Battalion, 18th Infantry and placed with an attached Infantry platoon into the blocking positions they had been in on the 4th, while the Infantry made another sweep through Tan Hiep. "A" Troop, minus the 1st Platoon, was given a search and destroy mission northeast of the Di An basecamp to hunt for any Viet Cong that may have escaped the fight on the 4th. "B" Troop was assigned a similar mission northwest of Di An toward Phu Loi. We searched the assigned area northeast of Di An, and checked every nook and cranny for signs

LT Ivan Prichard
A-36

of the VC, who might still be hiding in the area. Unfortunately, there was no trace of them.

But we did have a great opportunity to exercise the 3rd Platoon through the formations we had been using, which was one of my goals for the morning. LT Ivan Prichard's platoon was well disciplined, and they learned the Box formation quite easily. Around noon we stopped to eat lunch in a large open area. It was quiet. Too quiet.

We weren't used to no civilians and no enemy at the same time. It seemed like the calm before a bad storm. I had anticipated seeing signs of Charley making a hasty retreat through this area, or of being holed up in some convenient place until they felt safe to move on. We searched everywhere, but no Charley, although this was clearly a likely escape route from Tan Hiep.

While eating our C-Rations I studied the map to see if there was any place we had missed, or perhaps somewhere that Charley might be lying quietly waiting to ambush us as we passed his position. He was a master at that. He just might be in some previously prepared tunnels or spider holes where he could try to fire off an RPG as we passed. But it became clear that we were not going to flush him out if he was in this area.

The second and third platoons, as well as the headquarters platoon was with me. LT Prichard was a very intelligent officer, and in just a few hours I was completely comfortable with his leadership abilities. His platoon had been on an independent mission. I remembered what it felt like the first time I worked with the Troop after four months at Quan Loi. I felt quite awkward having a Cavalry boss.

It was wonderful to finally have my own full Troop together. The entire Alpha Troop was now ready for any challenges that were to come. I would miss Joe Birindelli, C-36, and his platoon, but I was also sure he would be a good asset for Bravo Troop and significantly add to their combat power.

The Squadron Commander was overflying Bravo Troop. The chatter over the command net told me that an unmanned, enemy anti-aircraft machine gun had been sighted from the air. As "B" Troop moved in that direction I wanted to get up on the command radio frequency and warn them that I smelled an ambush. Charley didn't just leave that important weaponry laying around for the Hell of it. Almost immediately, as they approached that location the gunfire erupted from all directions. They apparently had driven into a huge ambush that I had anticipated from the radio chatter.

Monitoring the command net made it clear that we may be required to get into this fight, so I moved the Troop close to the east-west road that went into the Di An basecamp's east gate. And it wasn't very long before my prediction was acknowledged.

Alpha Troop to the Rescue

Sometime around 1500 the order came from LTC Tyree to move to the Xom Moi (2) battle site as quickly as possible. With the second platoon leading with 3 tanks we headed for the east gate of Di An as fast as the tracks would move. We charged directly through that gate and when we reached the center of the base camp we turned to the right and headed toward the north gate.

That's when we saw a military police vehicle and three Military Policemen in the road waving their arms to slow or stop our movement. When asked what I wanted to do about it, my response was *"keep moving."* It was only seconds before the jeep was flying through the air and the MPs were diving for cover in the same direction. I felt like my other family was under attack, after having been with "B" Troop for a full year and with C-36 for many battles, so we were not going to slow down for anyone.

As we sped toward the north gate, I was listening to discussions on the radio between the Squadron Commander and the "B" Troop Commander, which sounded like there was a lot of confusion at the battle site and nobody quite knew what they were dealing with. The enemy was firing at them from gullies and bamboo stands from all directions and one tank threw a track and a couple others took hits from RPGs. We couldn't get there fast enough. When we passed through the north gate a "D" Troop helicopter overflew our advance to help us find the fastest way to Xom Moi (2).

My 1st Platoon was released from the blocking force to move with its attached infantry platoon to the north end of the area to join the battle. They were there before the rest of the troop, and as they entered the area from the north, they received significant enemy fire. They were then placed into a blocking position.

As we approached the battlefield from the southeast, I could hear the gunfire and artillery explosions from the battle. The following is from an unpublished manuscript written by Joe Birindelli (2014 picture to right), whose platoon was now attached to "B" Troop.

> . . . *As we began moving towards the tree-line we started firing to the front. Startlingly, heavy RPG and machine gun fire came at us from the ditch [a gully to the right of the platoon]. As we pressed forward the resistance continued. Suddenly, an RPG round found a target. I saw a bright green flash from the cupola of Three-Five [Platoon Sergeant's tank]. One of the crewmen was blown off the back deck and neither the gunner nor SFC White was to be seen. I tried calling but got no answer. . .. After a few seconds or minutes - I could not tell which - Three-Five suddenly popped his read out of the cupola and fired a round. Then he disappeared. After a few more seconds he reappeared and fired again. His gunner and loader had both been hit and he was loading and firing by himself. . .. We had recovered the man from Three-Five who was blown off. He was bleeding badly, but he ran back to us and the new medic who had joined us the night before took care of him.*
>
> *After backing out of reach of the enemy firing, we gathered our wounded and got them on a dust-off as quickly as possible. Three-Five was blinded and deafened by the RPG blast. The round had penetrated one of the viewing prisms and traveled through the small cupola (only about three feet) before exploding. The blast on the back side of the cupola had wounded the gunner, while SFC White and the loader were stunned by the flash and blast. Later I learned that they all suffered temporary flash blindness and hearing damage.*

After evacuating the wounded, I rearranged the crews to re-man Three-Five, then we had to get back to work. Meanwhile, as we were regrouping, Bravo-Six had called in an air strike on the ditch. After the smoke cleared, there was nothing moving in the ditch and all firing had stopped.

As we neared the ditch to assess the damage, Bravo-Six got a call from Dragoon-Six [LTC Tyree]. There was activity spotted in the same trench about three-quarters of a kilometer south. . .. We began moving toward the ditch and started firing canister and .50-caliber. As we neared, return fire began. I saw several RPGs, with their green trail of fire, pass harmlessly over our heads. But suddenly I saw a bright flash and felt a terrific pain. Three-Five had been hit again, and I caught some of the flying shrapnel in my leg. So many of my men who had been wounded before had expressed shock when they were wounded. The shock was that in the heat of battle, they didn't know they had been hit until someone else pointed out their bleeding. Well, that's not what I felt. My knee felt like someone had hit it with a baseball bat.

The battle continued with two new crewmen wounded, SGT Pete Morones was hit in the arm by the shrapnel. I had to dismount my ACAV and ground guide Three-Five back until it was safe. I stayed in the battle even though Bravo-Six wanted me to be evacuated. We were already short-handed, so I refused.

About then, I saw the most beautiful sight imaginable. Alpha Troop was coming over the hill behind us - in the now famous box formation. I suddenly knew what the settlers out west must have felt when the cavalry came to their rescue. The only thing missing was the bugle call. We were finally getting a break.

When the helicopter pilot told me that we were about 100 meters from "B" Troop, "A" Troop was put into a Box formation and charged between the "B" Troop tracks which were returning fire but seemed quite disorganized. When my tracks were forward of "B" Troop and the C-36 tracks, I had them stop, take over the firing, and try to sort out what we were dealing with. I maneuvered my track around to the "B" Troop Commander and told him I was going to help him get his tracks out of this area as he had received an order to move to a blocking position to the south.

The "A" Troop medics went on various tracks helping the "B" Troop medics tend to their wounded. Alpha Troop's maintenance crew and VTR (Vehicle Tank Retriever) assisted "B" Troop to get the disabled tracks out. Joe Birindelli was on top of his ACAV trying to control his Platoon while he and his track commander, SGT Pete Marones, were patching each other's wounds. They had been injured by the hot metal splatter from the second RPG to hit his Platoon Sergeant's tank that was directly in front of his ACAV. Joe told me that he was hearing Vietnamese voices in the gully that was very close to his track.

That was the last time I saw Joe for nearly 40 years, as after he was released from the hospital it wasn't long before he returned to the States on compassionate leave. And it was too close to the end of his tour in Vietnam for the Army to justify sending him back. He was one of the best Platoon Leaders I ever worked with.

I didn't want to move forward until "B" Troop and C-36 were out of danger. It was only a few minutes when it became obvious that matters were coming under control and "B" Troop was pulling its tracks out of the hotspot they were caught in. But there was still that tank with the thrown track to the left side of their formation. My ACAV moved to the disabled tank's location with another of my headquarters tracks. The enemy was firing from positions within the bamboo about 50 feet to the front of the tank. There was another "B" Troop ACAV at that location returning fire and trying to make the enemy keep their heads down. My track commanders and M-60 machine gunners placed additional fire into the edge the bamboo.

The disabled tank had thrown its left track in a deep sand pit. It was clear that we had to get that track back on the tank before it could move out of this position. The tank had an inexperienced driver that was close to panic. The tank commander also seemed to be inexperienced, and he didn't know what to do. He was having communications problems, and if he stopped firing into the bamboo and got down to ground-guide the track back on, he would be killed, and it would solve nothing. Charley peppered the area with AK-47 fire just as soon as the fire eased up on their positions. I realized that it was going to take some experienced supervision to quickly get that tank out.

While my Headquarters ACAVs placed a barrage of machine gun fire into the enemy positions, I jumped down off my track and spoke to the driver calming him a little. He said he was afraid of being left to fend for himself because he had been there so long. I motioned for another tank that was close by and had the track commander pull in behind the disabled vehicle. A couple men hooked tow cables from the rear of the disabled tank and to the front of this assisting one. At the same time some troopers got down off their vehicles and unfasten the end connectors and center guide on the disabled tank track, so they could spread the track out and prepare it to be reinstalled.

This was a hot, hurried job with occasional bullets zinging by. One of these "B" troopers was experienced in breaking track and he took over the placement of the track. I silently wished that a tank crewman would have taken over my job, as having my back to the enemy was quite uncomfortable. From that point on I only helped by ground guiding the disabled tank to pull the track back over the sprocket and support rollers where it could be reconnected with the end connectors and center guide. I don't believe a tank track was ever put back on any faster. Relieved that no one was killed or injured during this process, I was very happy to climb back onto my own track and move back to the security of our Box formation. The formerly disabled tank and a couple other "B" Troop tracks headed to their new position.

Kick-Ass Time

Resuming my position in the Box, I consulted with the Platoon Leaders as to what they thought we were facing. From what we could determine the firing was all coming from the base of the large bamboo stands surrounding the barren fields and from the gullies. The 1:25,000 scale aerial photo type map showed a Buddhist temple to our right front and what appeared to be many abandoned fields about 200 feet square with heavy bamboo stands between them about 15 feet wide. Much of this bamboo was ancient growth as large as 4 inches in diameter and well over 20 feet tall.

Except for the 1st Platoon, we were at the south-east corner of the battlefield. Across the huge gully to the southwest was a large pottery factory. Considering that huge area of sand, my best guess was that we were located on top of ancient clay mines and the ventilation was inside the heavy bamboo separating the fields. The enemy was occupying large tunnels below the ground that were made by mining the clay over a very long period - perhaps centuries. It would be only too easy to expand the air ducts in the mine shafts up into the thick bamboo stands to create well camouflaged fighting positions.

What once were beautiful gardens surrounded by ancient bamboo stands belonging to the Monks at the nearby temple, was now actually deadly ambush positions waiting for the unwary. And if all this bamboo had enemy positions in them then it could accommodate a very large force. Size was immaterial. We were there to destroy them and destroy them we would.

I decided that it would be best to stay in the Box and swing the formation toward where the 1st Platoon was located, so we could build the largest Box possible with 9 tanks up front. Our Box went into the first garden area and turned to the right, centered on the wall of bamboo we were approaching. The tanks opened-up with canister ammunition weakening the bamboo and then pushed the bamboo down when we got to it. All the ACAVs on the interior of the Box watched for enemy holes to drop grenades into. The tracks on the flanks and the rear fired into the bamboo on the sides and to the rear of the formation.

The firing was intense, both the enemy's and ours, but our ability to gain fire superiority grew quickly. We determined that these were North Vietnamese regulars by the uniforms on those who jumped to the surface to get an RPG shot, and we had a new ambush to fight with each successive field we entered. An artillery forward observer in a helicopter over the battle was keeping the enemy from leaving the clay mines and escaping through the deep gully.

The high-performance aircraft were called in and they laid waste to many bamboo stands with 1,000 to 2,000-pound bombs and napalm bombs, as well as strafing the bamboo before going back to reload. And the "D" Troop helicopter gunships got into the act as well, especially when we had a heavy volume of fire from a specific location. We took over the battle at about 1600 or 1630 and we wanted to smash down as many enemy positions as we could while we had daylight left, so we pushed hard.

As we advanced, an occasional enemy soldier would jump out of a hole with an RPG Launcher or an AK-47. We had no idea how many we were fighting. It is somewhat demoralizing to concentrate your fire at the base of bamboo where someone was shooting at you, though we generally never knew if we were killing any of them or if they were just relocating underground. Were they pulling their dead down into the mines and replacing them, or were we being ineffective? I was betting on the former.

The 1st Platoon had to button up as we approached since they were subjected to our fire, but it was sure good to put them into the Box. Their attached Infantry platoon had a couple of their members killed from when they first arrived, and we put them in one of our tracks until they could be dusted off. Then we had the Infantry move from the area, as if they were on the ground, we couldn't guarantee their safety, and they would certainly get in between the Cavalry's enormous firepower and that of the enemy's.

We started south to north. Now we went east to west, then north to south, and then west to east. As we approached the deep gully the NVA had a concentrated force waiting for us and many RPGs were fired at the tanks, fortunately we received no casualties. Unfortunately, the tanks could not lower their main guns that far to feed Charley a canister dinner. The tanks made room for Zippo Reb, the flame thrower track. He coated the enemy over the edge of the gully with burning napalm which solved the problem.

Then we proceeded north, west, south and east again. And soon it was time to leave the battlefield as the sun was going down fast. It was dark when we quit fighting. The stress was extreme, and we were exhausted, and low on ammunition and fuel.

As we moved out of this area to head for Di An, the NVA tried their best to ambush our Troop, or to delay its departure so they could employ some of their night tactics. The Box was changed into a double column and we laid out a barrage of machine gun fire as we moved out of the area. Then we could hear the artillery start their time-on-target. Six batteries of artillery were to blanket the battlefield all night long to keep the NVA in the mines.

As soon as we entered the north gate of Di An, I was instructed to have all the vehicles line up along the road just as they would be leaving in the morning, but to make sure they were on the side of the road single file. The fuel trucks came along side of the tracks, and the men who had not gone to supper yet fueled their vehicles. As others returned from supper, they started pulling maintenance to get ready for a busy morning.

And then the real surprise came, as "B" troopers came to help get our vehicles ready to commence the battle first thing in the morning. The "B" troopers did a magnificent job in getting "A" Troop ready. They resupplied each track, cleaned weapons and replaced the basic load of ammunition. The "A" Troopers were able to get some rest because of the help provided by the "B" Troopers. *What a day.*

Chapter 59

XOM MOI (2) AGAIN
May 6, 1968

We were able to grab a quick hot breakfast at about 0430 and departed Di An at 0600 sharp. Time on target artillery ceased as we entered the battlefield in the box formation. Within a minute the ambushes started and one of our tank commanders, SSG Stanley J Vossen (no picture available) was killed by an enemy sniper.

We moved back and forth across the battlefield, firing into the base of the bamboo stands and destroying them one by one. The enemy played a great disciplined game of invisibility. They stayed underground except when they had a specific purpose. Unfortunately for them, they were outgunned and outclassed. But they were very disciplined. The "A" Troopers were at their best too, and there were many cases of heroism that went unreported - - probably because we were always on the move. We suddenly lost another talented Tank Commander, SSG Haywood Johnson, Jr. It was my honor to present a Society of the 1st Infantry Division scholarship to his son about a year later.

SSG Haywood Johnson, Jr.

I can't recall why I found myself next to a severely damaged bamboo stand at around 1000 hours. While I was looking down at the map, an NVA soldier standing about 10 feet from A-66 fired a burst from his brand new AK50 that tore my nice new map case out of my hands. I jerked my head upward pulling my 45-caliber pistol from my shoulder holster.

My firing at him was totally ineffective. He stood there in disbelief wondering why one of us wasn't dead. The shock of it all caused me to have what's called buck fever, and all the rounds coming toward this Charley scared him into inaction, but never hit him. When my pistol jammed, I realized that he could spray my ACAV killing me and all my crew members. My mind worked unbelievably fast. I had no choice but to throw the pistol at him and dive toward him off the top of the track. I hit the ground and rolled once knocking him off his feet and he lost his AK in the process.

Ouch! He came up in a very professional karate stance. I quickly led with a hard kick in his face and upper chest. While he was stunned, I picked him up by his throat applying maximum pressure. It suddenly occurred to me that this karate guy could disable me with one good kick to my family jewels. So, I squeezed all the harder and held him off the ground in front of me as far as I could in hopes that some clear-thinking trooper on my ACAV would shoot him. He got heavy real fast and I was fighting an awful cramp developing in my forearms. Eventually, looking at my track I saw my troopers sitting there like they had a front row seat in a championship fight. They were enjoying this far too much.

I was afraid to release the NVA soldier before he was dead and was searching for signs of confirmation. Then I had a weird flashback from my youth. My father and I had to kill a lot of mice in our chicken coop when I was a boy. He showed me that when you squeezed their necks, just before they died their eyes would nearly come out of their sockets. It sounds awful, but you can learn to rather enjoy such dumb stuff as a kid.

Finally, I had to let go and dropped the soldier to the ground. He was dead. I picked up his AK50 and my pistol and headed for my ACAV. While approaching the track, I heard LTC Tyree over the external speaker calling 1st SGT Escobedo on the radio. *"Dragoon A6 Romeo this is Dragoon 6, where's John? He's not on his track."* He was very excited. My 1st SGT replied calmly, *"Dragoon 6 this is A6 Romeo. A Charley shot a hole in A6's new map case, and he is on the ground strangling him to death."* I quickly got onto the track and called my boss to assure him all was well. There were 2 holes in my new map case, and since it was folded twice it was a mess. After giving the troopers on my track the ass chewing of their lives, we got back into the Box where we belonged.

SP4 Richie Guirene
(above and to the right)

A young trooper on the 1st SGTs ACAV, Richie Guirene, a Chicago native, told me recently that this was his first day in the field, and when he saw what happened, he thought: *"Now that's what I want to be when I grow up."*

No one knew just how scared I was. They thought their Commanding Officer was another John Wayne. And I couldn't tell them anything different. All's well that ends well.

Replacing the Basic Load

By noon we were running low on ammunition and I had the 1st Sergeant call for a resupply. Soon General Westmoreland was above the fight. As he had previously promised, he asked if we could talk, and I welcomed him to our Troop frequency. To paraphrase our conversation, The General said, *"John, I've given you six Batteries of Artillery around the clock and priority on both of the Air Wings."* I'm heading up country and wanted to see if there is anything else, I can get for you before I go."* I thought deep and fast, and answered, *"Roger, it's hot as Hell down here, and my troops could use a delivery of ice and some Pepsi Cola.* He complemented us on what we were doing and said, *"I'll see what I can do about the Pepsi."* And he was gone. I never spoke to the great General again.

In about 20 minutes a full basic load of ammunition arrived in a Chinook helicopter. When the back ramp was lowered, we saw the most amazing sight. The left side of the helicopter held the complete basic load of ammunition we requested. On the right side there were pallets of Pepsi Cola and large blocks of ice. The Headquarters Platoon hauled the ammunition, Pepsi and Ice to each track. There was enough Pepsi to last two and a half weeks. That was well received by the troopers and a shot in the arm to their morale during a tough battle.

And of course, that put a feather in the Troop Commander's hat. I always had the belief that the troopers are as important as the mission. If you take care of the troops, the mission will take care of itself. It's a matter of loyalty, and it works from top to bottom and from bottom to top. We've been out of that Hell hole for a half century and I still get favorable comments from my former troopers on being well taken care of.

As dusk was approaching, we were getting heavy resistance. An air-strike came in to help. The bombs were appreciated. But then the pilot turned and came in for a strafing run. He made the run right over our formation instead of in front of the tracks. At the same time an RPG exploded directly over my head driving me from my standing position down onto my track with a shock wave that literally jammed my teeth together and flattened my face into the metal of the track. As I got back up there was the roar of the 20mm Gatling guns overhead and the scream over the radio for a dust-off. The Red Barron fired too soon and fortunately only one little finger was shot off. It could have been much worse with the projectiles bouncing off the tracks.

Of course, I got super pissed instantaneously and gave the pilot a bit of my harshest vocabulary. In short, I told him to get the f_ _ k away from my fight and never come back. He apologized and accommodated.

Shortly after this incident, fighting practically stopped, so we broke contact and headed back to Di An. It was a long day. Artillery time-on-target hit the area again until about midnight and stopped.

Chapter 60

A Trooper's Perspective

We all see these battles through a different lens. The following is the recollection of Trooper Bill Butler of the battles of Tan Hiep and Xom Moi (2).

The way I remember the location is that there was a road North out of Di An. Another road intersected going East and West to Phu Loi. The biggest fire fight took place Southeast of the intersection.

Bill Butler

On May 4th we were sent to support an infantry unit, I think it was the 1/18 Infantry, which had been ambushed in some rice paddies south of the village of Tan Hiep. The infantry had been mauled, and they had taken a lot of casualties. We ended up forming a laager with tanks and personnel carriers to secure an area to evacuate the casualties by helicopter medivac. Our field of vision was obscured by a tall rice paddy dike, so we could only hear the sounds of the fire fight, I watched the same two medics carry casualties out for hours. They made the trip so often, that it became obvious that they were exhausted. Finally, they made a trip back, and it seemed to me that they weren't dragging as badly. I realized the body they were carrying on the stretcher was gone from the chest up.

When my platoon entered the area of the fire fight on May 5, we were on line in almost a half of a circle, and we stopped. We were in a field with a ditch at its edge that had a narrow tree line in it. There was a burning tank from B Troop in the field beyond the tree line. There was an infantry squad on our left flank, and they were advancing towards the tree line. The infantry took fire from the ditch, and they hit the ground. We took fire from the ditch and from our rear from VC who were dug in. Some of the VC were in holes inside our perimeter. The vehicles in my platoon backed together, tightened up, and returned fire. We also received supporting fire from an observation helicopter which had a mini-gun. It had fired on the VC inside our perimeter.

During the fire fight we were in the Box Formation a lot of the time. What that meant was the tanks were on line and the personnel carriers were lined up in rows behind the tanks. [B Troop was moved to a blocking position after A Troop took over the fight.] We maneuvered in that formation. The following vehicles would fire between the vehicles in front of them. That was the only time I had seen that many vehicles together at one time. The firepower was tremendous. At one time we were told to quit firing our .50's because bullets were dropping into Phu Loi. The NVA were dug in camouflaged holes. The area also had a lot of ditches. I have often wondered how many people might have been smashed into caved in positions while we were maneuvering in that massed formation. [1,200 bodies of the 165th NVA Regiment were dug out after the 7th of May and the Regimental Commander surrendered to ARVN]

We didn't leave the area until after dark. We bivouacked that night in Di An in a company area of an infantry unit that was out in the field. We used their mess hall. We resupplied the vehicles. We had shot up practically everything we had down to and including our M79 and M-16's. We were issued Ml6 tracer ammo, so that's what we loaded our M-16 magazines with, and we had a bunch of them. That ended up being extremely fortunate for me.

That night we also stole a driver's escape hatch off a tank from the division's engineer unit. During the fire fight that day, our driver had to shit, so he dropped his escape hatch to do it. Our tank commander went off on him that night when he found out. He asked the driver what would have happened if someone would have rolled a grenade under the hatch. The TC told the driver that he should use his steel pot if that ever happened again. Somebody from our platoon told us the Engineers had at least one tank. A personnel carrier took us to their area, and we took a hatch off a tank to replace ours.

The next morning, we lined up at the North Gate at Di An. We were going back to the same area. It was obvious to us that we were going to get into another fire fight. A Catholic Priest gave last rights to anyone who wanted them.

When we returned to [the] area, we assumed the Box formation again. Contact was made immediately. Someone fragged some VC who were dug in. At one point during the second day, we were told to button up, so the Air Force could bomb close to us.

We had hit some bamboo which we could not penetrate. We backed up about 10 meters and fired canister into the bamboo to soften it up so we could go through it. When we went through the bamboo there was a dead VC between two fighting holes. He had probably been killed by the canister we had fired into the bamboo.

My tank commander radioed the platoon leader who got

the whole element to halt. I was told to search the body which was fine with me because we had heard the night before that the VC carried ID cards in their shirt pockets, and I wanted one. I grabbed an M-16 and jumped off the right front fender of the tank and landed about three feet from the first hole. The two holes were in a straight line to my position with the dead VC lying at 90 degrees to the line and about halfway between the two holes. The holes were about five feet apart.

I was squatted down. I held the M-16 in my right hand by the pistol grip. I fired a couple of rounds into the first hole. I had no idea how deep it was, but it was extremely shallow, and debris blew back on me and stung my face. I inched towards the body. I still held my rifle by the pistol grip but parallel to the ground and pointed at the other hole. I was reaching towards the dead VC's shirt pocket with my left hand trying to find his ID card when another VC popped up out of the second hole holding his rifle straight up, parallel and close to his body because the hole was so narrow. I began to fire my rifle, stood up, and grabbed the hand guard of my rifle with my left, and I emptied the magazine shooting from the hip. The VC was knocked down falling backward.

I turned, tripped, fell flat on my face, crawled around the left side of the tank, stood up, and ran around to the back of the tank. I got a full magazine for my rifle from a crewman who was on the back deck of the tank. While I was getting to the back of the tank, the tank commander fired one hundred rounds with the .50 caliber machine gun into the hole which was the entrance to a small bunker.

Another VC was in the bunker, and he was also killed when my tank commander fired his .50, the whole line of tanks began to fire their weapons, the noise was deafening, and it took about ten minutes for a cease fire to take effect. I went around the right side of the tank back to the hole and saw that it had been the entrance to a bunker that went back about six feet. The top of the bunker had been camouflaged, but it had caved in from the .50 caliber machine gun fire.

The original dead VC looked like hamburger. His legs were skewed in a grotesque manner. I also saw that there had been a second VC in the bunker behind the one I had killed. I picked up the AK47 that had belonged to the VC I had killed. I jerked it up in the air in a gesture of triumph showing it to my crew members and anybody else on the other vehicles who could see me. I threw the rifle on the fender of my tank.

I pulled out the AK47 that belonged to the VC that the tank commander had killed and handed it to one the crew members on the CO's track which had pulled up next to the bunker. I also gave them two packs which were filled with rice and had one mortar round in them and two red clear plastic canteens.

I remounted my tank, grabbed the rifle off the fender, climbed back onto the turret, and sat on the loader's hatch. There was a bullet hole in the hand guard of the rifle, and it was smeared with blood. I figured one of my bullets had gone through the VC's hand. There was also a bullet hole in the stock. I must have raked down his chest with one of the first bullets going through the hand guard, and one of the last bullets going through the stock of the rifle. I took the magazine out and pulled the bolt back. A bullet was ejected.

I was suddenly stunned and terrified. The rifle had been locked and loaded. I realized it had been ready to fire when the VC I had killed had come out of the hole. I realized that if 1 had not been ready to fire, or if 1 had waited just split seconds, I might have been killed. We had only been a few feet apart when we faced each other. I also realized that the first rounds that I had fired had gone over his head. If the rounds had not been tracers, I might have missed him.

The element was maneuvering in another area. The steering on our tank malfunctioned. We could turn right, but the tank would not turn left. I got on the back deck of the tank and opened the grill door above the left side of the transmission so I could push the lever on the transmission that turned the tank to the left with a tanker's bar. The nut and bolt that connected the steering linkage to the lever had fallen off. I was standing above the grill door watching the tank commander to take his direction. He would signal me when he wanted to turn left and tell the driver over the intercom when he wanted to turn right. I had been looking at the tank commander, he signaled me to turn left, so I turned my head back to the left to look down at the lever on the transmission to push it with the bar when another tank pulled up behind us at 90 degrees and fired his main gun.

The blast deflector on the barrel was on line with me, and the other tank was only a few yards away from me. The concussion that came out of the side of the blast deflector deafened me. The concussion rocked me so violently that my helmet was knocked off my head. We maneuvered back to an area where some vehicles had set up to secure an area to dust off dead and wounded personnel. Most of the vehicles were from Headquarters platoon, so one of the mechanics was able to repair the steering linkage while we were there. 1 got off the tank to help put the stretchers on the helicopters when they started to come in to evacuate the casualties. One of the people I may have helped put on a dust off was Sergeant David George who had his right leg blown off by an RPG. Sergeant George had been my platoon sergeant from about the middle of February to end of April when he was assigned to another platoon. I was on his tank. We had become good friends. He was a great soldier, and he had trained me constantly.

The element was again in the Box formation with all tanks forward and the armored personnel carriers following in rows behind the tanks. We had maneuvered into an area that had sparse vegetation with a wood line about 50 meters distant facing the element. We started taking small arms tire. The Zippo track was pulled up on line with the tanks and soaked the area directly in front of the line of tanks with napalm. The napalm was sprayed as far as possible into the wood line. After the fire from the napalm burnt down, the element was supposed to advance through the area. Our tank had a fuel leak, so the tank commander radioed the platoon leader. Another tank maneuvered into our position, and my tank was not supposed to advance with the rest of the unit.

When the fire died down, the element moved forward even though the area was still smoldering, and small fires were still burning. The tank that took our place maneuvered directly in front of us, it had moved forward about 10 meters on line with the rest of the line of tanks when the tank commander jerked back violently, his back seemed to have been blown out, and his whole back had turned to blood. I thought he had been hit with a rocket propelled grenade. That tank stopped advancing. The rest of the line of tanks started firing their .50 caliber machine guns and their main guns as they advanced across the open area towards the tree line. After the personnel carriers had maneuvered around us and the tank that had taken our place, the three other crew members on the dead tank commanders tank climbed on the turret and pulled him out of the hatch and laid him on his back on the back deck of the tank After the tank commander had been put on the back deck, the tank turned around, and went closely by us to the secured area where the casualties were being med-evacted. There was blood all over the back of the turret. I was confused because the dead tank commander only had a small wound in his chest. 1 thought he had been hit by a rocket, but I learned later that he had probably been hit with a communist .51 caliber machine gun. As the tank went by, my tank commander and I looked at each other in amazement, realizing how lucky we were. We commented that it could have been us. We usually rode on top of the vehicles, or if we were in a fire fight, we would be standing in the hatches exposed from about the waist up like the dead tank commander had been.

One of the personnel carriers in my platoon had the Playboy cartoon character, "Annie Fannie" painted on the side. The track commander had only been out in the field for a few days. He was shot in the head and killed. We saw his crew pull him out of the cupola.

My tank was on the left flank of the formation. Some infantry personnel were to the left of my tank and about 20 meters to the rear. We had taken some small arms fire from the front and left flank. We had suppressed the fire from the VC with machine gun fire from my tank and the personnel carrier to our rear. There was a VC pack on the ground about 15 meters to the left of the tank. One of the infantrymen must have thought the pack was a VC and threw a hand grenade at it. I yelled grenade, and 1 ducked inside the turret.

As I ducked down, I realized that the crew member who was on the back deck of the tank didn't hear me because he didn't react. The gunfire was constant at that time, and the noise was deafening. I raised back up to warn him, the grenade exploded, and a small piece of shrapnel hit my cheek and embedded in my left jaw; I was knocked off balance, my feet slipped off the loader's seat, I fell to the turret floor, and landed painfully on my knees. I climbed back up. I wanted to see if the crew member on the back deck was all right. He had been sitting on some C Ration cases that were strapped to the end of the back-deck loading M-16 magazines. He was completely oblivious to what had happened. Later we found that some of the cans in the C-Rations had small holes in them from the shrapnel from the hand grenade. He had been pretty lucky.

That night we went back to Di An. We had a hot meal in the mess hall. The colonel who was the squadron commander asked me how I was doing. I had a thick gauze bandage on my jaw that the medic had wrapped tape around the top of my head and under my jaw to keep the bandage on. I had no idea the colonel even knew who I was, but he knew that I had been on Sergeant George's tank, he told me that Sergeant George had been flown to the hospital at Long Binh, but he did not know what his condition was. I was devastated. It was hard for me to believe that Sergeant George had been wounded.

The next morning, I was sent on sick call and walked to the dispensary which was on the far side of the base camp with a jaw that had become swollen and a lot more painful. There were a lot of other people who had minor wounds at the dispensary, so we had a long wait to see a doctor. The doctor that saw me tried to probe for the shrapnel through the hole in my cheek. He tried to pull it out with tweezers. All he did was hurt me. He sent me on my way with a prescription of Darvon with codeine, and told me to come back the next day, so they could send me to the hospital in [Long Bien].

I walked back to the company area where we had bivouacked. My jaw hurt so bad that I ate most the Darvon I had on the way back, and by the time I reached the place, I was completely out of it from the codeine. The area where the vehicles had been the last two nights was full of trash. Most of it was the result of resupplying the vehicles with ammunition. The area was littered with ammunition cases and cans. I saw an almost new flak jacket on the ground. I thought someone had probably dropped it. I reached down to pick it up, and in my stupor all I did was flip it open. It was full of blood. The blood was coagulated and almost an inch thick. It was like jelly. I flipped the front back to cover the blood. Someone had written an A and the vehicle number of a personnel carrier on it with magic marker. The flak jacket had belonged to the track commander from my platoon who had been killed.

I felt sick from what I had just seen, the codeine, the pain, and the sun which was blinding me. I found a bunk in one of the barracks, laid down and fell asleep or passed out from the codeine. I slept until someone from my platoon found me and woke me at dusk. I was groggy, but I felt a sense of relief when I was told my unit had not gotten into a fire fight that day, and everyone had returned safely. I had assumed we would probably return to the area, and establish contact with the VC again, but they had withdrawn from the area.

The next day I went back to the dispensary, and I was sent to Long Bien on a truck. I went to an oral surgeon, and he cut the shrapnel out. It seemed bizarre to be sitting in dentist's chair, in a clean air-conditioned office. I could have been back home. Except I was filthy. The left shoulder of my fatigue shirt was stiff with dried blood. I smelled awful.

A few days after the fire fight, part of my troop returned to the area. The area was flat, the rains had started, the low areas were soft, so the tanks were left on higher ground while the personnel carriers searched the area. I started walking around the area. Different reports of the incident said the body count was anywhere from 200 to 600 dead VC. I have no idea what is correct, but I did see a lot of dead VC. I was in an area that had been burned by napalm that just reached into some bamboo. A VC was sitting inside the bamboo and the napalm had burned him up to his waist. He was leaning back against some bamboo like he was in a recliner. His hands where on the sides of his head. I got the impression that he had been pulling his hair in agony when he died.

I walked up on another VC who was lying on his back. His fatigue shirt had popped open because his body had swollen so much. There were maggots in his mouth. I was stunned. It was a scene out of Norman Mailer's "The Naked and the Dead" which I had read in high school. One of the characters in the book had walked up on the body of a dead Japanese soldier lying on his back with his fatigue shirt split open because his body was swollen, and he also had maggots coming out of his mouth. The only difference was the VC wore shorts and rubber sandals. Like the guy in the book, I was both fascinated and repulsed. I kept thinking that I had read about this. It seemed so bizarre, so unreal. The loader on my tank started yelling at me to come back. When I got back to the tank, he pointed out someone in the distance he had been watching and thought might be a VC. He turned out to be a VC who had been wounded in the shoulder, and eventually he walked towards the tank. He was in bad shape because the wound had not been treated.

We went back to the area one more time. We took a bulldozer loaded on a low boy. The tank retriever from

Headquarters Platoon was with us. The bulldozer dug a deep trench next to the burnt tank from B Troop. The bulldozer and the tank retriever got on the opposite side of the tank with their blades down, and they flipped the tank over and it fell into the trench upside down, the bulldozer covered the tank with dirt.

That's pretty much the way I remember what happened.

Chapter 61

A PLATOON LEADER'S PERSPECTIVE

The following are some comments concerning combat operations in Vietnam put together by Lieutenant Joseph Scates, the 1st Platoon Leader of Alpha Troop, and a damned fine Officer and Cavalryman.

One of the things that I remember was the amount of time the Cavalry spent in the field. While I was a platoon leader, I remember working with many different Infantry units. After a while I realized that they were rotating back to base camp after pulling a stretch of field duty. In my 8 months as a Cavalry platoon leader, other than the camps along Thunder Road (QL-13), I can remember only two occasions where I was in a division base camp.

The first was to Phu Loi with the Troop on my way to and from R&R in Australia. I remember well the road march going to Phu Loi. I was the lead platoon. The S3 was in a helicopter, on my Platoon radio net, giving me directions at every turn. I had a map and compass and had been using them effectively to travel throughout the III Corps Area of Operation. I didn't need or want the constant oversight and made a snide remark to that affect over the Troop's radio net. Apparently the S3 was monitoring that network as well and let me know that he had monitored my comments. At the gates to Phu Loi the S3 signed off the radios, leaving me to find the way to the Squadron's area. I had no clue where the Squadron area was located, and our terrain maps didn't have a street map of Phu Loi.

The second time I was in a division base camp came as a surprise. I was notified that the division was starting a new program to bring in for an overnight in the rear, officers who had spent a great deal of time in the field. I was selected as the first officer given the opportunity to take advantage of that program. I was picked up at our field location by a helicopter and flown to Di An where I spent the night in a 1st* *Aviation Battalion officers quarter. I was able to take a shower with soap and hot running water, dine at an officer's club and sleep between clean white sheets in a bed with a mattress. The next morning, I was returned to the platoon's field location.*

About 40 years later, reading copies of the Squadron's daily operation's logs found on the internet, I saw frequent entries of Bravo and Charlie Troop departures and returns to base camp but very few entries with information about Alpha Troop and our numerous contacts with the enemy. Only then did I realize how differently Alpha Troop had been operating.

REMEMBERING LIFE IN THE FIELD

Meals: *Frequently operating independently or with the Troop (-), the platoon lived mostly on C Rations. The Troop's mess section rarely operated in the field. Hot A Rations were occasionally "helicoptered in" in mermite cans. Frequently, the Infantry units, to which we were attached, allowed the platoon to eat hot A Rations cooked in their field mess. However, when A Rations were available, it was always for an evening meal.*

Troopers became very good at improvising recipes. "Tankers Stew", made by combining several C Ration meals in a pot and adding a good measure of Tabasco Sauce was very popular. C Ration pizza was also a hot item. Place half of a biscuit in the bottom of a can. Add half a can of spiced beef. Sprinkle on a little Tabasco Sauce if desired. Top it off with cheese whiz. Close the lid on the can, place the can in the C Ration box and set the box on fire. Almost every item in the C Ration carton was used. The exception was the Ham and Lima Beans which everyone hated. The troops would toss the cans to children gathered along the sides of the road. After a while the children started throwing them back. For most items, the preferred heating method was a C4 stove. Punch several holes in the side of a short C Ration can. Tear off a small hunk of C4 and place it in the bottom of the can and light it with a match. My eyes were probably as big as a saucer the first time I saw that done.

Showers: *Hot showers with soap were far and few between. My first shot at a hot shower was at Ton San Nhut Airbase on the first day of Tet 1968. Early in the morning on the first day of Tet, the Troop was awakened by an American gunship who was making a gun run followed by a rocket run on our perimeter north of Saigon. Following that we were ordered to road march to Saigon to help with the defense of Ton Son Nhut. Once in the city, I was ordered to take one tank and two PCs to help recover the bodies of several MPs who had been ambushed by the enemy. The remainder of the Platoon stayed with the Troop and continued on to the airbase. Finishing the recovery mission, we completed our travel to Ton Son Nhut. Arriving and rejoining the rest of the platoon I noticed how clean they appeared. When asked, they informed me that the airmen were so happy to see them that they offered them the use of the showers in their barracks. We were elated but just as we started towards the barracks the Troop Commander called me for a mission briefing. After the briefing I had just enough time to return to the platoon and give the order to mount up and move out. Hot shower opportunity* *missed.*

The next opportunity came a few days later when we were ordered to secure the Thu Duc Water Filtration plant north of Saigon and secure the supply route between Saigon and Long Binh. The filtration plant had an open room with numerous shower heads with hot water and soap. The Vietnamese, who showered wearing shorts to cover their privates, were not happy seeing American males in their showers wearing nothing more than what we were born wearing.

Most of the time we depended on field showers. These came whenever we had water to spare in our 5-gallon water cans. A canvas bag with attached shower head was hung by a strap on a tank gun tube and filled with water from one of the 5-gallon cans.   Water temperature depended on time of day and where the 5-gallon can had been stored on the vehicle. On occasion we used water from one of the many streams/rivers for our showers. Since we always rode atop of our vehicles, rain helped to contribute to a minor degree. Although I must say the rain hitting your body while riding atop a moving vehicle always felt cold at any time of year, rainy season or not.

Fatigue exchange: *The first thing you learn is that it was a waste of time and money to have name tags, rank insignia and unit patches sewn on to your first set of uniforms. Dirty fatigues were sent to the rear to a laundry facility on one of the many supply helicopters. When clean fatigues were returned to the unit, they were void of everything except the division patch and the US Army tag – sometimes not even that.*

Most of the Infantry units with whom we operated with were able to exchange fatigues after being in the field after just a few days. The Cavalry units -- not so frequently. We learned that fatigues will rot quickly if not cleaned regularly. Dirt mixed with sweat and the rays of the sun seemed to accumulate on the fatigues just above the knees and cause the fatigues to rot. When that happened, we pulled out a set of clean fatigues that were being saved for just such an occasion.

Resupply: *Our major resupply items were ammunition, fuel, repair parts, C Rations, Sundry Packs, sodas and water. Unless we were operating on one of the Thunder Bases or with a major headquarters in the field most of our resupply was accomplished by helicopter. The Platoon would set up a secure perimeter for the resupply helicopters to land and push out the supplies.*

As the helicopter approached it was often necessary to pop green smoke grenades so the pilot could clearly identify the landing zone. This was especially necessary if we were operating near hostiles. The landing area had to be selected carefully. Obviously as far away as practical from any suspected hostile activity but also in an area free from debris that could be picked up by the rotor wash from the helicopter.

Flying in a Command and Control aircraft on one mission I saw a helicopter attempt to land in an area where trees had been knocked down. The rotor wash picked up a downed tree that was still attached to its roots and stood the tree almost vertical before the pilot saw it and managed to pull up before it struck the rotor blades.

I must say that I would give resupply operations an A+ rating. This is especially true for critical combat items such as ammunition and fuel. On one particularly heavy day of fighting we were resupplied with fuel and ammunition by helicopter twice in the battle area during the fight and again when we closed into the night perimeter.

Maintenance: *In the field there was no formal by the book maintenance system. Formal documentation, such as, log books, 2404 daily inspection reports, etc., were not high on our list of to do items. A formal written documentation system was much too slow to meet the immediate needs of rigorous daily operations.*

When something needed to be repaired it had to be handled quickly. Oral communications were immediate 24/7 as soon as a problem was discovered. Living on and around their vehicle 24/7, every crew member developed a sort of sixth sense for differences in noises, vibrations, handling, appearance and operational capability of the vehicle.

We added fluids and lubricants, tightened nuts and bolts, checked the vehicles for damage and did whatever was necessary to maintain the capability of the vehicles to shoot and move in the environment in which we operated. Rarely did a vehicle leave the field for 2nd echelon or higher maintenance. When something broke or was about to break beyond our capability to repair, we notified Troop maintenance personnel. They ordered the necessary parts. The parts were delivered to our field location by helicopter and Troop maintenance personnel, assisted by vehicle crew members made the repairs. Heavy items like engines were brought to the field by helicopter. The Troop's M88 would lift out the old engine and lower the replacement engine into place. Occasionally a Super Crane Heavy Lift Helicopter would be required to lift out a M113 (sans engine) that couldn't be repaired in the field.

Medical: *Troop medics traveled with each platoon. Our medical personnel endured the same hardships and* *danger as our troopers and were outstanding in every regard. I personally witnessed one of our medics sitting in the open completely exposed between vehicles working on wounded troopers while the platoon was under intense machine gun and rocket propelled grenade attack. I give them an A++ for their bravery and willingness to put themselves in harm's way to save lives. Many of our troopers are still with us today because of their efforts.*

MEDEVAC: *As with resupply operations the Platoon would set up a secure perimeter for the MEDEVAC helicopter. But this was usually accomplished nearer to the battle area because of a need for speed and potential hazards of moving the patient. MEDEVAC missions were called as soon as we started taking casualties whose wounds required procedures beyond the capability of our own field medics. Consequently, the MEDEVAC helicopters were almost routinely exposed to hostile fire as they tried to get as close as possible to the collection point. I would give the MEDEVAC pilots and crew an A++ for their bravery and willingness to put themselves in harm's way to save lives.*

End of Day/Night Laagers: *At the end of daily operations the platoon would settle into a defense position for the night. These night time laagers were either into an established perimeter or a hasty perimeter. Whether established or hasty, the procedures were similar. The biggest difference was who established and maintained perimeter security.*

<u>Established Perimeters:</u> The division had established defensive perimeters all along Thunder Road (QL-13). At one time, I believe there were as many as ten such perimeters. They were named by number i.e., Thunder 4 or Thunder 10. These were multi-unit perimeters. Normally with one or more battalion size or smaller units

operating from the base daily.

Usually an Infantry Battalion Commander or sometimes a Brigade XO was designated as fire base commander. Infantry provided perimeter security outside the wire by sending out ambush patrols and out posts. Artillery units were included at each base and provided direct fire support for day and night time operations within their assigned zone and indirect fire support for units operating from other fire bases or field locations but within the range of their weapons. If a Cavalry unit was in the perimeter they would be assigned as a Ready Reaction Force to respond to the ambush forces and outposts if needed.

Hasty Perimeters: Because of operational missions we often had to set up hasty perimeters wherever we stopped operations for the day. Sometimes these were platoon level perimeters but more often they were Troop (-) perimeters. Each vehicle carried one or more rolls of concertina [wire].

We would select a location based on best defensible terrain and fields of fire. Higher headquarters were notified including the supporting artillery units. The vehicles would roll into the area and form a wagon wheel and face outward, making sure that each vehicle had overlapping fields of fire with the vehicles on either side. Once the vehicle locations were established the rolls of concertina were laid out to the front and connected to form a complete circle around the perimeter. Outpost positions with egress and ingress routes were selected. Claymore mines were set up – some with trip wires and some not. Chain link fences were set up in front of each vehicle to help protect the vehicle and crew from Rocket Propelled Grenades (RPGs).

Recover: Having established perimeter security, whether in an established or hasty perimeter, the priority was to rearm, refuel, clean all weapons, inspect and start maintenance on all vehicles, take care of the evening meal, review the day's activity and plan for the next day's mission.

Security Inside the Perimeter: Whether in an established or hasty perimeter, a rotating watch was required on every vehicle while in the perimeter. This required one man to be awake behind the 50 Cal on every vehicle. The person on watch had to monitor the platoon radio network at all times. SITREPS were called for by the Platoon Leader's vehicle throughout the night – usually at 15-minute intervals

Light and Noise Discipline Inside the Perimeter: The Division policy did not allow personal radios while operating in the field. This policy was followed by all units. Unit radios were monitored 24/7 but the volume turned down very low while in the perimeter. Communications requiring only an acknowledgment by the receiver were made by a double click on the mike. Wherever possible red lenses were used on flashlights. Exterior vehicle lights were turned off. Interior vehicle lights were either off or shielded as best as possible. Smoking and cigarette lighters were discouraged while outside of the vehicle at night.

Of course, 100% compliance is not always possible. The night before the TET Offensive of 1968 the Troop was in a hasty perimeter North of Saigon. The Troop mess Section was with us. Just before daylight the cooks started a cook stove to prepare the morning's coffee. U.S. helicopters saw the cooking fires and mistook us for part of the enemy forces who had just launched the TET Offensive. They made two runs at the perimeter, the first with machine guns and the second with rockets.

Night Operations: *Although night operations were frequently required, the pucker value was always higher at night time. This was especially true when other units were involved in the operation. When your unit receives incoming fire the first reaction is to return suppressive fire. When you operate in an area where there is no defined "front line" that incoming fire can come from any direction at any time.*

As a small unit leader, you know where your vehicles are, and you know roughly where other units are located. However, that does not guarantee avoiding casualties from friendly fire. I have been on night operations where the enemy was located in a tree line between you and following units. If you are fired on by the enemy at your rear and you return that fire, you risk hitting the other unit. In turn that unit may interpret the incoming fire as being from the enemy and return that fire. A lose, lose for both units and probably the enemy as well. If you don't return the fire the enemy can keep shooting without worry of being hit by return fire. A win for the enemy and a loss for the friendly unit. If the other friendly unit is dismounted infantry, it could be especially bad.

An armored unit, even if it is only M113s [ACAVs], will take fewer casualties than dismounted infantry. Some night operations were not as bad as others. After TET 68 Alpha Troop had the responsibility to keep open the supply route between Long Binh and Saigon. That involved reducing the number of ambushes on nighttime convoys.

After dark we would load up infantry units and drop them at various times and locations along the route. To disguise the locations, we would stop at various intervals and sit long enough for the infantry to dismount but keep them onboard for an actual drop at another location. Frequently we would run up and down the road empty but faking drops along the way. We were ambushed frequently, while doing this but we knew where our own infantry was located and were able to respond immediately to the threat without fear of endangering our own infantry.

USE OF ARMORED CAVALRY WITH THE AIR CAVALRY

I didn't feel like the division appreciated the value of the Armored and Air Cavalry operating together. It always seemed like our Air Cav flew mostly in support of the divisions Infantry units. While I am sure the Infantry was glad to have the support, it seemed to me a mostly defensive role.

The value of having Armored and Air Cav operating together was in an offensive role. Armored units caused great fear with the enemy. Typically, it was hit and run when the enemy was faced with an Armored unit. The Air Cav had the ability to see the enemy fleeing from the confrontation and take them on the run rather than trying to find an enemy dug in and resisting the infantry units. This was especially true in the less forested areas away from the heavily forested area near the border areas.

STRATEGIC VIEWPOINT

From my perspective it didn't take long to realize the war could not be won the way it was being fought strategically. When I first arrived and until TET68 we were told not to load a round in the tanks main gun. The reason was an accident that had killed innocent civilians when a round went off as it was being loaded. I asked myself, why are we fighting a war in the presence of innocent civilians? Why do I have to wait until I am shot at before I can put a round into the main gun tube?

TET changed all of that. But the questions lingered. While at Thu Duc securing the supply route an enemy soldier was killed during an ambush. We learned that he was a well-liked South Vietnamese soldier by day. When we encounter a person carrying a weapon how do we know if that person is a friend or a foe? In this case he was both, but we lost favor with the local population.

When I looked at the lives of civilians killed, and the destruction of buildings and farm land caused by our forces and enemy forces I asked myself why are we destroying what we have been here to protect? How long can the South continue losing people and resources before giving up and asking us to leave? How long before they lose confidence in the U.S. ability to protect them? Are we losing the hearts and minds of the people we were sent to help? What would happen if we took the war to the enemy? Wouldn't everyone we encountered be a potential enemy? If a person was carrying a weapon wouldn't they be considered an enemy combatant? Would the Hanoi regime shift support of the war effort in the South back to the homeland? Couldn't we take the battle to the enemy instead of waiting for them to bring it to us in the South? Wouldn't we be able to decide when and where to mass forces instead of waiting for the enemy to make that decision (i.e.: TET 68).

The elephant in the room – China. Could our politicians at the time work with our allies to stand up to any potential threats from China? Did they even attempt to do any of the above? In a book titled "The Presidents Club" I was shocked to read that candidate Richard Nixon had consorted with the North Vietnamese to not honor the peace talks occurring in late October 1968. Rather, wait for him to be elected President of the United States. It really hit me hard to read that. I was at Fire Base Rita on the Cambodia border the night of 31 October 1968. We were hit hard that night by an NVA sapper battalion. They managed to penetrate the perimeter and get inside the wire. The battle was intense, lasted several hours and supported with a large number of RPGs, mortars and possibly 120mm rockets. 12 U.S. soldiers (Infantry, Cavalry and Artillery) were lost that night. The number of wounded, also high, was never provided. The book also points out that our President entered a similar arrangement with the North Vietnamese while running for a second term.

Chapter 62

TO THE WATER PLANT .. A NEW MISSION
May 7, 1968

In the morning we headed back to the XOM MOI (2) battlefield expecting to be back into the fight. But except for one wounded NVA walking around they appeared to be gone. We thoroughly searched the area and found a tunnel entrance in the bushes to the West of the fighting fields surrounded by the crushed bamboo. We killed one VC and the second tried to escape. I suspected as much and circled the bushes on foot to intercept him. It worked, and he came out of the bushes right in front of me and surrendered rather than die.

After the prisoners were flown out by helicopter, we were ordered to move to the Thu Duc Water Purification Plant a little north of Saigon. That was about a ten-kilometer drive and a welcome relief from the past three weeks of fighting. And the water plant had hot showers. That was fantastic. We secured the water plant and enjoyed a well-earned quiet night.

VC Colonel Defects To South

5/5, 5/6 1968

SAIGON (AP) — A Viet Cong regimental commander has defected to the South, Vietnamese government officials said Monday.

He was the second highest-ranking man ever to defect and the second top officer to come over in less than a month, officials said.

The defecting officer was identified as Lt. Col. Truong Trung Doan, commander of the 165th Regt. of the Viet Cong 7th Div.

Officers said the colonel was being questioned. His initial reports to intelligence specialists said his regiment had been decimated in fighting north of Saigon.

The colonel said his regiment had been assigned the task of pinning down the 5th South Vietnamese Div. north of Saigon while a companion Viet Cong regiment, the 101st, slipped by to enter the capital.

In the process, said the colonel, his four battalions which normally numbered 400 men each had been cut down to about 100 men each.

The regimental commander defected May 9 to elements of the 5th South Vietnamese Div. about 30 miles north of Saigon. Further details were not immediately available.

The officer said he was originally a South Vietnamese Communist party member who had gone to North Vietnam with Red forces after the Geneva Conference of 1954.

His defection followed the similar defection in mid-April of a full colonel and political commissar who turned himself in and brought vital intelligence outlining the latest Communist attacks on Saigon.

The colonel, a North Vietnamese, was the highest-ranking officer to ever defect.

In the afternoon of the second day we received a visit from the Assistant 1st Infantry Division Commander, Brigadier General Emil Eschenburg. He came straight to me and asked where we could have a private conversation. I suggested behind the building where the water was filtered. Once there he told me the reason for his visit was that *"the Division Commander (Major General Keith Ware) sent me to chew your ass for reporting such a small body count. The 300+ dead enemy soldiers you reported was ludicrous for the expenditure of five basic loads of ammunition. The ARVN soldiers were sent into the clay mines and pulled out over 1,200 dead enemy soldiers of the 165th VC/NVA Regiment and all of their weapons, before putting the bodies back into the clay mines and blowing them shut."* He said they were going to cover the area with granular tear gas to make it inaccessible. Then he waited for a reply from me. General Officer or not, I couldn't help but climb on top of this issue.

"General, I only had my men count the enemy dead that were on the surface. I would not allow them to dismount and go into those mines. If it's a job for anyone, that would be an infantry job. And you may

know General, I'm a dumb ass High School dropout with a GED. Although I know how to fight like Hell, I agree that my shortcoming is in higher mathematics. Let me make a suggestion, sir. I've been to the Generals' dining facility and you have a couple Infantry Second Lieutenants at the front door with those little chrome counters. As people enter you hear; click, click, click, click. I suggest that the next time I get into a good fight that you attach these Second Lieutenants to me. I'll do the fighting and they can go through the enemy positions going click, click, click, click."

He looked at me and thought deeply. Then he said, *"Well Captain, it doesn't appear that I'm going to rattle you today, does it?"* I said, *"No sir, you just told me that we had the highest body count in this war, and there isn't any way I can be rattled after such good news."*

After a chuckle he suggested he address the troopers, and after relating very strong complements from the Division Commander he got onto his helicopter and was gone.

The 1st Infantry Division never bothered to change the recorded number of enemy that were killed, and I will never understand that. On the prior page

Relaxing at Water Plant

I inserted a supporting interview that a Pacific Stars and Stripes reporter had with the Regimental Commander of the 165th VC/NVA Regiment.

As a side note, Brigadier General Eschenburg gave a fine endorsement on my efficiency rating. I guess my failure to humble myself to his criticism didn't "rattle" him either.

> ***"I had the opportunity to observe Captain Conley
> move from staff to command his troop after a previous
> commander was killed. I then further observed him in***

his first battle. In this battle, as well as all subsequent ones, his performance was outstanding in every respect. Additionally, he is cheerful, responsive and eager to respond whether on the battle field or in [a] non-combat environment. He is a superb officer and an exceptional all-around leader."   *(21 AUGUST 1968)*

As a side note, following Vietnam, when I was attending the Armor Officer Career Course at Fort Knox, KY, I received a telephone call from the Colonel at the Officer Assignment Branch telling me that a General Officer had contacted him about sending this "dumb ass" Cavalry Officer to college, so he can learn his mathematics. It could not have been MG Ware, as he was killed the day I left Vietnam. It could only have been Brigadier General Eschenburg. I, then in 2 years obtained my baccalaureate degree from the University of Tampa., Graduating on the Dean's List.

And I do know my mathematics now.

Chapter 63

F-100 SUPER SABER RESCUE
& TANK RECOVERY

The hot showers and the well-earned rest didn't last very long. We were suddenly called out on a mission to rescue a pilot from a F-100 Super Saber high performance aircraft that crashed in a jungle area that could only be reached by crossing a single road from QL-13, about three or four kilometers north of Saigon. As we rushed down QL-13 to the turnoff, I studied the map and determined that the road we had to take crossed between rice paddies and that part of the road was about 600 feet long. One way in and the same way out. After the rice paddies, the dirt road went for roughly 50 meters before it became a jungle trail. This was like a jungle island, and the wreckage would be found somewhere in the middle of the forest. And it could be full of VC/NVA.

As we turned to cross between the rice paddies, we were single file with the tracks spaced about 100 feet apart. The VTR (Vehicle Track Retriever) and the Maintenance ACAV stayed at the top of the hill on QL-13 for safety purposes.

When we had almost all the troop across the rice paddies the road was deteriorating. When it was reported that the road was turning to Jell-O, I had the trailing Platoon leave its last two tanks on the high ground to secure the crossing. They likely would have sunk into the rice paddies anyway. I notified the Squadron Commander that when we came out, we would likely have a recovery problem to deal with.

As we approached the wreckage, I was advised that the pilot had been rescued by a helicopter, and that we should secure the burning wreckage until the Air Force recovery crew arrived. There wasn't much of the aircraft on the surface. It appeared that most of it was under the ground, although there were pieces of the plane spread all around. The bombs that it carried were nowhere to be found. We weren't there when the plane crashed, so they may have exploded. There were only 2 other possibilities. They may be underground or were carried away by Charley to make impressive mines. The Air Force was quick to get a helicopter in the air over the wreckage, so it was unlikely that the bombs were carried away. Everything was extremely hot from the full load of burning aviation fuel and it could be expected to burn for a very long time.

Within a couple hours the Air Force security troops and recovery unit were on site. This allowed us to move back toward the rice paddies and the soggy piece of road. Soon we were carefully moving tracks across what was left of the road between the rice paddies. Four tanks were still to cross when the road became impassable. The maintenance troopers had the VTR move as far down the hill toward the rice paddies as it safely could. Then the VTRs wench cable was extended across the paddies to the first tank. After hookup, this tank was able to come across the remaining road under its own power, with the VTR backing up providing assistance.

The second tank was harder as there was very little traction. The main gun was turned over the back deck and placed into travel lock. The tank's transmission was placed in neutral and the men were brought across after closing the

Huge VTR

hatches and hooking up the VTR's cable. Two tanks were placed behind the VTR and hooked to the VTR with tow cables. The wench was activated as the tanks and VTR backed up the hill together. I became concerned that the single cable might snap as the tank being towed was going deep into the muck. So, we pulled the VTR a lot closer and doubled the cable through a pulley and restarted the wench and backing up process. About 20 minutes later that tank was on high ground. Two down and two to go.

A second VTR from the Headquarters Troop arrived. This allowed the third tank to be brought across the rice paddies with the two VTRs using their wench capabilities. This time the tank being towed completely disappeared for about five minutes and the towing process took about 40 minutes.

Thankfully a third VTR showed up from "C" Troop so we could hook them all together with cables going through pullies to gain as much mechanical advantage as possible. The first VTR was moved to the edge of the rice paddies. As they began to pull, the tank went into the rice paddies and disappeared. I looked around and saw three General Officers and several Colonels watching the recovery process. I was surprised that they didn't put their noses in, and screw things up. Our Squadron Maintenance Officer was now supervising the recovery and it was very interesting.

Powerful VTR Towing an M48A3 disabled Tank

The last M48A3 Tank **completely** disappeared for forty-five minutes and the applause was tremendous when it resurfaced.

Better yet, it cranked right up. It was getting dark fast. Within thirty minutes we were on our way toward an open field where we laagered and spent a quiet night.

Chapter 64

ANYONE FOR SOME SCHOOLING?

The next day we were going to get a day to pull maintenance. I was told to move the Troop just outside the northern end of a village on QL-13 and set up an NDP. As we turned off QL-13 several ladies of the night (or day) showed up on the back side of the school yard. They were showing a little too much skin to be doing anything but planning to lure troopers from their work. And what they were flashing made me nervous. Remember, most of my troopers were between the ages of 18 and 20. And I knew that if there was a will, there was a way. But this could get them killed at night.

I knew that these little sirens could entice some horny young man through the wire at night and this would likely result in his being shot as he came back into the NDP. These men had been in the field for far too long to leave this to chance. The issue was discipline versus horny trooper. So, I ordered the Troop to circle the school house and include it in our perimeter. As soon as we stopped, I sent our interpreter, SGT Quan, into town with instructions to bring back some healthy gals interested in making a few bucks the old-fashioned way. I knew this was wrong, but my men were too valuable to leave it to chance.

About the time we finished fortifying our perimeter, SGT Quan showed up with several whores and put them in the school house as instructed. I then got on the radio and had all the tracks put their radios on the Troop command frequency, so I could talk to them all at one time. Once I was sure that this was done, I told the men that some ladies were in the school house and they could send one man at a time from a track to get educated. I told them that I wasn't twisting their arm to do this, but I was doing this only to make sure they had no excuse for going through the wire that night. And I made it perfectly clear that anyone coming into our NDP through the wire after dark would be shot dead.

Granted, this wasn't the moral thing to do on my part, as their Commanding Officer, and I've regretted it somewhat ever since. But at the time I saw it as the better choice between two evils. Was this so much different from giving them a pass to go to the village for recreation from a basecamp or going on R&R. In either case they weren't going to church. Once the schoolhouse festivities began, I set my mind on other important matters.

I needed to have a talk with the Squadron Commander, so I took the Medic Track, A-63, which needed medical supplies, my ACAV and a couple Tanks, and hit the road. It was only about eight to ten kilometers to the Phu Loi basecamp. When we were about half way there, I heard the Squadron Command chopper lifting off at Phu Loi, as LTC Tyree was keying his radio to inform that he was flying to my NDP. I replied that he could set the chopper down as I was about half way to his location. He replied that he always enjoyed talking with the "A" Troopers and he would continue to the NDP and see me when he returned.

Oh my, it would not do for the Squadron Commander to see the "A" Troop educational activities and I knew he had a habit of monitoring my command frequency, so I was careful. I called 1st SGT Escobedo and said, *"A-6 Romeo this is A-6, school is out. Do you understand? School is out."* 1st SGT Escobedo said, *"Roger Out."* And according to LTC Tyree everyone was either pulling maintenance or behind their guns when he arrived.

When Dragoon 6, LTC Tyree, returned to Phu Loi he said that he never visited a more professional unit. *(The rest of this story will continue in the chapter of LTC Tyree's going home party.)*

Chapter 65

♫ Oh where, Oh where has Charley gone? Oh where, Oh where can he be? ♫

It appears that when time-on-target was stopped at midnight on May 6th, the Regimental Commander escaped from Xom Moi (2) along with about 400 of his soldiers. This is based on what the Commander said after he surrendered. In an interview with Pacific Stars and Stripes he said that his Regiment had a strength of 1,600 soldiers when the battle began (4 Battalions of 400 men each and only had 100 men left alive in each Battalion). The ARVN soldiers counted 1,200 bodies. So, whenever we got the chance we hunted for more of his Regiment. I expected that most of them would be headed toward Cambodia to regroup.

On May 11, 1968 we left Phu Loi in the early morning, planning to end the day at Di An. We were searching the area to the west and south west of Di An. In the early afternoon as we were passing a dry rice paddy area, we received rifle fire from about 75 meters away on the bank of a rice paddy dike. This was not the smartest thing Charley could do as we might have passed by without detecting them. The Troop turned left, on line and started to cross the dry rice paddy toward where the firing was coming from. In the center of the dike two men were standing. One's appearance was that of an officer and he was waving a white rag indicating a surrender. The soldier next to him was holding an AK-47. Apparently not everyone was surrendering. It reminded me of what happened to the "B" Troop Commander, CPT Ed Bryson. I sensed deception. The firing never ceased from the enemy positions all along the dike.

One of the Platoon Leaders asked what to do about the white flag. My order was to commence firing and not to deliberately kill the man holding that flag. With the Tanks and ACAVs bouncing around as they moved forward, and considering the normal dispersion of the machine guns, it would be a miracle if the white flag waving officer survived. In any case, he had a lot of nerve to stand there with all the armor firing around him.

To our surprise, when we over-ran that dike everyone shooting at us was dead, 32 of them. Only their Company Commander, holding that white rag, was still standing and uninjured. He was as surprised as I was, maybe more. He was brought aboard A-66 and put in front of me to sit on my grenade box. His hands were tied behind his back.

We interviewed him and went through his wallet. He had a picture of his wife and two daughters, who were the same ages as my own girls. He had a Catholic scapular around his neck, like the one I wore. (I suddenly realized that in my haste to move out this morning I forgot my own scapular, bible, horse shoe, and tiny Buddhist prayer book.) Using the interpreter, I asked him why he surrendered, but not his men. He said that his men decided to fight to their death, but since they liked him so much, they wanted him to get home to his family. I asked him why he was here, and he asked me the same thing. Here-to-fore I saw my enemy as evil animals, but suddenly I realized that ***'but for the grace of God, there went I.'***

I couldn't help wondering if roles were reversed, would my men have such an extreme concern for me and my family. It was, however, impossible to understand why he didn't surrender his entire unit and save the lives of all his men. They must have decided this suicide among themselves in advance. The overwhelming power that they were facing surely would justify such a decision for all of them to give up. I suspect it was an issue of Honor. The Oriental mind sees Honor different than we do. As it was, they didn't even wound any of the "A" Troopers. They tried, but they failed. These were brave soldiers. They certainly had grit, and my respect for their Alamo style stand.

We continued our hunt but didn't find more NVA before the helicopter landed in about an hour. When the chopper arrived, I spent some time telling the Master Sergeant on board what was learned from this NVA Officer, and that he had earned my respect; and no harm should come to him. Based on what happened, hopefully he would get home to his family in one piece. This NCO gave me his assurances and departed with our prisoner.

We started back toward Di An. When we were about 3 kilometers from the basecamp, a man in black pajamas was running to the left of A-66, I threw a hand grenade right behind him as he dove into a hole. There was a huge explosion, and my left thigh felt like it had been hit by a hammer. Blood was significantly running out of a hole in my fatigue trousers, so I called for SGT Mims. He was there in less than a minute to put a compress bandage on my leg.

Dragoon 6 radioed the Operations Center at Phu Loi to have the Troop Executive Officer flown to the field to take command. Unfortunately, my XO was very inexperienced and had never even commanded a platoon in the past. This sudden submersion was patently unfair to both the XO and my troopers. With the short distance they had to go, a better choice would have been to simply have one of the Platoon Leaders already in the formation command the Troop into Di An. All the Platoon Leaders had very capable Platoon Sergeants to command their platoons, and this would have only required a couple frequency changes on the radios. As it happened, my XO was dropped onto my command track by surprise and caught Hell from those over-flying the troop's movement all the way to Di An.

The dust-off chopper had arrived in about ten minutes and I was delivered to Di An. As the dust-off chopper lifted off, I was able to get a good look at the hole that I threw the grenade into. It was about 15 feet wide and about that deep. Apparently, I tossed the grenade into an enemy ammunition storage area, and the ammo was ignited by the explosion of my grenade. I felt no sympathy for the Charley. On arrival I was met by my jeep driver at the helicopter pad who delivered me to the Squadron Surgeon.

CPT Leon Cantor did a field x-ray on my wound and it looked like there was a tooth about an inch from the femur in my upper left thigh. He said that it was not against the bone or any other thing he was concerned with. His first inclination was to have me evacuated to the hospital to have the item that looked like a tooth extracted. I objected as this did not seem like a good reason to turn my Troop over to anyone else with all the combat we were facing. He agreed, so long as he could clean out the wound without my screaming bloody murder.

Then he took three long handled cotton swabs and covered the ends with 4"X4" cotton squares, dipped it into Merthiolate, and ran it in and out of my wound several times. I clamped my teeth down on a couple tongue suppressors covered with 4X4s and came very close to yelling. The pain was excruciating but I didn't scream. My driver got excited and pointed his M-16 rifle at the good doctor and I remember his stern warning, *"Your hurting my Daiwe (Captain)!"* I had to restrain him by spitting out the tongue suppressers and yelling **"NO, NO!"** Thank God that worked.

By this time the Troop had arrived, and I limped to my track. I got into my Jeep seat on top of the ACAV and relaxed. CPT Cantor spoke with LTC Tyree and he went to visit MG Ware. I knew nothing of this at the time. In about a half hour LTC Tyree came walking toward my ACAV with a big smile on his face. I jumped off the top of A-66 and landed with most of my weight on my right (good) leg. That hurt, a lot.

LTC Tyree's greeting was *"How's the gout John?"* He informed me that he had just spoke to MG Ware and it was decided that my Headquarters would get three days off in Phu Loi for much needed maintenance and the platoons would be given separate missions during this period. The Headquarters Platoon troopers made comments that they hoped their boss would get hurt more often, as they never had a break since I was commanding the Troop. It wasn't long before we were on the road headed for Phu Loi, escorted by one of the platoons that would work out of that location. The Troop Executive Officer rode in my jeep in the column.

When we arrived, it was time to get cleaned up at the steam bath and get a good massage. Covered by white dust, I crossed the parade field, headed for the steam bath, and forced myself not to limp. Mr. Chin was headed my way and was panicking. Apparently, information about my injury, or worse, had already arrived. He said *"Diawe, you dead!"* He was very alarmed. Apparently, he thought he was talking to a ghost. I told him it wasn't that easy to kill me.

I told him I was there to get cleaned up, and he escorted me into the steam bath. I undressed in the shower room and sat on a stool covering myself with a towel. My favorite massage therapist, Hien, entered and gave me a good scrubbing. I finished the job in appropriate areas and washed the wound which had swollen shut with no leakage.

Then I went to the massage room and lay on my back covering myself with a towel, and a sound sleep overtook me. While being massaged I awoke, but to my surprise there was a long line of Vietnamese women approaching me, one at a time, to lean over me and look at the wound in my left thigh. They were surprised that there was no pain. But of course, I was faking it. You never know where a VC might be, so it was best for them to believe I was invincible, if possible. Hien had to chase them away, so she could finish her work.

What a day. Being exhausted, the break was great. It was needed - a lot. There were three visits to the steam bath, three nights in the Officers Club, several relaxing chats with Major Forbes, hot food and a lot of rest. It was exhilarating - - like being on R&R.

Chapter 66

CLEARING AROUND DI AN

Combined Arms Team

On occasion someone would try to create a combined arms team of a Cavalry Troop and a Vietnamese Infantry Company. I didn't particularly care for that. Confusion wasn't needed on the battlefield, as to who was friendly and who was enemy.

On one memorable occasion, I was sent by jeep to a Vietnamese Army post west of the Di An basecamp to coordinate the use of an ARVN Company the next morning. Upon arrival at a little before dusk, I was led into a small sandbagged bunker complex to discuss the attachment. I was not prepared to sit in an audience of four other officers including an American advisor and watch two Vietnamese Officers humping a couple whores. I was also not agreeable when asked to partake in the fun, and everyone seemed a bit put out by my refusal to join in. I heard of eating or having a drink before business discussions, but this was inappropriate. I was far from a prude, but this was just too much. I gave the map coordinates where I would meet the Infantry company at 0600 and departed wondering just what the Hell I was getting involved with.

Six o'clock came quickly and we found the ARVN Infantry company ready and enthusiastic about riding on a mission. They were just a bit surprised that they had to sit on top of the tracks. It was for their own safety in the event a track hit a mine. They appeared jittery and concerned that they were not being trusted in the protective confines of the tracks. If we hit a mine they would be killed.

I showed the Company Commander the plan of attack on the map, a jungle area that surrounded an old graveyard. There had been reports that Charley had been sighted at the edge of the mixed trees, brush and bamboo stands and we were going to pull up to the tree line in the Box formation to test the area with some 90mm canister rounds before pushing forward. As soon as we got to the tree line, I wanted the ARVN soldiers to deploy between the ACAVs to the rear of the tanks and move forward with the Cavalry as the tanks probed the wooded area by fire, and advanced.

The Vietnamese had a different concept of this operation and as the tanks began to fire and move forward, the Infantrymen began to fade backwards toward the rear of the box formation. Some small arms fire was received from the trees, but it was clear that this was not going to be a combined arms effort. Furthermore, I was worried as to whether these infantrymen were friendly because of their conduct. About that time, I was hit on the index finger knuckle of my right hand by a metal object and it hurt bad and was bleeding all over the place. Later I determined it was a ricochet of a cannister round pellet. It was about a half inch in diameter and almost a half inch long and flat on the ends. The ARVN Commander saw me get hit and became terrified.

I told the Company Commander that if he did not get his men under control and moving forward as planned, I was going to believe they were VC, and blow his friggin head off. By this time my pistol was slid out of my shoulder holster. My gut quickly told me that these ground troopers could not be controlled in a fight, so I directed the ARVN Commander to get them over a rise about 100 meters to the left of the armored vehicles and to keep moving back to their basecamp, which would take the rest of the day. He was all too happy to comply.

The focus returned to the front and the tanks moved forward without further delays. Charley disappeared. When the graveyard and surrounding jungle had been secured, I called in a report and was instructed to inspect the tombs we encountered to see if any weapons were hidden at that location. That began the dumbest exercise I ever conducted to search for enemy weapons.

Inspecting the old stone tombs was non-eventful, except for one slab that had clearly been recently moved on the top of a cement grave site. It took four strong men to slide the slab to where the contents could be examined. Inside there was a green plastic container which perked our interest and it was lifted out for examination. Nothing else was in the tomb. As the heavy plastic was opened, it quickly became apparent from the nostril wrenching stench that this was a container for the decaying remains of some poor soul who did not deserve to have his grave desecrated. Quickly the remains were restored to its resting place and the lid placed back where it came from.

There was not going to be more grave searching. If Charley wanted to hide his weapons among the dead, he was welcome to it. The stench of rotting flesh is not something to be forgotten and discussing it in the future brought facial winces and gaging to those who participated. We searched everywhere for the enemy and his weapons caches, but no more tomb openings.

Chapter 67

JUST WHO WAS OUR ENEMY?

Soon we were given the task of improving Di An's security. Perhaps no experience we had was more devastating to our lives over the long haul than when we received the mission to spray defoliant (Agent Orange) outside of the north perimeter of the Di An basecamp. One morning my Headquarters Platoon and one of the line platoons arrived in Di An to pick up Engineers along with several drums of defoliant and hand sprayers.

The drums were loaded on the Headquarters Platoon's ACAVs, including my own track, and after leaving the basecamp we spread out on line while the line platoon provided security for the operation. We sprayed the chemicals as we slowly moved through the heavy brush and secondary jungle growth outside the Di An perimeter. There was no concern that this chemical would give us cancers and other serious maladies throughout the rest of our lives.

In many ways this was like the poison gas that was used in World War I. The big difference was that the serious harm would occur over the next two decades or more. When we used deadly gas against our enemies in WWI, and the wind blew the poison onto our own soldiers, the injuries from this "friendly fire" were immediately apparent. They were awarded the Purple Heart medal and received appropriate medical care. That's not what happened in our case.

We stood in the back of our ACAV's beside the 55-gallon drums and sprayed these dangerous chemicals in complete trust that the mist from the spray, that was getting all over our arms, faces, necks and clothing, was harmless. We took no precautions whatsoever, and no one gave us any reason to be concerned.

Don't get me wrong, I believe that this defoliant <u>may</u> have been necessary to clear the jungle away from the roads to give us half a chance against ambushes. But we could have brought in more Engineer units with Rome plows to push the jungle away from the roads and keep the foliage knocked down outside the basecamp perimeters. The sick part of this story is that the manufacturer had an obligation to advise our civilian government as to the inherent dangers of Agent Orange. Or did they do this, and it was hidden from us??

This Agent Orange defoliant was also "friendly fire." We just didn't know what it was doing to us or what it could do to our yet to be born children. It was bad enough that we breathed the dust that was kicked up by our tracks in areas that had been previously sprayed from aircraft. But spraying it directly from our ACAVs was even more devastating to our health. Would our military commanders have created such missions that exposed us to such awful health problems if they knew the risks? I doubt it.

Many of my soldiers were severely wounded by this "friendly fire." And the Veterans Administration was terribly reluctant to recognize and treat the cancers and other illnesses they've suffered from these wounds. Additionally, when these chemical wounds are recognized as resulting from service in Vietnam the veteran should receive the Purple Heart medal. To not do so is adding insult to injury.

Our country should be able to do better. The Purple Heart creates a right to receive State benefits, VA benefits and treatment, and be buried in the Arlington National Cemetery as defined in 32 CFR § 553.12. All combat wounded veterans with Agent Orange injuries deserve this as well - - without exception. Who's the Jackass that's holding back on approving these awards?

I've had many of my former troopers die from Agent Orange related cancers and others are suffering from multiple cancers and other devastating illnesses.

All veterans have seen the belated public appreciation shown by politicians thirty or more years after the war. Should we believe they are sincere? I for one am a bit tired of disingenuous gestures. The latest "talk" is that they are going to "fix' the Veterans Administration. I do hope the effort is successful this time.

Even the South Vietnamese government in exile has recognized the injuries caused by Agent Orange by awarding an Imperial Cross of Gallantry with Bronze Star to all Vietnam veterans. Why can't our own government show genuine appreciation? Perhaps it has something to do with the amount of Vietnam War protestors that are in our government.

I'll sum this chapter up with my own very genuine: "Welcome home Vietnam veterans." "Welcome home."

We did receive something special from the Engineers while spraying defoliant outside Di An. It was ten E8 Teargas Launchers. They were a perfect size to mount on the tank searchlights. They had a lanyard and could be used as a counter ambush weapon. There were 60 40mm tear gas grenades that would fly out in an impressive pattern into the face of an ambushing enemy. I was told that they were removed from our searchlights in 1969 after one was hit by an RPG.

Chapter 68

THE 11TH CAVALRY REGIMENT ARRIVES

We often went back to the Catcher's Mitt, to conduct Search and Destroy missions. We kept searching for Charley, but he didn't want to be found. One night we saw the headlights of a huge unit moving through the jungle in a single column. I couldn't believe my eyes. I never saw anything like this. I was informed that this was Colonel George Patton Jr. (son of General George Patton of WWII fame) and his 11th Cavalry Regiment, and the other Squadron elements would be departing at daybreak. "A" Troop would stay behind to act as support to the Regiment. It didn't seem necessary, but orders are orders.

At daybreak everyone departed, and we found ourselves overwhelmed by this huge Regiment of armored units and wondering what our mission would be. It wasn't long before the Regiment's TOC was set up and we were told when the tactical meeting would take place.

Before the meeting, Colonel Patton noticed the E-8 Tear Gas Launchers we had obtained from the Engineers after spraying Dioxin along the northern perimeter of Di An. I told him about the tear gas launchers, and we were ready for any further gas attacks or ambushes that Charley wanted to deal us. We hadn't had an opportunity to use them yet but were looking forward to it.

Colonel Patton asked if we had any extra launchers, so I gave him my extra one. He flew back to his basecamp to check the effectiveness of this weapon. I learned later that he fired it on his own perimeter guards.

A couple months later I came across a Captain from his perimeter guard and he was still pissed that I gave him this weapon. Hell, I didn't know he would do that.

When COL Patton returned, he called all his subordinate Commanders to his TOC. An Australian unit on the southern side of the Catcher's Mitt was under attack. His order was to have "A" Troop lead his Regiment south down LTL-16 past the 2 villages and then to the left on a road to the Aussie NDP. I told him that this road appeared to be heavily mined, but I could lead him there through jungle clearings a lot faster and safer. He exploded, locked my heals, and made some very vulgar and threatening comments. We would be leaving in roughly a half hour.

Bullshit! There was no way I was going to kill or maim a bunch of my troopers. I went straight to my radio and called Dragoon 6 suggesting I contact the Division Commander. He agreed, and I radioed Major General Keith Ware, a level-headed officer who had won the Medal of Honor in Korea. I told him that if I was to obey Colonel Patton's order, we would likely become combat ineffective. He told me that he was detaching "A" Troop and gave me a map grid coordinates to move to immediately, to get us away from the Regiment.

I never called the Division Commander previously and didn't know if I would be successful in solving this problem. But, in my mind I saw a choice between getting detached, taking my unit down that mined road, or moving fast in a different direction. That's a bad position to be in. *Thank you so very much, General Ware.*

Chapter 69

BACK TO THE CATCHER'S MITT

Our Troop was frequently sent back to the Catcher's Mitt to secure the Rome plows. Rome plows are bulldozers made in Rome, Georgia with a special cutting appendage on the side of the blade to rip trees apart. The Engineers were ripping the jungle apart where we did battle in April, and where Captain Serio, SSG Wescott SP5 Lawson and SP5 Bainey and several "B" Troopers and LRRP troopers were killed.

Several plows were ripping down the jungle section by section, and we were making sure that Charley left them alone while they left fallen trees everywhere. It was difficult to move around the area. We had to be very careful. It was easy to get logs stuck in the sprockets of a track when changing directions, with the result of throwing a track. To put it back on was difficult among all the debris.

Soon the Rome plows uncovered huge bunker complexes about 100 feet from the basecamp we over-ran on April 18th This was clearly where COSVN Headquarters had been located. The complex had a series of large rooms, some as large as 10 feet by 10 feet. Above the rooms were up to 5 layers of logs in alternating directions with over a foot of dirt between each layer of logs. At the surface the entrances were invisible, covered like spider holes with vegetation growing over the top of the complex. The NVA left nothing behind. They had cleared out everything when we decimated their guard unit.

Suddenly, an animal dashed out from the underbrush. It looked like a little deer. I told my driver to take chase and soon found the little creature off the side of my ACAV. I pulled off my flak jacket and dove

Vietnamese Mouse Deer

through the air landing next to the animal while wrapping my flak jacket around it. It was a little deer. No sooner had I brought it into the track and climbed back to the top of my ACAV, when another tiny deer ran across our front. The chase was back on, and I bulldogged this little critter from the top of my ACAV as well. It turned out that I had a mated pair of the smallest deer in the world.

I now had my own pair of Vietnamese Mouse (Mice?) Deer. They were about the size of a wild rabbit and close to the same color. The male had small tusks and their hooves were as sharp as knives.

On the few nights we spent in Phu Loi I would put a lawn chair next to their home and enjoy them. They would lick the salt on my sweaty hands and project some peace into my spirit. They were lovely little animals.

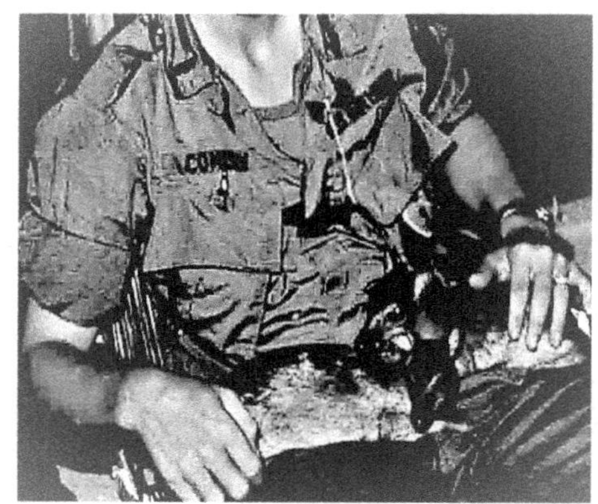
My Babies

When the Rome plows finished their job, we headed for Phu Loi. I turned my deer over to my jeep driver, and he built a great corral, so they would have a proper home. This trooper was from Wyoming and he knew how to take good care of them.

This was perhaps the most unusual and loyal soldier I ever met. He had a steel plate in his head from a combat injury. He was operated on in

Japan and refused to go home, but he successfully returned to "A" Troop and said that he told the doctors he would not go home until his Captain was safely out of Vietnam.

He said I saved his life in a battle. It might have been Fred Shirley, but he was long gone. I don't remember helping him, but things happen fast in combat and it could have happened. This trooper could not be in the field because he could not wear a helmet. I made him my jeep driver, and this jeep was the best looking and best running one in the Squadron. When he would hear that the Troop would be staying overnight in a major base camp, he would wrap a towel on his head, turban style, and with the helmet on top (with extended chin straps) he would get into a convoy, to be in that base camp before we arrived. To see him in that jeep was a sight to behold. What a trooper.

He was wonderful. He became attached to the little deer and it broke his heart when someone left the gate to the corral open and they were gone one morning. This was my fortune down the drain. I could have found a way to get them to the States when I left. But it was best this way, as they would likely become prey to a cat or dog.

Chapter 70

BEST MAINTENANCE CREW ANYWHERE

I've had a lot to say about the efficiency and heroism of our line troopers, but haven't said much about our maintenance troopers. Well, we were about 10 kilometers north of Phu Loi when a tank's engine totally died. Fortunately, we were in a huge open area and a decision was made to let us remain there and pull maintenance for a while. But there was no tank engine in the supply line all the way back to Detroit, Michigan. It was flown out immediately and there was very little preparation we could do while we waited.

CPT Ray Rosenberg our Supply Officer (S-4) had been tremendous in the past. Most memorable was the immediate replacement of forty warped 50 Caliber Machine Gun barrels in a one-week period of heavy fighting, when we were engaged in almost daily heavy combat. Could he get that engine to us before we had to leave that area?

Within a day we were notified that the engine was now in country. Since our VTR was in Phu Loi doing maintenance on another tank, we were on our own to remove the tank's back deck; remove the huge engine and transmission; separate them; attach the new engine and transmission together; put them back in the vehicle; make the attachments; put on the back deck; and start the engine. We were told that a large Chinook helicopter with the engine hanging underneath was on its way from Saigon, and we could use the Chinook to do our heavy lifting. The catch was that we only had an hour to do the work and then we had a mission to go on.

The four troopers on the Maintenance ACAV and the tank crew had everything ready when the Engine arrived. The Chinook sat the engine on the ground and hooked its cables to the tank's back deck. It was lifted and removed, followed by the engine and transmission. We had the Chinook land while the engine and transmission were separated. The Chinook then lifted and switched the old and new engines, and the process was reversed until the engine and transmission were in the vehicle and the back deck was in place. The total time elapsed until the new engine was installed and started, the old engine was flown away, and the vehicle moved forward was 45 minutes. That was phenomenal. What great troopers we had. That was awesome work.

A couple additional comments on these maintenance troopers. They also manned a huge M-85 VTR (Vehicle Tank Retriever) and an ACAV. The VTR is a monster tow vehicle with a heavy-duty wench, lift, dozer blade, and a welder and cutting torch. They were able to do most of the needed maintenance on the Tanks and ACAVs in the field. And they were equipped with 50 caliber machine guns and other weapons making them a formidable force in a battle and in an NDP.

Chapter 71

THE TROOPERS BESTOW A TITLE!

One morning the three Troop Commanders were flown in from the field to participate on a promotion board. I recall that the others on the Board were the Squadron Executive Officer, Major Forbes, and Command Sergeant Major Walter Laverty. All of us Troop Commanders were taken by surprise to be brought in from the field for this event.

The XO's favorite question for each trooper was *"what is the name the troopers call your Troop Commander behind his back?"* This was dirty pool. He had to assure each trooper that he would personally protect them from their commander's wrath, but it still made them very nervous to respond.

In my case the two prevalent answers were "Killer Cong Conley" and "Kick Ass Conley." I've always considered these handles as very complementary badges of honor, although I always preferred "Killer Cong Conley" because I felt that this was as close to a Trooper efficiency report as I was going to get. And a pretty good one at that.

After 50 years that's the name that keeps popping up. Among the nice actions that showed my Troopers' appreciation, in addition to that handle, Doc Dayton ("Steve") Determann carried a pretty red ostrich feather all the way from California to New Orleans to present to me for wear on my Cavalry Stetson. The justification was that Jeb Stewart wore one in the Civil War, and that I had more very successful battles and my unit killed more of the enemy than he did. That was a very nice gesture.

Then when my son, who is a Navy Commander, Ear Nose and Throat Surgeon, came to our reunion in Washington, DC, I overheard Richard ("Richie") Guerine tell my son, *"George, to many of the men at this reunion your father is our all-time hero"*. And my son responded, *"you know Richie, he's always been my all-time hero."* It sure was great to have a son of my biological and extended families express such admiration. And they had no idea I was eavesdropping until I turned around and gave my biological son a big hug.

Chapter 72

WHAT???--INTERCEPT AN NVA ARMOR BATTALION NORTH OF PHU LOI

A big surprise!!   One night an intelligence report came to the Squadron that an NVA Tank Battalion was headed south on LTL-1A, slowly moving through Dog Leg Village. Alpha Troop was selected to intercept that unit.

A big problem existed. There had never been an armor threat in this area and the American tanks were not properly prepared to do a night battle. The sights on the tanks had never been purged with nitrogen since the Squadron was in Vietnam. Therefore, using the sights in conjunction with the search lights at any distance would be suicide. You can bet the NVA sights would be working just fine.

The only other alternative would be to move the Troop into An My village, spread out on one side of the road between the houches (houses) and ambush the enemy column. We would be outnumbered and outgunned, but we would have surprise and our tank's High Explosive ammunition on our side. We would hit them point blank.

God it would be a mess. So many innocent villagers would die, not to mention my own troopers. But the armor unit had to be stopped. It was headed straight for Phu Loi. I advised the Troop on the move what the plan was and the urgency of the matter. Artillery was planned along the road, as we quickly moved into An My and spread the roughly 25 ACAVs out between our 9 tanks. We backed all the tracks off the road between the homes on the east side of the road and shut our engines off. A slight breeze was going to the west which would help us better identify our targets.

All weapons were off safety and poised for battle. Our skin crawled. We knew that in these positions we were also vulnerable to attacks from VC in the village. We waited, and we sweat. We mentally prepared ourselves for the carnage that was about to come. Time slowed. We waited in silence.

Soon we could hear the clank, clank, clank of tank tracks. There was no light, but we could make out that each tank was led (ground guided) by a man on foot. They started to pass my position one at a time, completely unaware of our presence. The tanks were very close together. As they approached the track which was farthest to the south end of the village, I was given the pre-arranged signal.

I then said, ***"ON MY COMMAND - READY."*** The next word that the entire Troop was expecting was ***"FIRE."*** I took a deep breath. Suddenly there was a scream over the Squadron Command frequency that they were a friendly ARVN unit. I knew what the men were expecting and said, ***"STAND DOWN - THEY ARE FRIENDLY."***

No one fired. I quietly thanked God for the discipline of my troopers. I told the Troop to turn on all their headlights. Then I jumped off my ACAV and went onto the road with our interpreter to find the Battalion Commander. They were all very shocked. They were scared. The whole battalion was within our killing zone. The adrenaline in my body was surging. When I found the Battalion Commander he was shocked at the near ambush, and just hadn't considered it important to let anyone know that his unit was on the move.

I replay all of this in my mind on a regular basis. I can't help but consider what would have happened a split second after I said *"FIRE."* I've seen and read of many battlefields with horrendous carnage, but I could only imagine the innocent civilians who would have been slaughtered in their sleep or waking panic. But once started it is unlikely that it could have been stopped.

Thanks be to God. If we had survived, it would have been awfully hard to live with that memory.

Chapter 73

BACK TO PHU LOI

The Troop was finally back home. Our daily activities included convoy security, Rome Plow security, rescuing infantry, and search and destroy missions. Charley decided that it was foolish to tackle the Cavalry and stayed away, although we had to contend with mines and occasional snipers. Life was a lot like mid-1967.

It was nice to get some maintenance time on our equipment and people. Although we were always on alert and ready to move out, Charley cut us some slack and practiced his art of invisibility. I enjoyed sitting in front of my hooch in the evening enjoying my little deer until they departed.

Platoon Leader Training

After the battles in April and May, and the short break after being wounded, LTC Tyree decided that I should break-in all new Platoon Leaders and this continued for a long time. It also meant that all current Platoon Leaders who hadn't received training in the Box Formation were cross attached long enough to be ready to use the new formation regardless of what Troop they were with.

For the new Platoon Leader this normally meant that I had to get the Platoon Leader to meld with his Platoon Sergeant and understand how the formations worked together. Once the Platoon Leader and his Platoon Sergeant worked together and could execute the new formation, there wasn't much more I could accomplish.

I would take them hunting for Charley with my Headquarters and one or two of my own platoons. After taking the attached platoon through the formations including the "Box," I would try to find a small scrap to get into, where I could initiate the new Platoon Leader. I generally could do that during this period. But finding Charley was getting harder and harder and not always possible.

Once a fight started, I would engage the attached platoon. The Lieutenant would usually get a little flustered and indecisive at first. I would ride him to the point where he would get very nervous and aggravated. I would monitor his platoon frequency on my auxiliary receiver, and his Platoon Sergeant could hear what was going on between me and his Platoon Leader.

Eventually his Platoon Sergeant would invariably tell his Platoon Leader on their radio frequency *'why don't you tell that SOB to get off your back?'* If the Platoon Leader took his advice, I would back off and he was ready to be on his own. Being able to take advice from one's Platoon Sergeant is absolutely essential for an Officer to succeed.

Once this happened, I would let the platoon finish their job without interference, and act as their backup. I only had one Lieutenant who was bone headed enough to not be able to meld. I understand he went to an Infantry unit.

The Phu Loi Gate

It's very dangerous for a combat unit to stop at a gate and wait for the Military Police to open it. And the Military Police seemed to see a delay at the gate as a show of their strength and authority. *'We will let them out when we are darned good and ready to do so.'*

To stop at a gate gave Charley the opportunity to be ready to nail the 1st Tank out the gate when the column moved out. I always wanted the gates open at SP Time, so we were not delayed regardless of the amount of dust the tracks kicked up making the turn onto the roadway.

But the Troop and the Platoons were continuously delayed waiting for the gate to be opened. I warned them on several occasions that the gate was not something that could hold us back. LTC Tyree brought our demands to the nightly Phu Loi commander's meeting. Finally, I was not going to wonder if the gate would be open on our arrival. It was time for action.

So, we arrived at the gate about 5 minutes early and herring boned the tracks. It completely covered the road. No one could easily get by the formation. I had the lead Platoon Leader have the lead tank put his radio on the troop frequency, so I could talk to the driver and Tank Commander. I had the Tank Commander lift the main gun above the gate and had the driver ease the tank up to the gate.

1st SGT Escobedo, who was near the rear of the formation called to let me know that MPs in their jeep were trying to get around the tracks, and he asked if he should allow them through. I told him to do nothing to help them, which meant the MPs had to drive their jeep first into one ditch and then into another after crossing the road or drive up the ditch.

In any case, when the time was 0600, I ordered, *"Move Out."* I knew there would be Hell to pay but the morale tradeoff was worth it.

It wasn't long before LTC Tyree flew out to our field position. He didn't appear angry, but he said that the Phu Loi Base Commander was furious and wanted my head. And he wanted our VTR to repair the gate. I told him I couldn't do that for morale reasons and suggested that "B" Troop do this. I could only guess what would happen.

The "B" Troop mechanics made a functional gate out of the scraps, but it wasn't very pretty. And we got a lot of pleasure seeing the gate they put together. It took about a month for a new gate to be acquired. And of course, "A" Troop was not allowed on Phu Loi until the gate was replaced. Was it worth it? ***Hell yes!*** And after that no one had to wait when they got to the gate. Problem solved.

Chapter 74

RESCUING THE AMBUSH PATROL
TRAPPED IN AN ORCHARD

It would be wrong not to account for the worst day in my life. It was after midnight when "A" Troop was called on to assist an Infantry platoon.

We headed out of Phu Loi and dashed north on LTL-16 until we came to a village, which was south of Tan Uyen on the right side of the road. North and south of the village were wet rice paddies. The east side was bordered by the Song Dong Nai river. The west side had high ground by the road.

The tanks could not get in to assist the Infantry as the platoon was in a small orchard with their backs to the river and their front to the open end of a horseshoe of houses. And they came under fire from the houses in this horseshoe.

One platoon, minus the tanks, and my Headquarters ACAVs went along the south side of the village on the higher ground between the village and the rice paddies. The Artillery was coming in on the village when we arrived. They were firing air bursts to minimize the damage to the homes. The helicopter gunships were also attacking targets in the village. The rest of "A" Troop became a blocking force along the road to prevent any VC escape.

We reached the river and turned left into the orchard. The Infantry platoon was spread out across the side of the orchard facing the horseshoe. We quickly joined the infantry, inserting the ACAVs in between their positions. A few of our Headquarters ACAVs including A-66 were spread out behind the Infantry and ACAV line.

Once in position I assumed command of the Infantry platoon, requested the Artillery and gunship support to be suspended and called for a med-evac helicopter. Soon we were evacuating the Infantry dead and wounded.

There were several fires blazing in the village. We waited and waited and there was no enemy activity. We were awaiting a counter attack. About 0300 my platoon leader saw a crouched over person walking very slowly across the open area of the horseshoe toward his track. He was watching this movement through his starlight scope and when he reported I immediately thought that it could be a sapper with a satchel charge. He would toss it into an ACAV and that would be the signal for a VC attack.

Anticipating the worst and hoping for the best, I called the Infantry platoon leader on the radio and asked him to verify that all his men were between the ACAVs. He called back and affirmed that they were all accounted for within our perimeter.

My platoon leader reported that the individual was still approaching directly toward his ACAV and still hunched over. Although my suspicion was telling me that this was the enemy, I once again called the Infantry platoon leader and asked if he had all his men accounted for in the perimeter. He called back again and claimed they were all in the perimeter.

My Lieutenant reported again that he was getting close to the perimeter. I made one final demand that the Infantry Lieutenant verify that all his men were inside the perimeter. He called back and said they were.

Then my platoon leader reported that the man was approaching his track. I said: ***"Kill him NOW!"*** He fired on the man with his M-16, and as he fell, the man said loudly ***"I'm an American!"*** My God what have I done? As it turned out, his friends were covering for this soldier. They knew he went off with a whore before the enemy attacked and kept giving false reports to their platoon leader.

Soon after this I received a report from a track commander on the left side of the perimeter that he was watching a house about 25 feet to his track's front through his starlight scope. He could see people moving around and doing something by the window facing the perimeter. I knew that the non-combatants had been instructed to stay in their hiding spaces under their houses until daylight during fighting, so these were presumed to be enemy soldiers preparing to launch an attack. One of the tracks was within an easy shot by an RPG and I couldn't let that happen.

I ordered the ACAV Commander to fire a burst from his 50-caliber machine gun. He did, and I heard screaming. These were not soldiers. Soldiers would not be screaming like this. He immediately ceased fire. We had killed a young lady and her brother and wounded the Grandmother. They likely felt secure with the Cavalry present and did not appreciate the risk; and it all went wrong. We dusted the Grandmother and her husband off with the American's body when dawn finally arrived. But we listened to the screaming and crying until daybreak. This was the worst night of my life.

After this incident I walked from track to track to talk with the troopers and Infantry. When I arrived at one ACAV I saw three very pale faces and asked who they were. It turns out that SSG Nestor from the S-1 and two other administrative personnel were in the EM Club when we were alerted to move out on this mission. They were dared to come along and did so. I called Major Forbes to be sure they wouldn't be carried as AWOL (Absent Without Leave) when they didn't show up for work in the morning. That took guts, having never been in the field before. I looked at this as an honor that we had stowaways going into a night rescue mission. I'm glad they were not hurt pulling a stunt like this, but I was very proud of them.

Chapter 75

LTC TYREE'S GOING HOME PARTY

I was called in from the field to attend LTC Tyree's going away party. When the helicopter arrived, they dropped off four Red Cross Donut Dollies to visit with the troopers. They were supposed to be picked up by the helicopter that later brought me back to the field. We were also going to send the old barber (Mr. Chin's father), that we kidnaped to give everyone a good trim back to Phu Loi, as his job was done.

I called the Armorer in our basecamp to prepare a nice gift for Dragoon 6 - - a nearly new 9mm Russian Luger that we captured. I got cleaned up and wrapped the Luger and went to the Officers Mess/Club. So, I started out with a few drinks to wet my whistle and clear the dust from my throat. That mellowed me out, so I took a couple drinks to my table and soon started to eat my steak dinner. Oh, the booze was hitting me hard. I wasn't used to it.

LTC Tyree gave a nice speech and then entertained questions. It wasn't long before I was standing and presenting "A" Troop's gift. Tyree happily accepted it. Then I did something stupid. With BG Emil Eshenberg sitting at the head table, I proceeded to thank Tyree for his type of leadership. which allowed "A" Troop to do their thing without excessive command interference, and for providing very appreciated support when we asked for it. Chaplain Doug Bol was tugging on my trouser leg to get me to back off. I finally did, after I made a royal ass out of myself.

Then Dragoon 6 asked me a question. He related to the day we were at the school house (previously discussed). He stated that he knew all his

Troop Commanders had certain codes that he prided himself on figuring out. But the one he couldn't crack was *"Schools out, Dammit, Schools out."*

The room was very quiet. Very, very still. I responded that it would not be a good idea to disclose this. He pleaded and pleaded and said he had finished my officer efficiency rating and told everyone that no matter what the code meant he would not change it. Finally, with those assurances repeated, I relented. I told him that it served two purposes. It alerted my men to look sharp and be sharp. Then it got the whore house in the school closed before he got there. It really wasn't used much at that point anyway.

He was in shock. For a moment his jaw dropped open. Then he said he had a mind go to his office and make significant changes to my efficiency rating. Immediately, General Eshenberg spoke up loudly and said: *"No you won't Tom."* Then Tyree turned and returned to his seat. I'm sure he didn't make any changes (see the Forward or Appendix).

This concluded the dinner and we moved into the Club. I had already drunk too much, but the night was still young.

The party moved into the bar area and the Squadron Surgeon played great rockabilly on the piano. He was hot. It wasn't long until some moron shouted: *"Prepared and Loyal, Sirs"*. This required all the Officers to clamber up onto the bar and sing the 4th Cavalry song (see Appendix). No sooner would everyone get off the bar and he would again yell *"Prepared and Loyal, Sirs"*. This got old after about five times.

So, I just stayed on the bar and had a conversation with the Assistant-Adjutant. Unfortunately, in my less than sober condition, after our chat concluded I forgot I was on the bar, faced left, and took a bold step into the wild blue yonder. On the way down a bar stool with a wooden slat back went under my rib cage on the right side. My breath was knocked out of me and despite the alcohol in my system, the pain was awful.

I doubled over next to the bar to catch my breath and the Squadron Surgeon came over. He determined that I had badly injured some ribs, and he could not wrap them because of the heat and humidity. The choices were to go to the hospital and lose my troop, or to put on my big boy pants and tough it out. I chose the latter.

I was flown back to the field about 0100 and flopped on my cot behind A-66. At 0530 I was awoken because we had to intercept some VC who had attacked a village. I had forgotten that we had some USO girls and a civilian barber in our encampment. But I hadn't forgotten the pain in my side. I wished I could.

We called for a chopper to extract them as we moved out, and before we got to the potential battleground we were able to send the non-combatants on their way. I really didn't care about their being scared. I was in terrible pain.

The enemy had disappeared which didn't break my heart. The extreme pain stayed for a couple months. I cussed my driver for every bump he found - - which were considerable. I never felt so many bumps before the injury. Maybe he was messing with me! Fortunately, the pain subsided in about two months.

Chapter 76

ARTICLE 32 INVESTIGATION

It's awful to be in command when friendly deaths occur. It broke my heart and will haunt me until I die. Why was that platoon put in such a location where they were so vulnerable? And as expected the Brigade Commander initiated an Article 32 of the Uniform Code of Military Justice investigation to examine the matter, as he should have. A Major was appointed as the investigating officer who interviewed everyone involved. Thank God I had called that Infantry Platoon Leader on the radio three times to verify that all his troopers were inside our perimeter.

The findings and recommendations exonerated everyone. But the Brigade Commander sent a formal Letter of Reprimand to me through our new Squadron Commander, LTC John Faith. I sat down in his office to read the letter that was intended to cover the Brigade Commander's ass while destroying my military career. The letter read that "a copy of this reprimand will be placed into your Department of the Army Official Record. *'Chew my ass if you want. I have plenty of scar tissue there, or even whip my ass if you can, but don't ruin my career for something I couldn't avoid.'*

I rebelled by relinquishing my command and demanded a trial by General Court-Martial. I was not going to go home to the United States, with the crap that was going on there, and be hauled into a kangaroo court. I wanted the matter settled while I was with rational friends.

As one could guess, I felt like shit. I was broken hearted. I went to the

Officers Club and ordered a quart of Hague and Hague and started to drink. Chaplain Doug Bol, whose Chapel was next door, was told by someone that I was a mess and he joined me. I told him everything that had happened. He patiently listened. And, about the time I was ordering my second bottle of booze an ACAV pulled up outside the door. In stormed my Track Commander, SP4 Hubbard, to announce that one of my OCS buddies' unit was being attacked and "A" Troop was requested and ready to move out. I told him that I was no longer the Troop Commander, and he said *"Captain, you're not going to have us go into a fight under the command of your Executive Officer, are you?"* Since my Executive Officer was not combat experienced, I knew he was right. Doug Bol said, *"Okay John, what are you going to do now?"*

I got up and staggered my way to the door asking if he brought some coffee. He said he had a mermite can of hot coffee inside the track. It took two of the troopers to assist me into my seat on top of the ACAV. And the M-60 machine gunner spent the next half hour keeping me from falling off the track and filling me with black coffee. The Troop was headed for the Phu Loi basecamp's gate and our ACAV moved smoothly into the formation without any hesitation.

With all the bouncing around, my uniform was a mess by the time we got to the field location where the hostilities were supposedly taking place. The enemy must have got wind that the Cavalry was on the way and departed before we arrived. So, what to do now? I wasn't ready to head back to Phu Loi. My head hurt, and I needed some rest.

I laagered the tracks (like circling the wagons in the old West, but with a hell of a lot more defensive power) and had the Platoons pull maintenance for a while. Strange that no one told me that the Squadron had never sent us out on this mission. As we moved to the field, we reported all the check points as we passed them and no one at the Tactical Operations Center bothered to mention that they knew nothing about this mission. It appeared that my former classmate called directly to the Troop and asked for help. So, as to this deployment, LTC Faith was in the dark. I changed out of my coffee saturated cloths and tried to get a little rest.

In about an hour Dragoon 6, LTC Faith, flew into our circled tracks. I met him at his helicopter. He asked what I was doing commanding "A" Troop after resigning. I told him what happened and was told he had been talking to the Division Commander, Major General Ware, about my resignation and demand for a court martial. General Ware said he would send a Warrant Officer from Division out to collect all the copies of that letter before it left Vietnam if I returned to my command and dropped my request for a General Court-Martial. That ended that issue.

Chapter 77

R&R to Okinawa

It was August 1968 and my R&R was at hand. I was going to visit Okinawa. With my Vietnam experience drawing quickly to an end, I needed to make arrangements for my wife and daughters to return to the United States. How could this wonderful visit with my in-laws find a way to turn completely into shit!?

When I arrived on Okinawa I stayed at my sister-in-law's home and visited friends and family on Okinawa and the island of Hama-Higa. It was a wonderful experience.

We went to Yakina Harbor and caught a taxi boat to Hama to visit with my good friend Shinsho and his family. Shinsho was a teacher of Okinawan dance as well as a boat taxi owner and was in the fields training the men away from distractions of everyday life. There were local and national competitions in folk dancing and Hama had won more than one of the annual Japanese national championships.

Shinsho was surprised to see us, and we spent a lot of time with him and his wife Masiko and their two boys, who were my girls' ages. Then we were invited to the island's dance ceremony. It started just after dark and went late into the night. It was awesome. It was like a parade starting with dances of the old folks. Then the children and the men. Finally, all the men (except myself) were dismissed for the dance of the maidens. It was all so fantastic. This was followed by singing and dancing to the beating of the drums and music of the Samisams. It was delightful. The women and children eventually went home, and the Saki became more plentiful. The men danced and sang at full pitch until about 2 AM. Many just went to sleep in place. Some, including myself and Shinsho, made determined moves for his home. I don't remember any mosquitos, so you could drop anywhere and sleep. They wouldn't dare swallow the blood of any of these guys, if they were there at all. Shinsho passed out and I carried him home in a fireman's carry. He was like a rock, but I stumbled across the school yard and dumped him inside of his house.

The plan was for me to stop in Okinawa when I left Vietnam and gather my family up for the trip home. After completing the arrangements, I caught my flight back to Vietnam. I had not yet begun to hurt but didn't understand the depression that was deepening as Vietnam came into view.

Chapter 78

SAD RETURN FROM R&R

There was nothing exceptional about the landing and I headed for Phu Loi. As I got to the Squadron  Headquarters and saw the American flag at half-mast my depression was understood. Something awful had happened while I was away. Damn it! While I was gone my platoons were sent on independent missions, and that's when it  happened.

Gary G Pool

LT Robert Gillespie, Jr

I always taught never to use the same trail twice. Charley would plant  a mine hoping you would use the easy route at the end of the day. The trail you cut in one direction would be the easy way to return. And it could be your last. And that's what I was told happened. On August 11, 1968 my new Platoon Leader, First Lieutenant Robert James Gillespie, Jr., returned from guarding Rome plows on the same trail he went out on in the morning. His ACAV hit an anti-tank mine and he was killed along with his troopers Gary G. Pool and William L. Debo. Such nice young men with their whole lives ahead

William L. Debo

of them. Staying alive in Vietnam didn't allow for mistakes. I was angry beyond reason, and I wanted revenge.

324

Chapter 79

VERY CLOSE TO AN ATROCITY

The cowardly mine attack happened near the village not far from Phu Loi on the road to Di An. This is the village where the north-south trail from Xom Moi (2) intersects with the east-west road south of the Phu Loi gate. Xom Moi (2) is where we had the big battles in early May. This was Charley's payback and I wanted mine. I know *"vengeance is Mine sayeth the Lord."* But I wanted mine as well. I was too angry to think straight. My mind was scrambled. I took the Troop south of this village.

There I found a large group of Villagers in a field next to a wooded area. I moved the Troop into a perimeter next to the woods and had my troopers gather the villagers into a bunch for interrogation. After some miserable failures talking to the villagers, and sure that someone here knew who placed the mine that killed our troopers, I went to Plan B.

I moved the villagers (about 50+) on one side of a small rise. Then I had them brought to me one at a time. When the Interrogator failed, I had each villager kneel and place his/her head over a log. They were obedient. Then I threatened with my machete to lop off his/her head while the interrogation continued. Finally, I would sink the machete into the log to make a noise that could be heard by the rest of the group. I would then have the villager moved away and be replaced by another.

I did this repeatedly with no success. Then a villager, when his head was placed over the log looked at me and laughed in a sneering way. I drew back the machete and brought it down as hard as I could toward his neck. Suddenly, I heard my mother say, ***"No Johnny - don't do it."***

I stopped within an inch of his neck. He was no longer sneering, and I was in shock as to what I almost did. No one had stopped me, and it was good fortune that I pulled away from the demon that was driving me. I was shaken.

I called all the villagers together and sincerely apologized for my conduct, which had insulted their dignity and my own. They graciously accepted my apology and we went our way. I was ashamed, but wiser. Years into the future I was to be confronted by what happened in the life of Lieutenant Calley while under extreme stress.

But for the Grace of God there I did not go. But such sadness, such misery. It was clearly my time to leave this war. My mind was twisted, and the stress was winning.

Chapter 80

THE BIRTHDAY BASH

Never would there ever be a more fantastic Birthday Party. I would be leaving Vietnam on Friday; September 13 and it couldn't come too soon. I had mixed emotions, but for my biological family I would have stayed until the end of the war. The replacement Commander, CPT G. Gram Poole, was ready to take over the unit. I knew he would be a fine troop commander.

From left: LTC Faith, LT Prichard, CPT Conley, CPT Poole, MAJ Murchinson, LT Bache

It was September 10, 1968, and I was now 26 years old and to over 140 of our country's best warriors I was the "Old Man." I had reached the pinnacle of my existence here on earth. All else would be anti-climactic. And I felt like an "Old Man."

The Troop was at Phu Loi for the change of command ceremony. It was well organized including the presentation by LTC Faith of some awards. Lest I fail to mention it, it was a great honor to have served under LTC John Faith, who retired as a Major General after a very distinguished career.

This ceremony was followed by a terrific Birthday party. A jeep trailer was full of iced down beer and with a pile of fresh beer cases nearby. The barbeque barrels were putting out steaks as fast as they could cook. And our Cook had all the fix-ins, potato salad, baked beans, etcetera, etcetera. And there was the most fabulous Birthday Cake. Before the day was over, I was given a briefcase from the Troopers and a drawing showing the destruction of the Phu Loi gate. Very, very touching.

If you can't read the captions, I'm called

"DEVASTATOR SIX" and the caption says, *"I told those mothers to have it open!"*

I was talking with Gram Poole about how to set up and execute an Armor Cavalry ambush. We were well pickled when we approached LTC Faith with a plan. There was only one part of Gram's training that was incomplete. He never had the pleasure or fear of being on an ambush patrol yet and we felt this was necessary, so he could feel what the troopers felt like when he sent them out on an ambush patrol. LTC Faith agreed and we went into the planning phase. With only one day to execute the plan, we had to get right on it.

Chapter 81

One Last Ambush

Ambush training for Captain George Gram Poole went fast. On the morning of September 11th, I showed him how to make a couple Fu-Gas bombs with 90mm canisters filled with napalm. The canisters were then wrapped with 2 wraps of det (detonation) cord with an electrical fuse, wire and a hand clacker (not attached) from a claymore mine. These were put in an ACAV to be taken to the ambush site, along with several claymore mines.

After selecting ten good men who would be on the ambush patrol, we departed Phu Loi and headed to the area north of Xom Moi (2). We scouted around this area until we found a good spot to set up along the north-south trail.

We laagered the Troop and had C's for lunch. We left 2 troopers at this location in the bushes in a hidden position, and everyone was briefed on where we would be along the trail and where the Fu-Gas Bombs and Claymores would be setup after dark. We left the troopers with a PRC 25 radio, so in case they were detected they could call the Troop which would be scouting the area nearby.

When we left the cite, we searched for a place to put the Troop after the ambush patrol was dropped off at dusk. Then we had our dinner C-rations. We were fortunate to locate a staging area about 300 meters away, where the Troop could quickly get to the ambush patrol if contact was made. And then we plotted Artillery check points to quickly bring in Artillery fire if needed at the ambush site.

At dusk we drove past the ambush site and the ambush patrol left the tracks. The Troop moved out under the command of a platoon leader, and they went to the staging area to await their summons.

With the ambush set up, we lay along the side of the trail in silence, only periodically reporting our status by clicks on the PRC 25 handset.

It was a long night. All I could think of was going home and hoping for some payback one last time. We waited and waited.

I was not able to verify my recollection that we popped the ambush that night. But I am sure that the new Troop Commander, Gram Poole, ended up with an armor ambush as a part of his Commander's tool kit, and had an appreciation of what it was like for the troopers he sent on an ambush patrol.

Gram's break-in period was complete, and I was convinced that my mental faculties were of no further use to the war effort. Who in their right mind would go on an ambush patrol with only a day to go in Vietnam, and of my own volition. I spent September 12th doing the required signing out procedures and got a good night's sleep.

Chapter 82

MY FRIDAY THE 13TH

The Troop left early to accompany a convoy north to An Loc and beyond to the Loc Nihn area. I stood and saluted each track as they

A new A-6 (CPT G. Gram Poole and A-6R (1st SGT Natividad Escobedo) with Red Dog and Trooper

passed by. It hurt - - a lot.

About an hour after they left, I was ready to travel. It was to be my last Jeep ride in Vietnam. My driver had his M-16 rifle and I had my AR-

15 for company along with the radio mounted on the jeep and an Aux receiver. I put the Radio on the Squadron frequency and the Aux on the Division's.

It felt enjoyable and comforting to be going home. I felt spent. When we passed Di An and was nearly to the paved road to Bien Hoa there was suddenly a tremendous amount of chatter on the Squadron and Division frequencies. A helicopter had been shot down and all on board were killed.

It was too far away for a clear radio transmission. But there was radio talk from the choppers to Lai Khe and Di An. Finally, it became clear. The Division Commander's helicopter had been shot down north of An Loc. Major General Keith Ware was dead along with all the Staff members on his chopper and his beautiful white German Shepard companion. The Division would never be the same. Such a terrible loss.

Friday the 13th was awful for the Division. MG Ware was one of the finest Generals I would ever know. He was gone, but as the fortunes of war would have it, I was heading home. We both would be free but in different ways. May God Bless his immortal soul and all the others on his helicopter.

When I was at the Bien Hoa Officers Club waiting for my freedom flight home, three pilots sat down at an adjacent table. I thought I recognized a voice and approached them. Sure enough, I met the Red Barron in person, at last. We had some drinks together and if my recollection is correct, he bought them all. What a coincidence. Over a year and a half, first he brought news of my child being born, then he made a bad beginners mistake of strafing my combat formation, and finally I got to spend some time with him for a little reconciliation before going home. He's a good man.

Chapter 83

WELCOME HOME TROOPERS

At last my war was over and I successfully met my Right of Passage. I was and am proud of what we accomplished.

I was satisfied I had done the best job I could do. To stay longer would have either got me killed or mentally screwed up. And I already felt the pangs of mental wear and tear. It's odd that no one else saw that I was close to going off the deep end.

I carry the scars of some of my troopers being killed and severely wounded. But I don't feel like I personally contributed to that through stupidity or poor leadership. I fought my piece of the war as skillfully as I knew how and held nothing back. All the Cavalrymen I served with did the same.

Sometimes I was guilty of immature conduct. But none of my snap judgements got anyone hurt. Considering that like everyone else, I was growing up while on the job, and I sometimes acted quite shamefully, I thank the Lord for protecting me and my men through it all. Anyone who says that an Officer doesn't mature through this process is nuts.

And I can look back on the challenges and advice of my Officers, NCOs and EM for a great deal of my growth. Watching their astounding conduct and decision making rubbed off on me, and I hope they all benefitted from my ability to be decisive, flexible, deliberate and, as taught in the Marines, to improvise.

Much of our success was the result of inventing tactics that fit both the safety of the troops and the accomplishment of the mission. In short, we improvised and outsmarted an enemy that had learned how to outsmart us. It's interesting that former SP5 Bill Butler (a good trooper) recently discovered a Box or Block Formation that was used by a Cavalry unit to move a wagon train through hostile Indian territory. And of course the great Roman Legions had a Phalanx formation that was nearly impenetrable. I have been asked if I copied my Box Formation from History, but all I did was to determine what was safest and what would get the job done. Just common sense. My Box formation nearly got me laughed out of the Armor Officers Career Course, but those amateurs could go screw themselves. They needed to internalize the "Nine Principles of War" and not be afraid to improvise. Your enemy knows your tactical books. And winning is more than what's in those books. So, IMPROVISE!

Can you find the Box Formation in these Principles?

The Nine Principles of War

Mass…Concentrate combat power at the decisive place and time.
Objective…Direct every military operation towards a clearly defined, decisive, and attainable objective.
Economy of force…Allocate minimum essential combat power to secondary efforts.
Offensive…Seize, retain, and exploit the initiative.
Surprise…Strike the enemy at a time, at a place, or in a manner for which he is unprepared.
Maneuver…Place the enemy in a position of disadvantage through the flexible application of combat power.
Unity of command…For every objective, ensure unity of effort under one responsible commander.
Security…Never permit the enemy to acquire an unexpected advantage.
Simplicity…Prepare clear, uncomplicated plans and clear, concise orders to ensure thorough understanding.

I trust that my frequent colorful language didn't harm the sensibilities of our fine young men, but if it helped get the job done at times, I have no regrets. I never reached the height of profanity of some very successful Officers of the past, so if anyone's feelings were hurt, I really don't give a shit. The proof's in the pudding (dead enemy, and alive cavalrymen).

In writing this book, I was deeply saddened by the loss of so many fine young men. It has broken my heart that the fortunes of war took so many and maimed so many more.

I've reflected on the guilt and mental agony many have brought home, while many Americans never carried the scars of war, or avoided it in Canada. Many of us screwed up our relationships with others because of our PTSD. Just remember, you did your best for your country, and the Good Lord allowed us to survive, so be grateful and keep punching. Treat your mental scars as badges of honor. You earned them.

Nearly half the citizens of our country carry the twisted progressive beliefs of Fondaism. And they will control our country if we don't keep vigilant. Don't let these nincompoops take away what you fought for so gallantly.

And feel free to contact me. I have lost contact with so many wonderful warriors and sincerely miss you all.

As I said at the beginning of this book, I may have got some matters wrong that I've written about. But I have done my best considering that these events took place a half century ago. I am grateful for everyone who aided my recollection.

And of course, *'Thank You'* to all who have read this story. I hope you enjoyed it.

And **WELCOME HOME TROOPERS!!**

End of Part II

THE CAVALRYMAN'S

RITE OF PASSAGE

PART III

APPENDIX

Wrapping It Up

For the experiences I had in Vietnam, and throughout my life, I am thankful for the memories.

For those I have helped, I am eternally grateful for that opportunity.

For those I have harmed, I sincerely beg your forgiveness.

And as to my Lord Jesus Christ, I trust in Your mercy, and thank You for Your love and kindness.

AUTOBIOGRAPHY

It began on September 10, 1942. I came from humble beginnings. My father, George Ernest Conley, went to Fort Wayne in Detroit, Michigan to report for the Draft. He had in his hand a hand-written Birth Certificate for his first and only son, John Ernest Conley. Yes, I was born earlier that morning and I was his fourth child. There was an exemption from service for men with four children, and I was the magic ticket.

They sent him home with the instructions to keep sending those vehicles to the front. At the time my father worked at Eaton Springs Company, and his job was essential with the Country on a full-scale war footing.

Unfortunately, he lived with serious regrets over not being able to participate in WWII. This was obvious at many junctures in my life when he would tell me how I saved his life with my timely birth.

"When Johnny Came Marching Home Again" it was a "Big Time in the Old House" again, with heroes galore, the drums kept beating. My father carried guilt for not going, and I carried it for not allowing him to go.

That's how I grew up, with a good attitude toward military life and a deep respect for all my uncles and the fathers of my friends who served during WWII. I had a great attitude toward military men and held them high on a pedestal. I had three older sisters. Virginia was the eldest and our mother hen. She was the serious sibling. Eunice was about two years younger than Virginia and Clara about two years younger still. I was a couple years younger than Clara.

We all went to the Catholic School for grades 1 through 6 and developed a good appreciation for what was right and wrong. Getting religion would help me overcome fear throughout my life, and I could easily appreciate the difference between good and evil.

Don't ever get me wrong, I was no saint, but I did learn some basics like it's human to fall, and okay to get back up again; there is no compromising with evil; all people do wrong (not just me); evil can never be good; justification of evil is evil; and giving and getting forgiveness is virtuous.

I learned that I needed time alone to think deeply and grow. That, and my sisters wanting to use me as the baby in their girlie games, led me to seek aloneness in the fields near my home north of Detroit. And I learned there to appreciate nature and helping the helpless, which fostered my sensitivity and a desire to take a stand against evil in all its forms. Eventually, the fields of my youth weren't big enough and wander lust set in. I was starving for adventure.

I left the nest and experienced extreme loneliness as a seventeen-year-old US Marine. There, I prepared for war. "I learned to do so much with so little, I could do almost anything with nothing." I learned to improvise and to lead men. I built guts and that "once a Marine, always a Marine" attitude. I learned to destroy Tanks and Bunkers, and how my enemy thought. I became an expert with flame throwers,

106mm recoilless rifles, and the Ontos anti-tank weapon. And became thoroughly familiar with the Jungle and oriental people.

I married Toyoko, a lovely girl from the Island of Okinawa, and made many friends in the nearby island of Hama-Higa. I became a Marksmanship Training Instructor, SCUBA Instructor, Life Guard Instructor Trainer, Water Safety Instructor Trainer and First Aid Instructor.

As I promised my father, I obtained my High School GED and Diploma before leaving the Marines, but I had no college until after Vietnam.

Civilian factory life didn't suit me, so I joined the Army and became a Tank Commander in Germany. My first child, Irene was born while I was freezing my butt off in a German winter. After nine months in Germany, I returned to Ft Benning, GA to be an Officer Candidate. As a 2nd Lieutenant I went to Airborne School, then to Armor Officer Basic and on to the Cavalry in the 101st Airborne Division at Ft Campbell, Kentucky.

Nearly a year later, after becoming a Jumpmaster and visiting the Panama Canal Zone to become a Jungle Expert, I went to Vietnam to become an Armor Cavalry Platoon Leader in the 1st Squadron, 4th Cavalry ("Quarterhorse"), of the famous 1st Infantry Division. My second Child, Maria, was then born while we provided security for convoys along the Cambodian border.

After 1.5 years in Vietnam I went to the Armor Officers

Career Course. My father died 4 months after I returned from Vietnam and 5 months later my 3rd child, George, was born. Then on to the University of Tampa (major in History); Korea; Ft Hood, Texas; Jackson, Mississippi District Recruiting Command and retirement. While in Jackson I completed a Master of Science and Business Management degree from the American Technological University, aka University of Central Texas.

After retirement I lived in Miami and then Lynn Haven, Saint Petersburg, Clearwater, Brooksville and finally New Port Richey; - all in Florida. And I married my second wife, Stephanie.

I went to the University of Florida and obtained a Juris Doctorate Degree. This served me well until I was forced to retire because of medical issues in 2008.

That's about the long and the short of it.

The Cavalryman's Great Grandmother's home

Trooper Comments

"One thing to think about — there are a lot of other people out there whose lives you made possible by your leadership and the good decisions you made."
Carl "Skip" Bell, Colonel, US Army Retired
9/18/2017

"I think about you being a great combat officer . . . I'm really glad we had you for our troop commander. Some officers I ran across could not have come close to performing like you did."
SP4 Bill Butler
5/4/13

"I remember you saying something like: 'Today we are going after COSVN HQ's, then straight to Hanoi to kick some ass.' If only they had let you!"
SP4 Steve Row (deceased)
6/14/01

"There were a number of times I would've wished you were not quite so damned good at finding "Charlie" as it seemed you were, but that aside I had the highest respect for you, and I remember one conversation over there where some of us EM were talking one night and we mutually agreed, regardless of what we felt about the war we would have followed you most anywhere."
SGT Rob Ferguson (deceased)
7/3/00

VIETNAM AWARDS

INDIVIDUAL AWARDS:
Bronze Star Medal - for meritorious service from February 1967 to January 1968, (GO 358)
Army Commendation Medal - for meritorious achievement from November 1-9, 1967, (GO 843)
Bronze Star Medal, 1st Oak Leaf Cluster - for meritorious achievement from March - April 1968, (GO 4698)
Silver Star Medal - for gallantry in action on 18 April 1968, (GO 5874)
Silver Star Medal, 1st Oak Leaf Cluster - for gallantry in action on 4 May 1968 (GO 8163)
Silver Star Medal, 2nd Oak Leaf Cluster - for gallantry in action on 5 May 1968 (GO 8567)
Silver Star Medal, 3rd Oak Leaf Cluster - for gallantry in action on 5 May 1968 (GO 12227)
Bronze Star Medal, 2nd Oak Leaf Cluster with "V" Device for heroism on 6 May 1968 (GO 8455)
Purple Heart Medal - for wounds received in action against a hostile force on 11 May 1968 (GO 9813)
Vietnamese Cross of Gallantry (with Bronze Star) - for Excellent and Courageous actions, 7/10/68
Bronze Star Medal, 3rd Oak Leaf Cluster - for Meritorious service from 3/1968 - 8/1968 (GO 8780)

UNIT AWARDS:
Valorous Unit Award
Vietnamese Cross of Gallantry (with Palm)
Vietnamese Civil Action Unit Citation (with Palm)

PRIVATE AWARDS:
Imperial Nguyen Dynasty of Vietnam, Cross of Gallantry (with Gold Star) - February 18, 2007

Vietnam Officer Efficiency Ratings/Recommendations

Special Efficiency Rating as Platoon Leader

Lt John Conley has led his platoon in an outstanding manner. In combat situations, he has provided inspired and professional leadership. He has participated successfully in many types of ground tactical missions in the Quan Loi area, to include search and destroy, convoy security, search and seal of villages, road running operations, and perimeter defense. On several operations, he commanded not only his own platoon, but attached infantry and tank platoons as well. Twice, for three day periods, he commanded the company team in the absence of the company commander. His aggressiveness, tireless energy, and enthusiasm insured success on each mission.

His performance in combat has been faultless. During one reconnaissance, his elements received small arms fire from a heavily wooded area. Lt Conley rapidly assessed the situation, realized that his armored vehicles would be at a disadvantage in the heavy jungle, called for and directed artillery and light fire team support upon the point of contact. Following completion of the fire support, Lt Conley returned to the area of contact and reconed the area thoroughly. His conduct in the action had been cool, correct, and professional.

The trademark of an armored officer is rapid reaction. Lt Conley displays this attribute to the highest degree. He has trained and led his platoon in such a manner
(See Continuation Sheet.)

that they responded rapidly to any alert or special mission. In addition, Lt Conley insured that his men and his equipment were always ready to function. Lt Conley was fair and just in the discipline of his men. It was because of his leadership that his men attained the high standards he had set for them. In the field of maintenance, Lt Conley personally supervised the efforts of the crews to insure that the maximum number of combat vehicles were operational. Only the lack of repair parts caused a temporary deadline among his vehicles.

As a junior first lieutenant, 1LT Conley is an outstanding combat leader. I fully recommend him for advanced military schooling and for promotion ahead of his contemporaries.

CLAUDE J. CLARK, 090721,
CPT, Armor
Commanding
Co B, 2d Bn, 34th Armor

Regular Rating as a Platoon Leader

Lieutenant Conley was an outstanding cavalry platoon leader. He has a thorough grasp of cavalry tactics as applied to all facets of counterinsurgency operations. The employment of his platoon was characterized by professional thoroughness in planning and execution. In addition the standards of maintenance in his platoon were the highest in the troop, resulting in a consistently high percentage of operational combat vehicles. His platoon was frequently detached from the troop, and during these periods Lieutenant Conley was commended for his cooperation and advice on proper employment of his platoon by the commanders of those units to which he was attached.

Lieutenant Conley has shown that he is capable of operating for extended periods of time with a minimum of supervision and accomplishing assigned missions with limited resources.

16 ENDORSER   ☐ I AM UNABLE TO EVALUATE THIS OFFICER FOR THE FOLLOWING REASON:

I agree in general with the remarks in paragraph 15, above. I observed Lieutenant Conley closely on several ocassions when his platoon was operating separately in a forward combat area approximately 90 kilometers from the squadron base. He was forceful, resourceful, and in complete command of every aspect of his platoon from its operational readiness to the status of laundry service available to his men. He exhibited a grasp of the entire panoply of command considerations seldom found in officers of his grade. Only part of the reason for this exceptional performance is to be found in Lieutenant Conley's enlisted experience: Most of it is attributable to his inate initiative and aggressiveness.

Because of his outstanding performance as a platoon leader Lieutenant Conley was selected to be executive officer of his troop. His professional knowledge and high leadership qualities commend him for attendance at the career course and selection for command duty.

PART VII - AUTHENTICATION (Read paragraph 211, AR 623-105)

17 SIGNATURE OF RATER   DATE

25 Sept 67

TYPED NAME, GRADE, BRANCH, SERVICE NUMBER, ORGANIZATION, AND DUTY ASSIGNMENT

WILLIAM F. MURPHY, CPT, Armor, 090978, Trp B, 1st Sqdn, 4th Cav, 1st Inf Div, APO San Francisco 96345, Troop Commander

18 SIGNATURE OF INDORSER   DATE

4 Oct 67

TYPED NAME, GRADE, BRANCH, SERVICE NUMBER, ORGANIZATION, AND DUTY ASSIGNMENT

JOHN W. SEIGLE, LTC, Armor, 068710, Headquarters, 1st Sqdn, 4th Cav, 1st Inf Div, APO San Francisco 96345, Commanding

1st Rating as Troop Executive Officer

Lieutenant Conley's performance in an extremely demanding assignment has been consistently outstanding. He has been charged with coordinating all administrative support for the troop. This was complicated by having at least one platoon detached at all times, and was accomplished with extremely limited resources. When the troop replaced almost all its combat vehicles with new ones during a three day period, the uninterrupted combat effectiveness of the unit was evidence of the careful planning and attention to detail that are characteristic of all his undertakings. Due to the nature of the unit's employment, Lieutenant Conley operated with a minimum of supervision. He is capable of analyzing very general instructions, determining the requirements, and developing a logical plan. In addition he is not content to wait for tasks to be assigned, and frequently initiates worth-while projects on his own initiative. Lieutenant Conley should be considered for attendance at the Career Course as soon as possible, and is fully qualified to command a troop or company.

l INDORSER   ☐ I AM UNABLE TO EVALUATE THIS OFFICER FOR THE FOLLOWING REASON:

I agree in general with the rating officer's assessment of Lieutenant Conley's performance of duties. Lieutenant Conley is a "self-starter" who works diligently and well with an absolute minimum of supervision. He was selected to be a troop executive officer because of the high quality of his performance as a platoon leader. His work has lived up to the expectations which were placed in him. Without instructions or supervision, as an example, he recently organized the efforts of a detached platoon preparing for a CMMI with such skill and in such detail that the unit scored well over 90% in the critical areas pertaining to moving, shooting, and communicating. Lieutenant Conley should be selected for the career course as soon as eligible.

SIGNATURE OF RATER

DATE 6 Nov 67

TYPED NAME, GRADE, BRANCH, SERVICE NUMBER, ORGANIZATION, AND DUTY ASSIGNMENT

WILLIAM F. MURPHY, CPT, Armor, 090978, Trp B, 1st Sqdn 4th Cav 1st Inf Div, APO San Francisco 96345, Troop Commander

18. SIGNATURE OF INDORSER

DATE 8 Nov 67

TYPED NAME, GRADE, BRANCH, SERVICE NUMBER, ORGANIZATION, AND DUTY ASSIGNMENT

JOHN W. SEIGLE, LTC, Armor, 068710, Headquarters, 1st Sqdn, 4th Cav, 1st Inf Div, APO San Francisco 96345, Commanding.

2nd Rating as Troop Executive Officer

15. RATER

LT Conley's performance of duty as troop executive officer was that of a devoted professional. He was in charge of all rear detachment activities to include supply, maintenance support, laundry, administration, statt coordination and base camp development and defense. His discharge of his responsibilities in each of these areas was outstanding. LT Conley's knowledge of techniques utilized in the various fields of combat support, combined with his ability to organize men and materials to have them at the proper place at the proper time under combat conditions, contributed immeasurably to the accomplishment of the unit mission. His desire and ability personally stay abreast of the tactical and administrative situation and to react to change and to solve problems without supervision are his greatest assets. LT Conley is a very, very energetic and dedicated officer. I recommend he be considered for selection to the career course at the earliest possible date and integrated into the regular army.

16. INDORSER   ☐ I AM UNABLE TO EVALUATE THIS OFFICER FOR THE FOLLOWING REASON:

1LT Conley has performed his duties of Executive Officer of a Cavalry Troop in combat in an exemplary manner. This officer's loyalty, devotion to duty, and professional competence is outstanding. He was materially instrumental in transforming a somewhat lackadaisical, loosely run unit into one with high standards and invariably outstanding operational performance. Moreover, he has exhibited a detailed knowledge of vehicular maintenance seldom found to such an extent in young officers. He bears up well under stress and his personal valor and sound judgment under fire is beyond question. This young, clean cut, forceful, dedicated, professional officer has accomplished every aspect of his job with outstanding results.

17. SIGNATURE OF RATER   DATE

Edward B. Bryson   21 May 1968

TYPED NAME, GRADE, BRANCH, SERVICE NUMBER, ORGANIZATION, AND DUTY ASSIGNMENT

EDWARD B. BRYSON, CPT, Armor, 096334
Trp B, 1st Sqdn, 4th Cav, 1st Inf Div   Troop Commander

18. SIGNATURE OF INDORSER   DATE

Barney K. Forbes   12 Jun 68

TYPED NAME, GRADE, BRANCH, SERVICE NUMBER, ORGANIZATION, AND DUTY ASSIGNMENT

BARNEY K. FORBES, MAJ, Armor, 077022
HQ, 1st Sqdn, 4th Cav, APO SF 96345, Executive Officer

Letter of Recommendation

TROOP B
1ST SQUADRON, 4TH CAVALRY
APO San Francisco 96345

SUBJECT: Letter of Recommendation   30 January 1968

TO: Commanding Officer
         1st Squadron, 4th Cavalry
         1st Infantry Division
         APO San Francisco 96345

    First Lieutenant John E. Conley has served as a cavalry troop executive officer under my command for the past four months. During this period, I have observed him to be the most outstanding company grade officer I have served with, or known, during my six years of service in armor. He is a professional soldier and officer in every sense of the words. In military matters, his thought processes are fast, his judgement superior and his actions immediate and complete. I have never observed a man with more complete follow through and flexibility to accomplish a mission than Lieutenant Conley. His personal traits and moral posture are superior and without question in the eyes of his superiors, contemporaries, and subordinates. In short, Lieutenant Conley has the personal traits which make him an outstanding officer and leader.

    During his tour in Vietnam, Lieutenant Conley served his first five months as a cavalry platoon leader. The first three months of this assignment were spent on an independant mission for which he was highly praised for his initiative, resourcefulness, and responsiveness in finding and solving problems inherent to the employment of a cavalry platoon independently for a period of months. In August 1967, Lieutenant Conley was assigned as troop Executive Officer. Under the current situation, he is required to operate the base camp, orderly room, supply, mail, and base defense in addition to his responsibilities as the troop maintenance officer in the field. Lieutenant Conley has performed his functions in a highly efficient manner (most of this period was without a troop First Sergeant). In addition, he has constantly been tabed by the Squadron Executive Officer to perform time consuming tasks requiring a highly capable officer who could act independently. An example of this was the investigation and resulting evection of a civilian laundry operating on post. His investigation and recommended actions were complete, accepted, and executed in highly efficient manner and without repercussions.

    This officer is extremely capable and constantly works to improve himself and his unit. I have no doubt that Lieutenant Conley will earn his college degree in a minimum of time and with a very high standing. I highly recommend this officer for appointment and integration into the regular army at the earliest possible time.

EDWARD B BRYSON
CPT, Armor
Commanding

1st Regular Rating as Troop Commander

RATER

Captain Conley is a hard-punching, fearless officer who has commanded his Cavalry troop in combat in an outstanding manner. His predecessor was killed in action, so Captain Conley had no period of overlap or break-in. Yet he was completely in command of his troop from the moment he arrived on the scene. In fact, he received a congratulatory message from General Westmoreland (the first of two such messages sent to Captain Conley) for an action which occurred within a week of the time he took command. Captain Conley is cool under fire, is quick in reaction, and has good judgment. He has great potential for high rank and responsibility. I strongly recommend(Cont.

INDORSER — I AM UNABLE TO EVALUATE THIS OFFICER FOR THE FOLLOWING REASON:

I had the opportunity to observe Captain Conley move from the staff to command his troop after the previous commander had been killed. I then further observed him in his first battle; in this battle, as well as in all subsequent ones, his performance was outstanding in every respect. Additionally, he is cheerful, responsive and eager to respond whether on the battle field or in non-combat environment. He is a superb officer and an exceptional all-around leader.

SIGNATURE OF RATER	TYPED NAME GRADE BRANCH SERVICE NUMBER ORGANIZATION AND DUTY ASSIGNMENT	DATE
	THOMAS B. TYREE, LTC, Armor, 057111 1st Squadron, 4th Cavalry, Commanding	12Jul68
SIGNATURE OF INDORSER	TYPED NAME GRADE BRANCH SERVICE NUMBER ORGANIZATION AND DUTY ASSIGNMENT PHIL F. ...., BG, USA, 023469, HHC 1st Infantry Division, Assistant Division Commander	21 Aug 68

REVIEWER (Read chapter 5 AR 623-105)   MY REVIEW   INDICATES NO FURTHER ACTION   RESULTS IN ACTION STATED ON INCLOSURES

OFFICER EFFICIENCY REPORT (Rater's Comments)

Captain John E. Conley 05329329, Period Covered: 11Feb68–12Jul68

Part XIa continued

that he be given an assignment which will enable him to complete his education and then be integrated into the Regular Army at the earliest possible time.

THOMAS B. TYREE, LTC, Armor, 057111
1st Squadron, 4th Cavalry, Commanding

2nd Regular Rating as Troop Commander

Captain Conley has performed his duties as a reconnaissance troop commander in a truly outstanding manner. He is combat wise; mission oriented; absolutely devoted to his duty, his men, and the Squadron; original and imaginative; and thoroughly professional. He has passed on his knowledge to a large number of platoon leaders in the Squadron while they were operating under his control, and his technique of making a platoon leader's instruction period out of a combat reconnaissance in force or ambush mission is a superlative example of the depth of knowledge and natural leadership he possesses. Without reservation I recommend that he be afforded the opportunity to complete his education and tendered a regular commission.

PART III AUTHENTICATION (Read paragraph 12, AR 623-105)

SIGNATURE OF RATER

TYPED NAME GRADE BRANCH SERVICE NUMBER ORGANIZATION AND DUTY ASSIGNMENT

JOHN C. FAITH, LTC, Armor, 050590

1st Squadron, 4th Cavalry, Commanding

DATE

[Captain Conley has performed his duties as a reconnaissance troop commander in a truly outstanding manner. He is combat wise; mission oriented; absolutely devoted to his duty, his men, and the Squadron; original and imaginative; and thoroughly professional. He has passed on his knowledge to a large number of platoon leaders in the Squadron while they were operating under his control, and his tecnique of making a platoon leader's instruction period out of a reconnaisance in force or ambush mission is a supulative example of the depth of knowledge and natural leadrship he possesses. Without reservation I recommend he be afforded the opportunity to complete his education and tendered a regular commission.]

Vietnam mouse-deer

The **Vietnam mouse-deer** (*Tragulus versicolor*), also known as the **silver-backed chevrotain**, is a species of even-toed ungulate in the family Tragulidae that at present only is known from Vietnam.[1] Until 2004, it was generally treated as a subspecies of the greater mouse-deer (*T. napu*), though it more closely resembles the lesser mouse-deer (*T. kanchil*).[3] Recent records of this very poorly known species are missing, but this is more likely due to the difficulty involved in separating it from other mouse-deer and the general absence of field work within its presumed range than it being extinct.[2] The Silver-backed Chevrotain is among the 25 "most wanted lost" species that are the focus of Global Wildlife Conservation's "Search for Lost Species" initiative.[4]

References

1. Wilson, D.E.; Reeder, D.M., eds. (2005). *Mammal Species of the World: A Taxonomic and Geographic Reference* (http://www.departments.buck nell.edu/biology/resources/msw3/browse.asp?id=14200183) (3rd ed.). Johns Hopkins University Press. ISBN 978-0-8018-8221-0. OCLC 62265494 (https://www.worldcat.org/oclc/62265494).

2. Timmins, R.J.; Duckworth, J.W. & Meijaard, E. (2008). "*Tragulus versicolor*" (http://www.iucnredlist.org/details/136360). *IUCN Red List of Threatened Species*. Version 2008. International Union for Conservation of Nature. Retrieved 29 March 2009. Database entry includes a brief justification of why this species is of data deficient.

3. E. Meijaard, C.P. Groves (2004), "A taxonomic revision of the *Tragulus* mouse-deer (Artiodactyla) (http://www.blackwe ll-synergy.com/doi/abs/10.1111/j.1096-3642.2004.00091.x?journalCode=zoj)", *Zoological Journal of the Linnean Society* 140 (1), 63–102 doi:10.1111/j.1096-3642.2004.00091.x (https://doi.org/10.1111%2Fj.1096-3642.2004.00091. x) http://zmmu.msu.ru/rjt/articles/ther3_1%2009_13%20Kuznez_Borisenko.pdf

4. "The Search for Lost Species" (https://www.lostspecies.org). *Global Wildlife Conservation*. Retrieved 10 July 2017.

Vietnam mouse-deer[1]

Conservation status

Extinct	Threatened	Least Concern
EX EW	CR EN VU NT	LC

Data Deficient (IUCN 3.1)[2]

Scientific classification

Kingdom:	Animalia
Phylum:	Chordata
Class:	Mammalia
Order:	Artiodactyla
Family:	Tragulidae
Genus:	*Tragulus*
Species:	*T. versicolor*

Binomial name

Tragulus versicolor

(Thomas, 1910)

The Silent Column
Song of the 4th U. S. Cavalry

unknown

I am a Christian (author unknown)

When I say that "I'm a Christian,"
I am not shouting that "I'm clean living."
I'm whispering that "I was lost,
But now I'm found and forgiven."

When I say that "I'm a Christian,"
I don't speak of this with pride.
I'm confessing that I stumble
And need Christ to be my guide.

When I say that "I'm a Christian,"
I'm not trying to be strong.
I'm professing that I'm week
And need His strength to carry on.

When I say that "I'm a Christian,"
I'm not bragging of success.
I'm admitting I have failed,
And need God to clean my mess.

When I say that "I'm a Christian,"
I'm not claiming to be Perfect.
My flaws are far too visible,
But God believes I'm worth it.

When I say that "I'm a Christian,"
I still feel the sting of pain.
I have my share of heartaches,
So, I call upon His name.

When I say that "I'm a Christian,"
I'm not holier than thou.
I'm just a simple sinner,
Who received God's good grace, somehow.

GOD BLESS AMERICA

THE END

I hope you enjoyed my story as much as I enjoyed putting it on paper for you.

Don't forget to rate the book.

I can be contacted at TheCavalryman@aol.com

Always "Prepared and Loyal"

"Duty First"

John
The Author

CPSIA information can be obtained
at www.ICGtesting.com
Printed in the USA
LVHW030806201119
637820LV00001B/53/P